CliffsTestPrep®

Praxis II®: Principles of Learning and Teaching

by

Diane E. Kern, Ph.D.

WILEY
Wiley Publishing, Inc.

About the Author

Diane E. Kern, Ph.D. (Wakefield, RI), is Assistant Professor of Education at the University of Rhode Island. She serves on the School of Education's ad hoc committee on licensure tests.

I would like to acknowledge the many people who helped me craft this book. Johnny B.—it all started with you! Grace Freedson of Freedson's Publishing Network for seeking me out. Greg Tubach and Matt McClure for your leadership, encouragement, patience, and expert editorial assistance. Jim, Jimmy, and Tory for your comic relief and never-ending support, especially on long writing days. Our "Reading Team"—Jim Barton, Meg McGuire, Rebecca Schilke, Mary Hoyt, and Wendy André—for helping me to become a better teacher, educator, and writer. My teaching colleagues—I hope you'll enjoy finding little bits of your dedicated teaching throughout this book. My future teaching colleagues, especially those of you who have attended test-prep sessions, worked hard in class, taken careful notes, and dedicated your free time to becoming the best teacher you can be—thanks for the inspiration.

Publisher's Acknowledgments

Editorial

Project Editor: Matthew McClure

Acquisitions Editor: Greg Tubach

Production

Proofreader: Shannon Ramsey

Wiley Publishing, Inc. Composition Services

CliffsTestPrep® Praxis II®: Principles of Learning and Teaching

Published by:
Wiley Publishing, Inc.
111 River Street
Hoboken, NJ 07030-5774
www.wiley.com

Copyright © 2006 Wiley, Hoboken, NJ

Published by Wiley, Hoboken, NJ
Published simultaneously in Canada

Library of Congress Cataloging-in-Publication data is available from the publisher upon request.

ISBN-13 978-0-471-75212-7

ISBN-10 0-471-75212-6

8 7 6 5 4 3 2

WILEY

Table of Contents

PART I: DIAGNOSTIC PREVIEW TESTS

PART II: PREPARING FOR THE FORMAT OF THE PLT

PART III: PREPARING FOR THE CONTENT OF THE PLT

PART IV: FULL-LENGTH PRACTICE TESTS

PART V: CLOSING THOUGHTS

Introduction

Getting Started

As you know, teaching is a rewarding and challenging profession. One way you will show that you are ready for your teaching license is to pass your state's required Praxis II: Principles of Learning and Teaching (PLT) test. The way you will show that you are ready for your teaching career is to use this book to thoroughly prepare for your teaching licensure test. Successful teachers, like you, do their homework, so let's get started.

Format of the Test

Each of the PLT tests is designed to measure your knowledge of a broad range of teaching-related topics. Your knowledge of these topics is usually developed in undergraduate or teacher-certification teaching methods courses, as well as in educational psychology, human development, classroom management, and foundations of education courses. No matter which of the PLT tests you take, you will answer a total of 36 questions—12 short-answer questions (known as "constructed response" questions on the PLT) and 24 multiple-choice questions. There are four different PLT tests, broken down by grade (see the following table).

PLT Test	Test Registration Code
Early Childhood	0521
Grades K–6	0522
Grades 5–9	0523
Grades 7–12	0524

The constructed-response questions are short-answer questions that relate to four teaching situations (also called case histories) in order to provide real-life teaching context for your responses. For a preview of a case history/constructed-response question, turn to Chapter 5.

Each multiple-choice question includes a teaching situation, a question, and then four answer choices. For a preview of the multiple-choice questions, turn to the Chapter 6.

You will have a total of 2 hours to complete the PLT test. The constructed-response questions that accompany each case history will require more time. You'll want to plan 25 minutes for each constructed-response question in order to read each case history and to write your short-answer responses. The multiple-choice questions should require less time; plan for a total of 20 minutes to answer all 24 multiple-choice questions. There is no penalty for guessing, so be sure to answer every question.

Question Type	Total Number of Questions	Format	Pacing Suggestions
Constructed response	12 short-answer questions	4 case histories, each followed by 3 constructed-response questions	25 minutes per case history/ 3 constructed-response questions
Multiple choice	24 multiple-choice questions	2 sections, each with 12 multiple-choice questions	10 minutes per section

On the test, you will first be presented with a case history and three short-answer constructed responses. Then you'll read another case history and provide three short-answer constructed responses. Next, you'll answer 12 standalone multiple-choice questions that do not relate to one another or to any of the case histories. Then the pattern of test questions repeats—case history, three short-answer constructed responses, case history, three short-answer constructed responses, and finally 12 standalone multiple-choice questions.

Content of the Test

Now that you have a general idea of the format and pacing of the test, let's take a closer look at the content of the PLT test. The broad topics "Students as Learners" and "Instruction and Assessment" make up approximately 66 percent of the test. Clearly, this is where you'll want to spend the majority of your study time. In addition, the PLT test assesses your understanding of "Communication Techniques" and "Teacher Professionalism" in approximately 33 percent of the test questions, so these topics also deserve your review time.

	Students as Learners	Instruction and Assessment	Communication Techniques	Teacher Professionalism
Percentage of Your Score	33%	33%	11%	22%
	Student development and learning processes	Instructional strategies	Effective verbal and nonverbal communication	Reflective practitioners
	Diverse learners	Planning strategies	Cultural and gender differences	The larger school community
	Motivation and learning environment	Assessment strategies	Stimulating discussion	

Frequently Asked Questions

You've already started on the path to success by orienting yourself to the format of the questions, planning to pace yourself, and becoming familiar with the content covered on this test, but most likely you still have several questions about your licensure test.

Q. How do I register for the PLT?

A. Contact the Educational Testing Service (ETS) on the Web at www.ets.org/praxis or by phone at 800-772-9476. My students and I have found that registering online is easiest.

Q. How do I know which PLT test to take?

A. Contact the department of education for the state for which you seek teacher licensure. I recommend that you use your favorite Internet search engine to locate your state department of education's teaching certification office.

Q. What score do I need to earn my teaching license?

A. Each state department of education sets its passing score. Contact your state's department of education for this answer.

Q. Do all states require the PLT for teacher licensure?

A. No, but several do. Some states have created their own licensure tests. Some states use other Praxis II tests. Again, contact the state department of education for specifics. States that require the PLT will accept your PLT scores no matter where you took the test provided that you meet the state's passing score requirement and that you did not take the test too long ago (usually five or more years ago).

Q. How long does it take to get my scores back?

A. ETS usually mails your scores to you in four to six weeks.

Q. Are any accommodations available to test-takers?

A. Yes. Test-takers with disabilities and those whose primary language is not English may apply for test-taking accommodations. More information is available at www.ets.org/praxis or in the Praxis series registration booklet.

Q. What do I need on the day of the test?

A. You need:

1. Photo identification with your name, photograph, and signature
2. Second alternative identification with your name, photograph, and signature—just to be safe!
3. Admission ticket, printout of your online registration, letter of authorization, mailgram, or telegram showing your test registration
4. Several #2 pencils and an eraser
5. Two blue or black pens for constructed response questions
6. A watch without calculator functions (optional, but advised)
7. To wear layered clothing (optional, but you can't control the temperature of the testing room!)

Q. What's the best way to prepare for the Principles of Learning and Teaching tests?

A. Doing just what you're doing! Become familiar with the format, types of questions, and content of the test. After you're familiar with what will be on the test, it's best to complete several PLT practice tests, self-correct, and study the questions/content you get incorrect.

Suggestions for Using This Study Guide

CliffsTestPrep Praxis II: Principles of Learning and Teaching offers various levels of support to make your test preparation efforts successful.

Part I: Diagnostic Preview Tests

This section provides an introductory experience with the constructed-response and multiple-choice formats of the PLT. You can select your specific PLT test version (Early Childhood, Grades K–6, Grades 5–9, or Grades 7–12), complete the sample questions, and self-correct to determine areas you know and areas you need to study. Each item on the preview test has a detailed explanation that leads you to another section of this guide to help you gain deeper knowledge of the content covered in each test item.

For additional practice, you may also want to complete all the other preview tests in this section. While the teaching situations presented are grade specific (e.g., the Early Childhood test offers case histories about a first-grade classroom), the content of any PLT test follows a consistent pattern. In other words, each one tests your knowledge of the four content categories—Students as Learners, Instructional Strategies, Communication Techniques, and Teacher Professionalism—so completing the diagnostic preview tests from other grade levels still pays off!

Part II: Preparing for the Format of the PLT

This section provides specific strategies for answering each of the two question types on the PLT—constructed response and multiple choice.

Part III: Preparing for the Content of the PLT

As you know, the PLT tests have four categories of content: Students as Learners, Instructional Strategies, Communication Techniques, and Teacher Professionalism. In this section, detailed content outlines have been prepared to save you time (no need to scour all those methods and educational psychology text books!) and offer a concise overview of the key theories and practices used in teaching today. Each Diagnostic Preview Test question from Part I of this book is linked to a chapter in this section to provide the information you need to learn to be more successful on the actual test.

Part IV: Full-Length Practice Tests

This section offers you the opportunity to apply all you've learned. Complete the two practice tests for your grade level, self-correct, and then study the detailed explanations. You can even practice your pacing—remember, you have 2 hours for each practice test. If you'd like, you can make the most of your studying by completing any of the other six full-length practice tests to give yourself additional practice.

Part V: Closing Thoughts

This brief section includes a few final test preparation tips and resources to help you perform well on the PLT test.

PART I

DIAGNOSTIC PREVIEW TESTS

Early Childhood Preview Test

This preview of the PLT Early Childhood test (0521) is designed to give you an overall sense of the test's format and to help you determine the content areas you need to focus on in your studies. This preview test will *not* help you with your pacing on the test—this preview is approximately half the length of the actual PLT and may not represent the entire scope of the test in either content or difficulty.

After you complete the preview test, score your answers and use the explanations to self-diagnose content areas to study in Part III of this guide. You may also want to complete the preview tests in Chapters 2, 3, and 4 to aid you in determining which content areas to study. Even though these additional preview tests are written for other PLT test grade levels, the question topics—Students as Learners, Instruction and Assessment, Communication Techniques, and Teacher Professionalism—remain the same.

Case I

Directions: The case history is followed by three constructed-response questions. Read the case history and then respond to the three questions.

Scenario: Daniel

Daniel is a 7-year-old second-grade student who loves nature, likes classifying and organizing things, and enjoys attention from his peers. His teacher, Miss Whitcomb, uses a science-based, thematic unit approach to instruction but has found that Daniel is having difficulty completing his science log each day. She immerses her students in the lives of many living things by placing a variety of animal tanks around the perimeter of the classroom. She allows the students to move the animals to their desks in order to get close-up views of the animals. She has a variety of information sources about animals in the classroom, including nonfiction books, reference books, children's science magazines, and computer resources such as online encyclopedias and Internet access. Miss Whitcomb asks her mentor to observe Daniel so that she can offer teaching suggestions to help Daniel complete his written work.

Observation: Miss Whitcomb's Class

Pre-observation notes: Miss Whitcomb states, "The purpose of the science log is to make daily observations of a living creature in our classroom and to learn to express thoughts in complete sentences." She continues, "Daniel has not completed his science log for several days now. When Daniel remembers to turn in his log, or when he has not misplaced it, his log entries often have a drawing of the living creature and a few words, not complete sentences. I believe Daniel is capable of higher-level work than this, and I would like you to observe his work to make some suggestions so that I can better help Daniel achieve second-grade standards."

Mentor Classroom Observation Focused on Daniel

Miss Whitcomb begins the whole-group lesson by asking students to share what they wrote in their science logs yesterday. Daniel does not offer to speak. Instead, he whispers to a friend nearby and then looks at the tanks of living creatures near him.

Next, the teacher makes a KWL chart on the chalkboard and asks students to share what they want to know about the living creature they are observing. The teacher writes these facts under the K (Know) column. Daniel excitedly contributes that he knows that a hermit crab can move from one shell to another and that he has seen hermit crabs at the beach. After several students share, Miss Whitcomb instructs the students to turn to the next clean page of their logs and write a sentence about what they would like to know. Daniel appears to think during this time and then begins to draw a picture of a hermit crab. After a short time, Miss Whitcomb asks three students to share what they want to know, and then she writes these sentences in the W (Want to Know) column. Daniel does not offer to share his sentence, as he does not have a sentence written, only a drawing. He shows his drawing to a girl nearby, and she praises his artistic ability.

Next, Miss Whitcomb asks the second-graders to get their living creature's container, place it on their desk, and observe the creature quietly. After five minutes of individual observation, the students are instructed to spend ten minutes writing in their science logs about what they observed today. She also asks the students to write what they wanted to know about their living creature.

Miss Whitcomb moves to her desk to correct spelling papers while the students complete their science log entries. Daniel completes his drawing of the hermit crab with careful attention to detail, and then he writes "my hermut crabbe," "bech," and "ates?" on his paper. Once he has finished his work, he talks with a boy near him about the hermit crab and asks the friend if he knows what a hermit crab eats. The boys have a serious conversation about the crab's eating habits until Miss Whitcomb brings the students back together to share their entries.

Miss Whitcomb closes the lesson with time to discuss what the students learned about their living creatures. Once again, Daniel is silent and appears uncomfortable with the written work in his science log. When Miss Whitcomb calls on Daniel to share, he appears nervous and says that he does not want to. Miss Whitcomb reminds the students to place their science logs in the blue bin on their way out to lunch. Daniel puts his log in his desk and hurries to catch up with a friend in the lunch line.

Post-observation notes: Miss Whitcomb shares that she believes Daniel is a bright boy who loves science. She expresses her concern that Daniel does not complete his science log as instructed; instead, he draws, talks to peers, and then labels his page with words, not sentences. Miss Whitcomb also says that Daniel's talking to friends during class may be one reason he does not complete his work. Her mentor suggests, "Perhaps Daniel is completing the assignment to the best of his ability at this time. Let's talk more about strategies to help Daniel be more successful when writing in his science log."

Directions: Questions 1–3 require you to write short answers, or "constructed responses." You are not expected to cite specific theories or texts in your answers; however, your knowledge of specific principles of learning and teaching will be evaluated. Be sure to answer all parts of the question. Write your answers in the space provided.

---

1. Suppose Miss Whitcomb and her mentor discuss alternative ways to open this lesson.

   - Identify TWO alternative ways to open this lesson so that Daniel might be more successful completing his science log.

   - Regarding these two alternatives, explain how each could meet Daniel's learning needs. Base your response on principles of activating and developing prior knowledge before writing.

2. Next, Miss Whitcomb and her mentor discuss ways to support Daniel during the science log observation and writing time.

   - Identify TWO specific ways to actively engage Daniel in this lesson so that he might be more successful.

   - Explain how each way you have identified could meet Daniel's learning needs during observation and writing time. Base your response on best practice and principles of learning and teaching.

3. Finally, Miss Whitcomb and her mentor discuss ways to assess Daniel's work and ways to provide helpful feedback to Daniel and his family about his progress.

   - Identify TWO criteria for scoring the science log in this second-grade classroom and ONE way to share this information with the student or parents.

   - Explain how your assessment ideas will make the science log more successful for Daniel.

Case II

Directions: The case history is followed by three constructed-response questions. Read the case history and then respond to the three questions.

Scenario: Miss Elliott

Miss Elliott is a second-year first-grade teacher in a large urban school district. Miss Elliott's students have diverse learning styles and needs. Of her 25 first-graders, six students are English language learners, five have learning disabilities, four receive gifted and talented program services, and two have been diagnosed with attention deficit hyperactivity disorder (ADHD). In addition, one of Miss Elliott's students, Susie, was born prematurely with fetal alcohol syndrome. Of all her first-graders, this student is making the least progress academically and socially. As required in her contract, Miss Elliott must complete a professional portfolio that contains clear evidence that she is achieving her professional goals. She also will be evaluated by her principal this month.

Document 1: Professional Goals

The teacher evaluation process requires her to document two ways that she has demonstrated her achievement of three professional goals. Miss Elliott has set the following goals:

1. Create effective bridges between students' experiences and the first-grade curriculum goals.
2. Improve classroom discussions to help students share thinking in different ways, for different purposes.
3. Develop and utilize active partnerships with parents, colleagues, and school leaders.

Document 2: Unit Goals

Miss Elliott plans to collect all six artifacts for her professional development portfolio during the next unit of instruction, which involves the theme of friendship. The following are three curriculum goals for this unit:

- Students will express qualities of a good friend.
- Students will read about friendships to make comparisons/contrasts to their experiences.
- Students will write a story involving friendships with a beginning, middle, and end.

Document 3: Project Assignment: Family Book Bags

A key assignment in Miss Elliott's friendship unit involves the children and their families reading a book at home together in a project called "Family Book Bags." The book bag contains a quality and age-appropriate children's book, a toy or prop that comes from the story, a journal for the student and family to respond in, and a letter to the family explaining the project. Here's a sample letter from the *Baby Animals* book bag:

Dear first-grade friend and family,

Please enjoy reading the book *Baby Animals* with your child. You and your child can read the book together. It's also okay for you to read the whole book to your child. After reading, your child should write and draw on the notebook pages. You should write and draw on the pages labeled "family pages." Your child may want to draw a favorite baby animal, either a real or a stuffed animal. You should write down the child's retelling, as well as any comments or questions you have about reading *Baby Animals* with your child.

Good retellings include:

- The characters
- The setting
- The main events in the story
- How the story ends

If your child has a picture of your real animal or would like to bring a stuffed animal to school for the day, please put it in the book bag. Your child can share it with the class! Please have your child return the book bag the next day, if possible. You may have up to two school nights with the book bag, if needed.

Happy reading!

Miss Elliott

Document 4: Project Assessment

When the family book bag is returned to school, the child has the opportunity to show and tell about the book bag experience. The book bag reading experience is assessed on the following criteria:

- Retelling includes characters
- Retelling includes setting
- Retelling includes main events
- Retelling includes conclusion
- Student response includes drawing and words
- Student oral sharing is clearly spoken and connected to *Baby Animals* reading

Document 5: Transcript of Susie Sharing Her Book Bag

Miss Elliott: Susie, it's your turn to share the *Baby Animals* book bag that you read at home with your grandma.

Susie: Oh, good! I love share time!

Miss Elliott: Tell us about your favorite part of the story.

Susie: My favorite animal is a leopard. My grandma and I went to the zoo, but I could not see the leopard because it was hiding behind the rocks, and then we had an ice cream and I had to go home.

Miss Elliott: Did you see a baby leopard in the *Baby Animals* book?

Susie: No. I did not like this book because it did not have a leopard.

Miss Elliott: Oh, Susie. You will be so happy to know that I saw a baby leopard in the *Baby Animals* book. Look at this picture!

Susie: Yeah! That's a baby leopard. That's my favorite animal. I love the spots and her color.

Directions: Questions 4–6 require you to write short answers, or "constructed responses." You are not expected to cite specific theories or texts in your answers; however, your knowledge of specific principles of learning and teaching will be evaluated. Be sure to answer all parts of the question. Write your answers in the space provided.

---

4. Miss Elliott's first professional goal—to create effective bridges between students' experiences and the first-grade curriculum goals—will require her to consider her students' prior experiences and how these experiences relate to the goals in the friendship unit.

- Suggest TWO instructional techniques for creating effective bridges between students and curriculum goals.

- Explain how Miss Elliott can document her use of these techniques as part of her professional evaluation portfolio. Be sure to base your response on best professional practice and principles of learning and teaching.

5. Miss Elliott's second professional goal—to improve classroom discussions to help students share thinking in different ways, for different purposes—requires her to use effective communication techniques when teaching her first-graders.

- Suggest TWO communication techniques to stimulate discussion in different ways for particular purposes, especially for the diverse learners in her first-grade classroom.

- Explain how Miss Elliott can document in her portfolio the effectiveness of the students' discussions. Be sure to base your response on principles of learning and teaching.

6. Miss Elliott's third professional goal—to develop and utilize active partnerships with parents, colleagues, and school leaders—requires her to be a reflective practitioner and to connect with the larger school community. Miss Elliott is especially concerned about her student, Susie, who had fetal alcohol syndrome and who is making less than adequate progress in first grade. Miss Elliott would like to concentrate on supporting Susie's educational needs while she documents her achievement of this third professional goal.

- Identify TWO resources Miss Elliott can utilize to help her to achieve this third professional goal.

- Explain how each resource you have identified could benefit Susie's learning needs and could help Miss Elliott meet her professional goal. Base your response on best professional practice and principles of learning and teaching.

Discrete Multiple-Choice Questions

Directions: Questions 7–18 are not related to the previous cases. For each question, select the best answer and mark the corresponding letter space on your answer sheet.

ANSWER SHEET

7 Ⓐ Ⓑ Ⓒ Ⓓ
8 Ⓐ Ⓑ Ⓒ Ⓓ
9 Ⓐ Ⓑ Ⓒ Ⓓ
10 Ⓐ Ⓑ Ⓒ Ⓓ
11 Ⓐ Ⓑ Ⓒ Ⓓ
12 Ⓐ Ⓑ Ⓒ Ⓓ
13 Ⓐ Ⓑ Ⓒ Ⓓ
14 Ⓐ Ⓑ Ⓒ Ⓓ
15 Ⓐ Ⓑ Ⓒ Ⓓ
16 Ⓐ Ⓑ Ⓒ Ⓓ
17 Ⓐ Ⓑ Ⓒ Ⓓ
18 Ⓐ Ⓑ Ⓒ Ⓓ

---

7. Mrs. Dougherty's first-grade students work in small groups at the blocks center three days a week. Which of the following provides the best rationale for blocks center work?

   A. Direct instruction
   B. Discovery learning
   C. Independent practice
   D. Visual learning

---

8. A reading lesson plan that is organized with direct instruction, guided practice, and independent practice is likely to provide which of the following to students?

   A. Grade-level expectations
   B. Phonemic awareness
   C. Scaffolding
   D. Vocabulary development

Questions 9–10 are based on the following description of a class.

Mrs. Horton teaches a second-grade class of 20 students. She has a diverse group of children, including:

■ Five students identified as eligible for an IEP and placed in her classroom, which is considered each student's "least restrictive environment"

■ Two students whose primary language is not English

■ Two students who have been diagnosed with attention deficit disorder

■ Two students who are eligible for the gifted and talented program

9. One of Mrs. Horton's goals for the class is to have the students take turns and listen attentively to the speaker. Which of the following instructional strategies will best support the students whose primary language is not English?

   A. Practice taking turns and listening in a small group with support from the teacher
   B. Whole-class practice listening and speaking
   C. Listening to a tape-recorded conversation
   D. Brainstorming a list of rules for taking turns and listening

10. Mrs. Horton also has set a goal to teach each student to read at the second-grade level by the end of the school year. Which of the following methods is LEAST likely to support this goal for the diverse group of learners in her class?

   A. Language experience approach
   B. Independent reading of a book on the child's frustration level
   C. Whole group reading of a quality children's literature book
   D. Guided reading practice in small groups

11. During oral reading, one student reads the word *cape* as *cap*. This child most likely needs help with

   A. concepts about print.
   B. encoding.
   C. comprehension.
   D. phonics.

12. A student in Miss Cindy's kindergarten class loves to repeat the rhymes in poems, visits the listening center often, and has memorized the letters of the alphabet by singing the ABC song. Which of the following best describes this child's intelligence?

   A. Visual/linguistic
   B. Verbal/spatial
   C. Musical
   D. Interpersonal

13. Mrs. Antosh strives to make accommodations for the students in her kindergarten class who have short attention spans, have difficulty starting a task, and often appear distracted by the busy classroom. Which accommodation is LEAST likely to support these students?

   A. Providing a less visual, quiet area to work
   B. Providing short tasks with immediate positive feedback
   C. Moving the student closer to the teacher
   D. Seating the student in a group

14. As part of the district's assessment plan, Miss Webb gives a criterion-referenced assessment to her first-graders at the end of her Communities social studies unit. Which of the following types of information will Miss Webb most likely get from this assessment?

   A. Each student's grade-level equivalent compared to other first-graders in the district
   B. Each student's attainment of the unit's goals and objectives
   C. A better understanding of the student's attitudes about social studies
   D. Each student's percentile rank in social studies performance on the Communities unit

Questions 15–16 are based on the following teaching situation.

Mrs. Lahiri is a teacher assistant in Mrs. Campbell's primary grade-level resource classroom. During a time when Mrs. Campbell created a lesson plan in which Mrs. Lahiri works with a small group of students drafting a story, the principal asks Mrs. Lahiri to assist in the office because of an absence. Mrs. Campbell and Mrs. Lahiri are discouraged that their plans have been interrupted. Furthermore, their students will not receive the small-group instruction delineated in their Individualized Education Plans.

---

15. Which of the following is a professionally responsible and reflective way for Mrs. Campbell to approach this situation?

   A. Discuss concerns with Mrs. Lahiri and encourage her to file a complaint.
   B. Discuss concerns with the school principal and offer alternative solutions to the problem.
   C. Support the change in student services in order to be a team member.
   D. Discuss concerns with colleagues in the teacher's room and brainstorm solutions to the problem.

---

16. Which of the following best provides guidance to Mrs. Campbell when considering solutions to this teaching situation?

   A. Reading First
   B. Title VI
   C. Individuals with Disabilities Education Act
   D. Title I

---

17. Mr. Colombino, a second-grade teacher, has a student who has repeated difficulty following class rules. Which of the following approaches can he use to best change this student's behavior?

   A. Corporal punishment
   B. Regular communication with the student's family
   C. Negative reinforcement
   D. Formal operational development

---

18. The *Brown v. Board of Education* legal case of 1954 struck down which of the following doctrines?

   A. "Carpe diem"
   B. "Least restrictive environment"
   C. "Separate but equal"
   D. "Separation of church and state"

Answers and Explanations

Cases, or "constructed responses," are graded holistically on a scale of 0–2, with 0 being the lowest score. For details on this type of question, be sure to read Chapter 5. In this section, you'll find the content categories and suggested content to include in your case study responses. For more information about the content category, you can study Chapters 7, 8, 9, and 10. The suggested content is designed to help you get a sense of the type of response required, but it may not cover all the correct options in such an open-ended question. You may also find it helpful to share your constructed responses with an education professor, adviser, or educator.

Case I

1. **Suggested content:** Provide direct instruction as to how to complete a science log entry; share benchmark papers to demonstrate exemplary, acceptable, and not acceptable examples of the assignment; elicit specific observations from Daniel one-to-one and help him compose sentences in his science log.

   Each of these alternative strategies provides a higher level of scaffolding, or support, for this assignment. Daniel may be choosing to draw observations and write words because he is not clear on the assignment's expectations or because his level of literacy development is below the level expected by Miss Whitcomb. One key to opening this lesson is finding out what Daniel knows and is able to do and providing specific, corrective instruction.

2. **Suggested content:** Two strategies to use during this lesson might include: breaking the task into smaller chunks; providing more frequent, positive feedback to Daniel; having Daniel work with an equally able or more able peer; asking Daniel to verbally describe his drawing and then encouraging him to put this description in writing.

   Students such as Daniel benefit from differentiated instruction. Daniel's level of literacy development may be at an earlier stage than his peers. His behavior may be age-appropriate for his knowledge level. Daniel would benefit from positive guidance and timely feedback. These changes in the learning environment will likely help Daniel's self-motivation. Encouraging Daniel to explain his thinking probes for his understanding and may encourage his divergent thinking, which sends a message of caring and respect.

3. **Suggested content:** This response seeks your knowledge of assessment and professional ability to communicate with parents. Suggested content includes using a four-point rubric with specific indicators for what makes an exemplary science log. TWO criteria could include: Two detailed sentences describing what the animal is doing; a sketch of the animal with labels for the animal's habitat; sentences including a capital letter and end punctuation; or an "I wonder question," which is a question about the animal's behavior, habitat, or physical characteristics. ONE way to share information could include: a brief letter to parents detailing the purpose of the science log; an activity page for the family to complete with the child after reading the science log (for example, writing a note back to the child to praise his or her work); or extension ideas for keeping a science log with the family at home.

   Teachers should share the criteria for success on a task before the assignment is completed. Criteria should be measurable, free from bias, and understandable to the student. Teachers should regularly communicate with parents and guardians to develop and utilize active partnerships that benefit the child, as well as the larger school community. Communication should be respectful and reciprocal.

Case II

4. **Suggested content:** Based on principles of learning and teaching, there are several ways to bridge students and curriculum, including the following: modeling, guided practice, independent practice, appropriate homework, activating prior knowledge, and teaching predicting and verifying. For more information about this content, turn to Chapter 8.

   Teachers must actively teach students to connect prior knowledge to new curriculum content. Schema theory, scaffolding, and teaching to a student's "zone of proximal development" are three theories that provide a rationale for the techniques.

5. **Suggested content:** You might include the following techniques: helping students share their ideas and thinking processes; promoting risk taking and problem solving; or teaching students to question, such as those found in Bloom's taxonomy. It is also important to develop an example or two that describes how the technique you've chosen will best support a diverse learning environment in Miss Elliott's classroom. For example, four of her students attend gifted and talented programs. Asking questions at the analysis and synthesis levels of Bloom's taxonomy will challenge such students, while at the same time discussing a topic that can benefit the whole class. For more support on this content, see Chapters 7 and 9.

   Metacognition (thinking about one's own thinking) provides one important reason to promote the communication techniques detailed in this response. Teaching students a variety of ways to ask and respond to discussion questions provides an opportunity for all students to learn to think.

6. **Suggested content:** Miss Elliott might turn to the professional literature, the school nurse, or the child's family to help her make instructional decisions for her student who was born with fetal alcohol syndrome.

   Building partnerships to solve educational problems provides an opportunity for shared ownership and shared decision-making of the problem. Susie may need to repeat first grade or receive evaluation for special education services. When school and home are working collaboratively, a student's needs are met more effectively.

Discrete Multiple-Choice Questions

Answer Key			
Question	*Answer*	*Content Category*	*Where to Get More Help*
7.	B	Students as Learners	Chapter 7
8.	C	Students as Learners	Chapter 7
9.	A	Students as Learners	Chapter 7
10.	B	Students as Learners	Chapter 7
11.	D	Instruction and Assessment	Chapter 8
12.	C	Instruction and Assessment	Chapter 8
13.	D	Instruction and Assessment	Chapter 8
14.	B	Instruction and Assessment	Chapter 8
15.	B	Teacher Professionalism	Chapter 10
16.	C	Teacher Professionalism	Chapter 10
17.	B	Teacher Professionalism	Chapter 10
18.	C	Teacher Professionalism	Chapter 10

Explanations

7. **B.** Discovery learning is an instructional approach based on Bruner's constructivist theory. Students select and transform information, creating hypotheses relying on cognitive structures.

8. **C.** Scaffolding is an instructional technique introduced by Vygotsky. The teacher models how to approach a task, breaks complex assignments into smaller parts, and offers scaffolding, or support, for student learning. When the student is ready, the teacher provides independent practice.

9. **A.** English language learners benefit from working in small groups, where they can practice speaking in English and listening to peers.

10. B. Mrs. Horton will least likely achieve her goal of teaching her second-graders to read at grade level if her students read books independently at their frustration level. It is best practice to have students read books at either their independent or instructional level.

11. D. When a child reads the word *cape* as *cap,* he or she needs help with phonics or decoding. You may have chosen answer choice B, encoding, which is synonymous with spelling. The question states that the child is reading, not writing, so phonics is the credited response.

12. C. According to Howard Gardner's theory of multiple intelligences, there are eight different intelligences. Students who possess musical intelligence have sensitivity to pitch, tones, and rhythm. They are the students who like to hum, repeat chants, play instruments, and learn melodies.

13. D. The LEAST effective accommodation for a student who has a short attention span, struggles to begin a task, and appears distracted in the classroom is placing the student in a group. This student would be more successful with added structure and teacher direction until he or she can learn strategies to deal with these attention problems.

14. B. A criterion reference test compares a student's knowledge, as demonstrated on the test, to the goals and objectives in the curriculum.

15. B. Discussing concerns with the school principal and offering alternative solutions to the problem would be the most professional response to this situation. According to the No Child Left Behind Act, teacher assistants assigned to children as part of their Individualized Educational Plans are required to spend instructional time with students. Working professionally and collaboratively with the principal is the most desirable professional option presented.

16. C. Individuals with Disabilities Education Act became a public law in 1997 to ensure that students with disabilities and their families have access to a free and appropriate education. This law focuses resources on teaching and learning for students with Individualized Educational Plans.

17. B. Of the choices offered, regular communication with the student's family has the most potential for supporting the learning needs for a student who struggles to follow class rules. Corporal punishment—spanking or striking a student—is not an option in public schools today. Skinner's theory of negative reinforcement states that a student escape punishment by repeating desired responses, such as not following the rules in Mr. Colombino's class. Formal operational cognitive development does not make sense in the context of this question.

18. C. The *Brown v. Board of Education* legal case of 1954 struck down the "separate but equal" doctrine in public schools during this time. The Supreme Court determined that state-mandated segregated schools were inherently unequal and discriminatory.

Grades K–6 Preview Test

This preview test of the PLT Grades K–6 test (0522) is designed to give you an overall sense of the test's format and to help you self-diagnose content areas you need to study. This preview test will *not* help you with your pacing on the test—this preview is approximately half the length of the actual PLT and may not represent the entire scope of the test in either content or difficulty.

After you complete the preview test, score your answers and use the explanations to determine which content areas you need to study in Part III of this guide. You may also want to complete the preview tests in Chapters 1, 3, and 4. Even though these additional preview tests are written for other PLT test grade levels, the topics of the questions—Students as Learners, Instruction and Assessment, Communication Techniques, and Teacher Professionalism—remain the same.

Case I

Directions: The case history is followed by three constructed-response questions. Read the case history and then respond to the three questions.

Scenario: Miss Webb

Miss Webb knows that she is facing a challenging school year, so she is getting started on long-range and short-range planning in early August. Her neighborhood school has closed as part of a redistricting and consolidation plan, so her third-graders will not attend the same school that their older siblings attended. In addition, the district has adopted a new mathematics series that promotes problem-solving, higher-level thinking, and the use of manipulatives. Her principal has decided that she will be comparing last year's third-grade student performance in mathematics basic understanding and mathematics problem-solving to this year's students' performance in the same areas, so Miss Webb is feeling a bit anxious about her students' mathematics performance with all these changes in the district. The following documents provide samples of Miss Webb's short-term goals, long-term goals, and lesson plans for the start of the school year.

Document 1: Long-Term Goals

- My third-grade students will meet or exceed third-grade mathematics standards for problem-solving.
- Each of my third-grade students will have an older buddy or friend to make them feel a part of the school community.
- My third-grade students will show what they know about mathematics through written and oral work.

Document 2: Short-Term Goals

- My students will know the location of important places in the school building (such as the nurse's office, main office, emergency exits, restrooms, water fountains, and cafeteria).
- My students will meet weekly with a sixth-grade "buddy" for two main reasons: 1) to share mathematics problem-solving strategies and 2) to establish student relationships in order to build a positive school community.
- My students will explain "how they know" during mathematics problem-solving in order to demonstrate a variety of approaches to solving problems.

Document 3: Lesson Plan

Objective

Each third-grade student will learn the names of two sixth-grade students and be able to identify one interest of each older student.

Resources

Name cards, crayons, color pencils, photographs of sixth-grade buddies

Motivation

Today, we are going to meet our sixth-grade "buddies"! Before we do, let's think about three things you like to do. Perhaps you have a hobby, a talent, or a special interest that you like to do in the summer or after school.

Procedures

Warm-up: I really like to attend my children's basketball games, so basketball is one of my interests. What do you like to do? (Teacher asks for volunteers and then writes down contributions on a chart paper.) On this name card, you can see that I wrote my name in large, dark letters so that others can read my name from a distance. I have also drawn a picture of a basketball because it is one of my interests. I've also drawn a picture of my pet dog and another picture of flowers. I have three interests—basketball, pets, and gardening. I'd like you to write your name on your name card and draw pictures of three interests you have.

Preview

Your name cards look great, and it's so interesting to learn about all your interests! Now, let's bring our name cards and walk down the hall to our buddy classroom. Our sixth-grade buddies have also made name cards. You are going to have a chance to meet several sixth-graders and learn about their interests. By the end of our time in our buddy classroom, I'd like you to be able to tell us the name of two sixth-grade buddies and one interest that you learned about each sixth-grader. Our goal is to get to know older students who can be our buddies this year, help us learn more about our school, and help us solve both school problems and mathematics problems.

Teach

Miss Webb greets the buddy classroom teacher, Miss Orr, and both teachers discuss their interests, which are drawn on their name cards. After the teachers model the task, Miss Webb matches each of her third-grade students with a sixth-grade student and asks the students to introduce them and share interests. After a few minutes, Miss Webb asks the students to greet another student and repeats this procedure one more time.

Assessment

Third-grade students return to their own classroom and, using the photographs of the sixth-grade buddies that are posted on a classroom bulletin board, state the student's name and one interest. If more than one student has met this sixth-grader, more interests may emerge. Miss Webb uses a checklist with her students' names and writes in the sixth-grade buddy's name and interests as stated. She then reviews the name cards from the sixth-graders to verify accuracy of names and interests. In future lessons, Miss Webb will use this checklist to match up third-graders and sixth-graders who have common interests or appear to have made personal connections.

Independent Work

Students will be encouraged to look for and greet their buddies on the school bus, in their neighborhoods, in the hallways, and on the playground. When students find their buddies in school and in the local community, they can return to class and share this buddy connection by writing the places they saw the buddies on stickers and posting the stickers next to the sixth-grader's photographs.

Directions: Questions 1–3 require you to write short answers, or "constructed responses." You are not expected to cite specific theories or texts in your answers; however, your knowledge of specific principles of learning and teaching will be evaluated. Be sure to answer all parts of the question. Write your answers in the space provided.

1. Consider Miss Webb's short-term goals. Identify ONE short-term goal and write a lesson plan to help her students work toward this goal. Be sure to base your response in principles of instruction and assessment.

2. Consider Miss Webb's long-term goal "My third grade students will meet or exceed third-grade mathematics standards for problem-solving." Offer THREE suggestions to help Miss Webb attain this goal. Be sure to base your response in principles of instruction and assessment as well as teacher professionalism.

3. Suggest TWO ways in which Miss Webb can assess her students' growth as mathematical problem-solvers during their work in the classroom and during sixth-grade buddy sessions. Be sure to base your response in principles of assessment and communication techniques.

Case II

Directions: The case history is followed by three constructed-response questions. Read the case history and then respond to the three questions.

Scenario: Stafford

The Teacher Support Team (TST) is designed to support teachers' attempts to resolve instructional problems for their students with academic, emotional, social, or behavioral issues. The team is comprised of the school principal, the team guidance counselor, a reading specialist, a special education teacher, a school psychologist, a classroom teacher, and the teacher who refers a student referral. Caregivers, a school social worker, and the school nurse are invited to attend when appropriate. The goal of the TST is to offer instructional strategies to classroom teachers in an effort to provide education services in a student's least restrictive environment. For students who are not making adequate yearly progress, the TST may recommend further testing by specialists.

Mrs. King is an experienced second-grade teacher who has requested a meeting of the TST to discuss her student, Stafford. The TST reviewed the background information prepared by Mrs. King on Stafford, an 8-year-old second-grader in her classroom. Stafford lives with both his mother and father, as well as two older sisters. His primary language is English, and he appears to be in good physical health based on records from the nurse's office. Stafford did not attend preschool. He stayed home with his mother while his two older sisters attended school. He attended the public school district's half-day kindergarten, where he had limited success learning the alphabet, had trouble with concepts about print, and experienced difficulty with appropriate social and emotional behaviors when he faced academic or social challenges in the classroom. In first grade, Stafford lagged behind his peers in reading and writing development. Now in second grade, Stafford loves listening to stories read aloud but rarely reads independently. He enjoys the listening center and chooses the building or blocks center every opportunity he gets. He enjoys recess time where he can demonstrate his advanced gross motor skills and enjoys being chosen as the teacher's helper.

At the TST meeting, Mrs. King described the problems Stafford is experiencing in second grade. He is becoming a classroom bully; he has frequent outbursts when asked to complete his reading or writing work. In addition, Mrs. King has noticed that Stafford has difficulty hearing rhythm, rhyme, and syllables in poetry or language arts exercises. Mrs. King added that she has met with Stafford's parents, who share her concerns about Stafford's lack of reading progress and his increasing outbursts during homework time at home. Stafford's parents mentioned that they recently purchased a phonics-based home study program to help their child with reading and would appreciate any support Mrs. King can give them.

Mrs. King has tried the following strategies to support Stafford's reading and writing development:

- Moved his seat to the front of the classroom, near the teacher's instruction.
- Placed him in a reading group at his instructional level. Stafford is alone in this group and receives one-on-one instruction from Mrs. King for 15 minutes each day.
- Provided opportunities to read along with books on tape in the listening center.
- Asked Stafford to make signs for the blocks and building center.

After meeting with the TST team and Stafford's parents, Mrs. King would like suggestions for new strategies to try in the classroom, but she also would like the support of her colleagues' expertise. She has requested that a reading specialist or a special educator conduct an in-depth evaluation of Stafford's strengths and weaknesses.

Directions: Questions 4–6 require you to write short answers, or "constructed responses." You are not expected to cite specific theories or texts in your answers; however, your knowledge of specific principles of learning and teaching will be evaluated. Be sure to answer all parts of the question. Write your answers in the space provided.

4. Identify ONE strategy Mrs. King hasn't tried to support Stafford's diverse learning needs. Be sure to base your response in principles of learning and teaching.

5. Suggest ONE reason why Stafford may benefit from an evaluation for reading intervention or special education. Be sure to base your rationale in principles of student learning.

6. Suggest ONE way not already offered in the scenario that Stafford's parents can support Stafford's literacy development at home. Be sure to base your response on principles of teacher professionalism or communication techniques.

Discrete Multiple-Choice Questions

Directions: Questions 7–18 are not related to the previous cases. For each question, select the best answer and mark the corresponding letter space on your answer sheet.

ANSWER SHEET

7 Ⓐ Ⓑ Ⓒ Ⓓ
8 Ⓐ Ⓑ Ⓒ Ⓓ
9 Ⓐ Ⓑ Ⓒ Ⓓ
10 Ⓐ Ⓑ Ⓒ Ⓓ
11 Ⓐ Ⓑ Ⓒ Ⓓ
12 Ⓐ Ⓑ Ⓒ Ⓓ
13 Ⓐ Ⓑ Ⓒ Ⓓ
14 Ⓐ Ⓑ Ⓒ Ⓓ
15 Ⓐ Ⓑ Ⓒ Ⓓ
16 Ⓐ Ⓑ Ⓒ Ⓓ
17 Ⓐ Ⓑ Ⓒ Ⓓ
18 Ⓐ Ⓑ Ⓒ Ⓓ

7. B. F. Skinner and other behavior theorists recommend teachers first identify the student behavior they are trying to change, reward the positives, and then

   A. provide consequences for the negative behavior.
   B. reward the negative behavior.
   C. ignore the negative behavior.
   D. contact the parent/guardian about the negative behavior.

8. A fourth-grade teacher gives a spelling pretest for which of the following reasons?

   A. Vygotsky's "zone of proximal development"
   B. Ausubel's theory of advance organizers
   C. McCarthy's 4MAT with the pretest as the first of four activities
   D. Kohlberg's theory of moral development

9. Glen is a fifth-grader who appears to learn best through visual learning experiences. Which of the following techniques might help him learn best in his social studies class?

   A. Activity exploration
   B. Tape-recording teacher's lessons
   C. Using the overhead projector
   D. Completing questions and answers at the end of the chapter

10. A sixth-grade teacher offers "prizes" such as homework passes and pencils for quality work and good behavior. The primary rationale for such rewards is to improve students' behavior through

   A. humanistic motivation.
   B. internal motivation.
   C. intrinsic motivation.
   D. extrinsic motivation.

11. When planning a sixth social studies unit on immigration to the United States, the teacher hopes to introduce her students to primary source documents as required by state and national standards. Which of the following primary source documents will best support this unit on immigration?

    A. A letter from a soldier at Pearl Harbor

    B. An Army recruiting poster

    C. A medical screening form from Ellis Island

    D. A short story on coming to America at the turn of the century

12. Which of the following questions is an example of a "knowledge" question in Bloom's Taxonomy of the cognitive domain?

    A. What do you think is the author's message?

    B. Who can tell us the setting of the story?

    C. Where did the boy go to school?

    D. How would you rate this story and why?

13. Students who have difficulty working in cooperative groups and expect the teacher to provide answers to questions may be experiencing differences in

    A. mood.

    B. cultural expectations.

    C. intrapersonal skills.

    D. attention to directions.

14. A teacher-made multiple-choice test is an example of which of the following?

    A. Criterion-referenced assessment

    B. Norm-referenced assessment

    C. Performance assessment

    D. Embedded assessment

Questions 15–16 are based on the following passages, which are from a debate about the advantages and disadvantages of using published school reading program materials.

Why Published School Reading Program Materials Are Effective

Published school reading program materials are based on scientifically based best practice in reading instruction and are written by well-known researchers in the field. In order to receive federal funding in our K–6 school, we must use proven instructional methods as required by the No Child Left Behind Act (NCLB). Published school reading program materials offer an easy and effective solution to difficult curriculum revision decisions. Our school does not have the time or the resources to write a curriculum given all the other demands on our teaching staff. Published reading programs provide a detailed teacher's manual and a variety of instructional support materials that are very helpful to beginning teachers and those teachers who do not know how to use scientifically based reading best practices in classrooms today.

Why Published School Reading Program Materials Are Ineffective

Teachers should teach with a variety of materials and methods to meet the diverse needs of learners in classrooms today. Children should learn to read and read to learn with authentic works in order to achieve real, purposeful, and meaningful literacy tasks. Children have little opportunity to select their own reading, an important literacy strategy. The skills-based approach of these programs usually presents skills in isolation and become boring and meaningless for many children. Furthermore, the extraordinary expense of purchasing a published reading program and maintaining these materials usually prohibits inclusion of quality children's literature, big books, and trade books in the budget. Perhaps the most damaging effect of published reading programs is the disempowerment of the teacher as decision-maker in the classroom. The teachers' manual is designed to be teacher-proof—anyone can teach reading to any child because all the decisions are research-based.

15. The first passage advances the idea that published reading programs are scientifically based and contain ideas for best practice. In the view of the author of the second passage, if your district requires the use of such materials, which of the following is essential when teaching K–6 in schools today?

   A. Lesson plans are done for you.
   B. Well-known leaders in literacy wrote these materials.
   C. Teachers modify lessons to meet the diverse needs of students.
   D. These materials are teacher-proof.

16. The author of the second passage believes that

   A. teachers should take three or more courses in reading methods.
   B. teachers benefit from the teachers' manuals in published reading programs.
   C. teachers need to learn to teach reading well.
   D. teachers are decision-makers.

17. Which of the following is the name of the published reading program introduced in 1841 that had themed lessons on honesty, truthfulness, and promptness?

   A. Dick and Jane Series
   B. Spot and Dot Basals
   C. McGuffey Readers
   D. Exploration Series

18. Special education and related services specifically designed to meet the special needs of students are called which of the following?

   A. No Child Left Behind Act
   B. American with Disabilities Act
   C. Interdisciplinary Education Plan
   D. Individualized Education Plan

Answers and Explanations

Case I

Cases, or "constructed responses," are graded holistically on a scale of 0–2, with 0 being the lowest score. For details on this type of question, be sure to read Chapter 5. In this section, you'll find the content categories and suggested content to include in your case study responses. For more information about the content category, you can study Chapters 7, 8, 9, and 10. The suggested content is designed to help you get a sense of the type of response required, but it may not cover all the correct options in such an open-ended question. You may also find it helpful to share your constructed responses with an education professor, adviser, or educator.

1. **Suggested content:** Restate one of the short-term goals from Document 2 in the Miss Webb Scenario and then detail a lesson plan that would directly support that goal. The lesson plan should contain all the components from the lesson plan in Document 3—objectives, resources, motivation (or anticipatory set), warm-up (or review), preview (which contains a statement of the lesson's purpose), teaching methods/procedures, and assessment plans.

2. **Suggested content:** Three suggestions for attaining the long-term goal "Third-grade students will meet or exceed third-grade mathematics standards for problem-solving" include, but are not limited to, reading professional literature on mathematics problem-solving and using manipulatives to solve problems, setting grade-level benchmarks for exemplary problem-solving, and attending professional development offered by the district or local colleges.

3. **Suggested content:** Include two ways Miss Webb can study her students' growth as mathematical problem-solvers, such as teacher action research, comparing benchmark papers, examining student work from this year and last, and keeping a professional journal with reflections on student performance and problem-solving processes.

Case II

4. **Suggested content:** Strategies Mrs. King can employ to support Stafford's learning needs include, but are not limited to, trying a targeted intervention in phonics or phonemic instruction, asking the reading specialist to assess Stafford's literacy strengths and weaknesses, listening to Stafford read aloud and note his miscues and strategies, and including more kinesthetic experiences when teaching literacy, including role play and tactile experiences with letters.

5. **Suggested content:** Stafford might benefit from an evaluation by a reading specialist or special educator for the following reasons: he may have a learning disability, may have attentional difficulty, or may not have had the prior experiences to prepare him academically for reading and writing in second grade.

6. **Suggested content:** Stafford's parents can continue to support literacy experiences at home by reading aloud and discussing the reading with Stafford; playing word games; writing letters, lists, and other authentic documents at home; going to the library together; and modeling reading and writing.

Discrete Multiple-Choice Questions

Answer Key			
Question	*Answer*	*Content Category*	*Where to Get More Help*
7.	A	Students as Learners	Chapter 7
8.	A	Students as Learners	Chapter 7
9.	C	Students as Learners	Chapter 7
10.	D	Students as Learners	Chapter 7
11.	C	Instruction and Assessment	Chapter 8
12.	C	Instruction and Assessment	Chapter 8
13.	B	Instruction and Assessment	Chapter 8
14.	A	Instruction and Assessment	Chapter 8
15.	C	Teacher Professionalism	Chapter 10
16.	D	Teacher Professionalism	Chapter 10
17.	C	Teacher Professionalism	Chapter 10
18.	D	Teacher Professionalism	Chapter 10

Explanations

7. A. According to Skinner's behaviorist theory, providing consequences for negative behavior is the best response. Choices B and C are ways to provide consequences for the negative behavior but are too narrow and may not be best for certain behaviors and situations.

8. A. Vygotsky's "zone of proximal development" is based on a teacher finding the best information to teach a student next. The spelling pretest is one way for the teacher to find out which words to teach his students to spell next.

9. C. Visual learners learn by seeing information. In addition to using the overhead projector, the teacher could use graphic organizers, facial expressions, body language, and video to convey new content.

10. D. Extrinsic motivation is from without, or outside of the learner. Intrinsic motivation is from within and is the most desirable type of motivation. Teachers sometimes use small rewards or tokens to motivate students, but teachers should strive to help students realize the intrinsic rewards for learning.

11. C. Primary source documents enable teachers and students to get as close as possible to an actual historical event or time period. The best primary source document related to U.S. immigration is the medical screening document from Ellis Island.

12. C. Knowledge level questions require students to recall specific facts and terms from the material. Choice A is a comprehension level question. Choice B requires analysis. Choice D is at the evaluation level of Bloom's Taxonomy of cognitive development.

13. B. In some cultures, teachers are seen as the primary source of knowledge, and students expect the teacher to be the only one in the classroom to present information. Cooperative learning groups require students to rely on one another as sources of information and expect the teacher to facilitate, not lead, instruction. This disconnect between home and school cultures is the best reason presented for why the student is having difficulty working in the group.

14. A. A criterion-referenced test is made up of questions based on predetermined criteria, such as the teacher's lesson objectives or unit plan goals.

15. C. Even if required to use district-mandated materials, teachers must remember that they are instructional decision-makers who should modify lessons to meet the diverse needs of students.

16. D. The author of the second passage states, "Perhaps the most damaging effect of published reading program materials is the disempowerment of teachers." A person with this view sees teachers as decision-makers who know the needs of their students.

17. C. The McGuffey Readers, published in 1841 and very moralistic in tone, were one of the earliest published school reading program materials.

18. D. An Individualized Education Plan (IEP) is a document written for an individual learner who has documented learning differences. The IEP plans for all areas of difference, related services to support the child, and needed accommodations in regular and special education settings.

Grades 5–9 Preview Test

This preview test of the PLT Grades 5–9 (0523) is designed to give you an overall sense of the test's format and to help you self-diagnose content areas you need to study. This preview test will *not* help you with your pacing on the test—this preview is approximately half the length of the actual PLT and may not represent the entire scope of the test in either content or difficulty.

After you complete the preview test, score your answers and use the explanations to help you determine which content areas to study in Part III of this guide. You may also want to complete the preview tests in Chapters 1, 2, and 4 to help you determine content areas to study. Even though these additional preview tests are written for other PLT test grade levels, the topics of the questions—Students as Learners, Instruction and Assessment, Communication Techniques, and Teacher Professionalism—remain the same.

Case I

Directions: The case history is followed by three constructed-response questions. Read the case history and then respond to the three questions.

Scenario: Mr. Enright and Mr. Toll

Two middle-level social studies teachers at Plainville School couldn't be further apart in their approaches, but both teachers are well respected for their eighth-grade students' success. Mr. Enright involves students actively in learning content through history simulations, webquests, dramatic reenactments, and project-based learning. Mr. Toll uses lectures, worksheets, and textbook questions and answers to teach the same history content. Mr. Toll sees himself as an "explainer" of important historic events. He often uses an advance organizer to start a lesson and study guides to help students prepare for tests. The following documents show recent lesson plans on the Civil War written by each teacher.

Document 1: Mr. Enright's Civil War Lesson Plan

Objective

The student will discuss the primary causes of the Civil War from a variety of perspectives.

Resources

Costumes from Civil War period, music from the Civil War, primary source documents, chart paper, markers

Motivation

Mr. Enright opens the class dressed as President Abraham Lincoln and introduces his "guests," Robert Barnwell Rhett of South Carolina (the principal dressed as this political leader of the South) and Henry Ward Brown of Connecticut (the physical education teacher dressed as this abolitionist leader of the North). The three adults lead a dramatic reenactment of a discussion on the causes of the Civil War.

Warm-up

Mr. Enright thanks his "guests" to the students' applause and leads the students in creating a KWL chart to elicit their prior knowledge of the Civil War and to help students set purposes for learning more about the Civil War's causes from multiple perspectives.

Preview

Mr. Enright tells the students that they will learn about the causes of the Civil War and will be able to discuss the causes from various perspectives, specifically from Abraham Lincoln's view and from the view of leaders from the North and South.

Teach

Mr. Enright divides his class into three heterogeneous groups to read and discuss the primary documents found at their table. One group studies Abraham Lincoln's view of the war's causes; one studies Northern leaders' views; and the third studies Southern leaders' views. The students use chart paper and markers at the table to complete the following graphic organizer as a group:

Students discuss the quotes, who said each one, and meanings. Then, after giving them time to write at least three ideas on the chart paper, Mr. Enright has the groups change tables and read the information and contribute additional information to the other charts.

After the three groups have moved to all three information tables and have had a chance to make a contribution to the charts, Mr. Enright gathers the students as a whole group and the class reviews the charts. Mr. Enright closes the lesson by impersonating President Lincoln again. He summarizes what the students have learned so far and then assigns homework.

Assessment

Mr. Enright observes the students' participation in the group discussion and evaluates students' individual contributions in the closing discussion. He also individually assesses the homework for content accuracy.

Independent Work

The homework requires students to write three paragraphs summarizing the three different views on the causes of the Civil War as a review of the day's class work.

Document 2: Mr. Toll's Civil War Lesson Plan

Objective

The student will discuss and write about the primary causes of the Civil War.

Resources

- Social studies textbook
- Online resources

Motivation

Mr. Toll provides an advance organizer with an outline of the textbook chapter on the causes of the Civil War.

Warm-up

Mr. Toll uses a computer projector to show the class a credible source website that discusses the causes of the Civil War. The students take turns reading the information from the website out loud and discuss important or difficult material as they go.

Preview

Mr. Toll tells the students that they will learn about the primary causes of the Civil War and will be able to discuss and write about those causes.

Teach

Mr. Toll asks the students individually to read the social studies text chapter section on the causes of the Civil War and use the advance organizer to guide their reading. After the students finish reading, Mr. Toll leads a lecture on the causes of the Civil War and asks students questions to check for understanding. To close the lesson, Mr. Toll summarizes the primary causes of the Civil War and assigns homework.

Assessment

Mr. Toll observes student involvement in reading the online text and individual reading of the textbook. He informally assesses students' contributions to the discussion. He individually grades the homework for content accuracy.

Independent Work

For homework, the students individually write their answers to the four questions at the end of the chapter.

Directions: Questions 1–3 require you to write short answers, or "constructed responses." You are not expected to cite specific theories or texts in your answers; however, your knowledge of specific principles of learning and teaching will be evaluated. Be sure to answer all parts of the question. Write your answers in the space provided.

---

1. Identify ONE student learning style that may find success in Mr. Toll's room and ONE student learning style that may find success in Mr. Enright's room. Be sure to base your response in principles of student learning and instruction.

2. Suggest TWO ways Mr. Toll can learn more about Mr. Enright's methods for teaching social studies and communicate with his colleague. Be sure to base your response in principles of teacher professionalism and communication techniques.

3. Suggest ONE way Mr. Toll can modify his instruction to meet the needs of all learners. Suggest ONE way Mr. Enright can modify his instruction to meet the needs of all learners. Be sure to base your response in principles of students as learners and instruction.

Case II

Directions: The case history is followed by three constructed-response questions. Read the case history and then respond to the three questions.

Scenario: Mrs. Pendola

Mrs. Pendola is thrilled to have the opportunity to teach in the town in which she was educated more than 20 years ago. A few of her former teachers at Lincoln Middle School are still teaching, the building looks the same, and the principal is the same, but the school's student body has changed over the years—racially, ethnically, linguistically, and economically.

Fifty percent of the student body is Hispanic; 13% is white; 31% is African American; 5% is Asian; and 1% is Native American. Fifteen percent of the student body receives English language learner or bilingual education services. The students in Mrs. Pendola's seventh-grade class speak more than ten different languages besides English. Sixteen percent of the student body receives special education services. Forty-six percent of the student body at Lincoln School receives free or reduced lunch.

Mrs. Pendola has set three professional goals for the school year:

- To create a positive, respectful learning environment in which all of her students can achieve high standards
- To get to know each student and his or her family
- To actively engage students in meaningful learning experiences

Her first unit is called "That Was Then, This Is Now." The students will read S. E. Hinton's novel *That Was Then, This Is Now* in her reading/language arts class. The following activity demonstrates how Mrs. Pendola has chosen to kick off the unit and to begin to achieve her professional goals.

That Was Then, This is Now

Mrs. Pendola shares her seventh-grade class picture when she attended Lincoln School two decades ago. She tells a bit about her "favorites"—friends, subjects, activities, and teachers. She also explains a bit about the make-up of her nuclear family and some of their traditions. As she shares this information, she allows students to ask questions and adds the information to a large chart paper. This provides a model for her students. Next, she asks her students to think back to their lives one decade ago, to when they were around three years old. She smiles and adds that they weren't born two decades ago! She asks the students to write down information about friends, activities, teachers (if they attended preschool), or caregivers who taught them something, who they lived with, and what some of their traditions were. For homework, she asks the students to speak with adults at home and review baby books or photo albums to add more information to their visuals. She also asks each student to bring a photo or drawing from this period. The students share their work the next day, and Mrs. Pendola posts their photos next to each student's first day of school photograph she has taken.

Directions: Questions 4–6 require you to write short answers, or "constructed responses." You are not expected to cite specific theories or texts in your answers; however, your knowledge of specific principles of learning and teaching will be evaluated. Be sure to answer all parts of the question. Write your answers in the space provided.

---

4. Suggest ONE way Mrs. Pendola can achieve her first goal: to create a positive, respectful learning environment in which all students can achieve high standards. Be sure to base your response in principles of learning and teaching.

---

5. Suggest ONE way Mrs. Pendola can achieve her second goal: to get to know each student and his or her family. Be sure to base your response in principles of learning and teaching.

6. Suggest ONE way Mrs. Pendola can achieve her third goal: to actively engage students in meaningful learning experiences. Be sure to base your response in principles of learning and teaching.

_____

_____

_____

_____

_____

_____

_____

_____

_____

_____

_____

_____

_____

_____

_____

_____

_____

_____

_____

_____

_____

_____

_____

_____

Discrete Multiple-Choice Questions

Directions: Questions 7–18 are not related to the previous cases. For each question, select the best answer and mark the corresponding letter space on your answer sheet.

ANSWER SHEET

7 Ⓐ Ⓑ Ⓒ Ⓓ
8 Ⓐ Ⓑ Ⓒ Ⓓ
9 Ⓐ Ⓑ Ⓒ Ⓓ
10 Ⓐ Ⓑ Ⓒ Ⓓ
11 Ⓐ Ⓑ Ⓒ Ⓓ
12 Ⓐ Ⓑ Ⓒ Ⓓ
13 Ⓐ Ⓑ Ⓒ Ⓓ
14 Ⓐ Ⓑ Ⓒ Ⓓ
15 Ⓐ Ⓑ Ⓒ Ⓓ
16 Ⓐ Ⓑ Ⓒ Ⓓ
17 Ⓐ Ⓑ Ⓒ Ⓓ
18 Ⓐ Ⓑ Ⓒ Ⓓ

7. Mrs. Basel asks her seventh-graders to complete a collage titled "Who Am I?" during the first weeks of middle school. She is most likely supporting which of the following human development stages from Erikson's theory?

A. autonomy vs. doubt
B. integrity vs. despair
C. risk vs. safety
D. identity vs. role confusion

8. Mary, a student in a fifth-grade mathematics class, relies on her 100's chart to help her complete multiplication problems. She is most likely working at which of the following stages of Piaget's theory of cognitive development?

A. concrete operational
B. formal operations
C. preoperational
D. hierarchical

Questions 9–10 are based on the following passage.

Mr. DePasquale has three bilingual students in his eighth-grade social studies class and one student who is an English language learner. He works to build on students' language and cultural "funds of knowledge." He seeks the advice of the teacher of English language learners (TELL) to ensure that he is meeting the needs of his student still learning to learn in English.

9. Mr. DePasquale most likely sees the cultural and language differences of his students as

A. teaching differences.
B. sources of enrichment.
C. sources of difficulty.
D. an added challenge.

10. One important consideration for Mr. DePasquale to be mindful of when teaching English language learners according to the TELL is that ELL students may

    A. be absent frequently.
    B. be required to speak only in English in his classroom.
    C. be silent or contribute less to class discussion.
    D. need frequent breaks.

11. Mrs. Shackleton, a ninth-grade English teacher, has set the following objective for her students:

Students will demonstrate appreciation of the author's message and use of language in *Night,* by Elie Weisel, in a written essay.

Mrs. Shackleton's objective is best categorized by which domain of objectives?

    A. affective
    B. cognitive
    C. deductive
    D. psychomotor

12. Mrs. Munroe, a fifth-grade teacher, holds class meetings to discuss conflicts that come up in the classroom. She focuses on behaviors rather than students to help her students resolve conflicts. Her classroom management philosophy is based on which of the following theories?

    A. Canter's assertive discipline
    B. Glasser's control theory
    C. Kounin's management plan
    D. Hunter's direct instruction

13. Prior to calling on a student to respond to his questions about the Crusades, Mr. Edmonds asks students to think, pair with another student to discuss ideas, and then raise hands to share responses. Mr. Edmonds is using which of the following modifications to his lesson to help all students succeed?

    A. inquiry, response, inquiry
    B. hands-on experiences
    C. direct instruction
    D. cooperative learning

14. Miss Weeks, a sixth-grade social studies teacher, teaches a unit on the Medieval period in which her students are assigned the task of creating a village from this period that includes activities, dress, food, and occupations. She provides a rubric that includes criteria for achieving acceptable, exemplary, or unsatisfactory success on this assignment. This project can be described as which of the following assessments?

    A. local assessment
    B. self-assessment
    C. performance assessment
    D. standardized assessment

15. Miss Hoyt spends a lot of time after teaching her lessons thinking about her students' interactions and considers both the intended and unintended consequences of her instruction. One best describes Miss Hoyt as a

A. novice teacher.

B. cooperating teacher.

C. master teacher.

D. reflective teacher.

16. Mrs. Friedman's eighth-grade class is working on writing a poem when she notices that Jimmy is not working and is looking frustrated and angry. She offers to brainstorm ideas to include in the poem, and Jimmy says that doing so will not help because he's not good at rhyming anyway. Which of the following responses by Mrs. Friedman best demonstrates her ability as a reflective practitioner and teacher of writing?

A. "Everyone needs to write a poem for his or her portfolio. You can use the dictionary, but you need to get started."

B. "You can work with Mary, who is good at writing, Jimmy, but you need to get something written before the end of class."

C. "It is difficult to find the right words when writing poetry, Jimmy. I suggest we first brainstorm ideas together and then find a type of poetry that best matches your ideas. Not all poems need to rhyme."

D. "You can help me correct math papers now, and we will find another assignment for you to complete during recess."

17. Mrs. Smith is planning to meet with her students' caregivers for sixth-grade parent/teacher conferences. Which of the following is NOT something Mrs. Smith should plan to do?

A. be positive

B. share information about the rest of the students

C. be prepared

D. highlight students' strengths

18. This education leader organized annual education conventions and helped create the first U.S. schools for training teachers.

A. Horace Mann

B. John Dewey

C. Jean Piaget

D. Edward Thorndike

Answers and Explanations

Case I

Cases, or "constructed responses," are graded holistically on a scale of 0–2, with 0 being the lowest score. For details on this type of question, be sure to read Chapter 5. In this section, you'll find the content categories and suggested content to include in your case study responses. For more information about the content category, you can study Chapters 7, 8, 9, and 10. The suggested content is designed to help you get a sense of the type of response required, but it may not cover all the correct options in such an open-ended question. You may also find it helpful to share your constructed responses with an education professor, adviser, or educator.

1. **Suggested content**: Students who may find more success in Mr. Toll's social studies class may have a verbal linguistic multiple intelligence, may have an auditory learning style, or may have lots of background knowledge in this content area.

   Students who may find more success in Mr. Enright's social studies class may have a kinesthetic or tactile learning style, may have bodily-kinesthetic multiple intelligence, or may have limited background knowledge of this content, which is further developed through the social experiences in this classroom.

2. **Suggested content:** Mr. Toll could read professional journals, attend conferences, or join a listserv run by a social studies professional association. Ways to communicate include sharing lesson ideas, discussing student work, conducting learning walks, and sharing a visit to classrooms of other teachers using these methods.

3. **Suggested content:** Mr. Toll's students might benefit from more frequent check-ins, step-by-step instructions, graphic organizers on which to take notes, or additional kinesthetic, or hands-on, experiences with the content, such as concrete examples, making a TV show, or creating a visual representation.

   Mr. Enright's students might benefit from frequent check-ins (especially during long-term projects), guided discovery questions and discussion, and individual accountability during group work to ensure that students are retaining content objectives.

Case II

4. **Suggested content:** Ways to create a positive, respectful learning environment with high standards for all include, but are not limited to, cooperative learning, responsive classroom class meetings, conflict resolution modeling and discussion, Glasser's Control Theory, and Glasser's Assertive Discipline model.

5. **Suggested content:** Mrs. Pendola can get to know her students and their families in the following ways: holding monthly events in the classroom (both during the day and in the evening), conducting an interest inventory for students and family members, distributing monthly newsletters in English and in the family's home language, and goal-setting with the students with family input.

6. **Suggested content:** Mrs. Pendola can actively engage her diverse learning in the following ways: project-based learning, simulations, cooperative learning, and discovery learning.

Discrete Multiple-Choice Questions

Answer Key			
Question	**Answer**	**Content Category**	**Where to Get More Help**
7.	D	Students as Learners	Chapter 7
8.	A	Students as Learners	Chapter 7
9.	B	Students as Learners	Chapter 7
10.	C	Students as Learners	Chapter 7
11.	A	Instruction and Assessment	Chapter 8
12.	B	Instruction and Assessment	Chapter 8
13.	D	Instruction and Assessment	Chapter 8
14.	C	Instruction and Assessment	Chapter 8
15.	D	Teacher Professionalism	Chapter 10
16.	C	Teacher Professionalism	Chapter 10
17.	B	Teacher Professionalism	Chapter 10
18.	A	Teacher Professionalism	Chapter 10

Explanations

7. D. Erikson suggests that the stage of identity vs. role confusion is typically addressed during adolescence, ages 12 to 18, and is the single most significant conflict a person faces. Choices A and B are also stages in Erikson's theory. Choice C is a distractor—a choice not based on any theory.

8. A. Children 7–11 years of age typically operate in the concrete operational stage of cognitive development, in which they reason logically with familiar situations. Choices B and C are also stages of Piaget's theory. Choice D is a distractor.

9. B. According to Luis Moll, when a teacher considers students' culture and language as "funds of knowledge," he sees this diversity as enriching to a classroom community of learners.

10. C. Many English language learners experience a period of silence in the English-speaking classroom and may be less vocal in class discussions. English language learning takes time: usually up to two years for conversational literacy and five to seven years for academic English literacy.

11. A. The affective domain of objectives includes teaching and assessing students' values, attitudes, and beliefs.

12. B. Glasser's control theory suggests that teachers discuss behaviors, not students, in class meetings. In this constructivist approach, students listen to one another and arrive at compromises to resolve conflicts.

13. D. Cooperative learning instructional methods, such as think-pair-share, offer opportunities for students to talk to one another and to support one another's higher-level thinking.

14. C. A performance assessment is an authentic task that requires analysis and synthesis of information. Students must create a meaningful and purposeful response to demonstrate understanding of the course content. Students are given a rubric that delineates task criteria, and they are often asked to assess their own progress.

15. **D.** A reflective teacher or practitioner engages in thoughtful reconsideration of their students' behaviors and his or her instruction.

16. **C.** Mrs. Friedman responds reflectively by acknowledging Jimmy's difficulty emotionally and content-wise. She offers support and an alternative form of poetry as a possible solution to Jimmy's problem.

17. **B.** It is important for teachers to prepare for conferences with caregivers and to be positive and focus on students' strengths. Mrs. Smith should refrain from sharing information about other students in the classroom.

18. **A.** Horace Mann (1796–1859) attended Brown University, served as the first Secretary of Education in Massachusetts, and made significant contributions to teacher education in his lifetime.

Grades 7–12 Preview Test

This preview test of the PLT Grades 7–12 (0524) is designed to give you an overall sense of the test's format and to help you self-diagnose content areas you need to study. This preview test will *not* help you with your pacing on the test—this preview is approximately half the length of the actual PLT and may not represent the entire scope of the test in either content or difficulty.

After you complete the preview test, score your answers and use the explanations to help you determine which content areas to study in Part III of this guide. You may also want to complete the preview tests in Chapters 1, 2, and 3 to help you determine content areas to study. Even though these additional preview tests are written for other PLT test grade levels, the topics of the questions—Students as Learners, Instruction and Assessment, Communication Techniques, and Teacher Professionalism—remain the same.

Case I

Directions: The case history is followed by three constructed-response questions. Read the case history and then respond to the three questions.

Scenario: Jason

Jason is an eighth-grade student in Mr. Pope's health class. Jason shows great interest in the course content, actively participates in class, and responds well to Mr. Pope's enthusiastic and positive teaching style. Jason does very well with an assignment that Mr. Pope designed for a test grade and then repeats once a month throughout the marking period. Below is a brief synopsis of the assignment.

> Use the Internet or a magazine to find an article related to health and fitness. Write a summary of the article that includes at least three main health-related points and then make one connection between the article and your knowledge/experiences. Be sure to include the proper citation of your article and its source.

Mr. Pope introduced the assignment by providing a model and then offering direct instruction on how to write the summary. He also gave examples of personal connections between the article and his knowledge and experiences and showed the students how to add this information to the end of the summary. Mr. Pope modeled his writing process by thinking aloud and actually demonstrating his writing using the overhead projector. Mr. Pope's eighth-grade English teaching colleague teamed with Mr. Pope and planned to carefully teach how to cite Internet sources and periodicals. The two devised a guide sheet, which they provided to students and turned into a poster for both of their classrooms.

Jason earned a B on his first health summary because he misunderstood or did not read some of the directions carefully. In addition, the assignment was one day late. Jason got discouraged that he forgot his homework on his desk, which is a problem he often has with schoolwork. Mr. Pope has noticed that Jason's health binder is usually disorganized, and Jason frequently forgets to bring a pencil to class. Mr. Pope reviewed the second health summary assignment individually with Jason and checked with Jason to be sure he had an appropriate article a week before it was due. He also had his class work in pairs to discuss real-life connections to the topics of their articles during class time a few days before the next summaries were due. On the second assignment, Jason earned an A. He continued to earn A's on his other summary assignments, with the exception of one, which was submitted late. Jason became an active class contributor and appeared to be confident in his abilities to find health-related information on the Internet and in magazines, as well as in his ability to write a summary.

Directions: Questions 1–3 require you to write short answers, or "constructed responses." You are not expected to cite specific theories or texts in your answers; however, your knowledge of specific principles of learning and teaching will be evaluated. Be sure to answer all parts of the question. Write your answers in the space provided.

1. Identify TWO strengths of Mr. Pope's health assignment. Explain how each strength demonstrates aspects of effective planning. Be sure to base your response on principles of planning instruction.

2. Suggest TWO ways Mr. Pope could communicate to Jason to encourage him to achieve academic excellence. Be sure to include communication techniques based on teacher professionalism.

3. Identify TWO ways to make accommodations for a student with Jason's learning style. Be sure to base your response on principles of teaching students with diverse needs.

Case II

Directions: The case history is followed by three constructed-response questions. Read the case history and then respond to the three questions.

Scenario: Ms. Brousseau

Ms. Brousseau is a tenth-grade mathematics teacher of geometry. Her class has been grouped with average-achieving students, although, as one might imagine, her students have a wide range of knowledge, skills, and dispositions in mathematics. Several of her students have been identified as having diverse learning needs, such as attention deficit hyperactivity disorder (ADHD) and learning disabilities. She also has bilingual language learners in her class.

For a lesson on points, lines, and planes, she has the following objectives:

- The student will state whether an object suggests a point, a line, or a plane.
- The student will define the following terms: segment, intersection, and union.

She gathers the following materials and resources before her lesson begins: a replica of the Empire State Building, an art poster that involves lots of geometric shapes and repetition, a geometry textbook, an overhead projector, transparencies, and an overhead pen.

Opening of lesson: Ms. Brousseau shows a replica of the Empire State Building. She states, "We see geometry in the structures in which people live and work. Architects use geometry to create buildings. Artists use geometry to create art. Some of you may plan careers in these areas. Geometry is all around us. Let's take a look at the Empire State Building here." She asks students about their background knowledge related to this famous building and then asks them to identify points, lines, and planes using the replica. She continues the discussion and accessing of prior knowledge by sharing an art poster that involves lots of repetition of geometric shapes. She asks the students to identify points, lines, and planes in the art poster.

Middle of lesson: Ms. Brousseau uses direct explanation of points, lines, and planes as they relate to line segments, intersections, and unions. She uses the overhead projector to display examples from the geometry textbook and provides a definition of each term for students to write down in their notebooks. After trying a few problems together with teacher guidance, her students work alone to complete problems that require the application level of knowledge for each of these geometric terms.

Close of lesson: Ms. Brousseau asks students to review what they have learned today and how these terms are found in everyday life, besides her math class. She assigns homework that includes answering more application questions and finding a picture or replica of three real-life examples that suggest a point, a line, and a plane.

She assesses her students' participation in the lesson discussion and grades homework individually, making corrections as needed.

Directions: Questions 4–6 require you to write short answers, or "constructed responses." You are not expected to cite specific theories or texts in your answers; however, your knowledge of specific principles of learning and teaching will be evaluated. Be sure to answer all parts of the question. Write your answers in the space provided.

---

4. Identify TWO strengths of Ms. Brousseau's geometry lesson. Explain how each strength demonstrates aspects of effective planning. Be sure to base your response on principles of planning instruction.

5. Suggest TWO ways Ms. Brousseau could make additional accommodations for the diverse learners in her geometry class. Be sure to base your response on principles of teaching diverse learners.

6. Suggest TWO ways Ms. Brousseau can assess students' understanding of the lesson. Be sure to use the class experience and homework and to base your response on principles of assessment.

Discrete Multiple-Choice Questions

Directions: Questions 7–18 are not related to the previous cases. For each question, select the best answer and mark the corresponding letter space on your answer sheet.

ANSWER SHEET

```
 7  Ⓐ Ⓑ Ⓒ Ⓓ
 8  Ⓐ Ⓑ Ⓒ Ⓓ
 9  Ⓐ Ⓑ Ⓒ Ⓓ
10  Ⓐ Ⓑ Ⓒ Ⓓ
11  Ⓐ Ⓑ Ⓒ Ⓓ
12  Ⓐ Ⓑ Ⓒ Ⓓ
13  Ⓐ Ⓑ Ⓒ Ⓓ
14  Ⓐ Ⓑ Ⓒ Ⓓ
15  Ⓐ Ⓑ Ⓒ Ⓓ
16  Ⓐ Ⓑ Ⓒ Ⓓ
17  Ⓐ Ⓑ Ⓒ Ⓓ
18  Ⓐ Ⓑ Ⓒ Ⓓ
```

7. Carol Gilligan was a student of Lawrence Kohlberg who derived her own theories of moral development in people. Her theory is best known as

  A. feminist theory.
  B. an ethic of care.
  C. gender equity.
  D. cognitive development.

8. Mr. Robinson's 12th-grade student Danielle often demonstrates a genuine interest in the welfare of others in her classroom discourse, her involvement in community service, and her written work. Danielle may have achieved which level of Kohlberg's stages of moral development?

  A. Conventional
  B. Anticonventional
  C. Postconventional
  D. Preconventional

Questions 9–10 are based on the following passage.

Theresa is an 11th-grade student who has been at South High School for a year. Her parents recently filed bankruptcy because of a failed small-business investment and plan to move again next month in order to find work. Theresa's grades have begun to decline, and she is often alone at lunch and in the hallways.

9. According to Maslow's hierarchy of needs, which of the following may be affecting Theresa?

  A. Self-actualization
  B. Esteem
  C. Safety
  D. Synthesis

10. Theresa's new teachers have been informed by her former teachers that Theresa's family has a pattern of migration in pursuit of work opportunities. An accommodation that may best support Theresa is

    A. involving parents in planning and decision-making for Theresa.

    B. more time on tests.

    C. cooperative learning.

    D. independent study.

11. Which of the following is not teacher-centered instruction?

    A. Direct instruction

    B. Mastery learning

    C. Expository instruction

    D. Discovery learning

12. According to Canter's model, which of the following statements is true?

    A. Teachers must show their students they are "with it."

    B. Teachers must maintain a positive, caring, and productive classroom.

    C. Teachers must try to keep the whole class involved.

    D. Teachers must be aware of the "ripple effect."

13. A teacher with a laissez-faire approach to classroom management:

    A. Uses discussion to determine rules with students

    B. Uses rewards and punishments to change student behavior

    C. Establishes no rules, and students do what they want

    D. Establishes rules, and students do what they want

14. A test that measures what it is designed to measure is considered

    A. reliable.

    B. valid.

    C. usable.

    D. normative.

Questions 15–16 are based on the following passages, which are from a debate about student-centered versus teacher-centered instructional methods.

Student-Centered Instruction Is More Effective

Student-centered instruction involves more student input, self-monitoring, and responsibility. If teachers' primary goal is to teach students to learn to be reflective, responsible adults, then teachers should use student-centered methods. When students have opportunities to give input into what is taught and how, they develop more ownership, which motivates them intrinsically. Students who know how to self-monitor learning know what learning strategies work for them and know how to use information in a variety of ways. Responsibility for learning should be transferred to students by high school to help them learn how to learn without the direct guidance of an adult. Student-centered instruction methods are the most effective teaching methods in secondary schools today.

Teacher-Centered Instruction Is More Effective

Teacher-centered instruction methods are the most effective in secondary schools today. Students benefit when teachers use direct instruction, mastery learning, and meaningful homework. Direct instruction is scientifically research based and has been proven to be the best approach when a student has limited background on a skill or concept being taught. Master learning is systematic instruction that requires mastery of one concept before moving on to the next. Meaningful homework is essential to help students learn that they will be held accountable for their work. Teacher-centered instructional methods make the most of academic learning time and hold students to high standards of academic excellence.

---

15. The first passage advances the idea that student-centered instruction is more effective. The author of this passage most highly values which of the following?

    A. Students' areas of cognition, interest, and social adjustment

    B. Students' grades from last quarter

    C. Students' teachers from last year

    D. Students' completion of homework

---

16. Which of the following is least likely to be used in the classroom of the author of the second passage?

    A. Discussions

    B. Homework

    C. Lecture

    D. Guided discovery learning

---

17. Schoen describes teacher reflection-in-action as

    A. looking back on experience or action in order to change future teaching.

    B. observing action and thinking as they occur in order to adjust teaching.

    C. analyzing teaching after a lesson observation by an administrator.

    D. discussing teaching with a colleague to improve future lessons.

---

18. John Dewey established which of the following periods of education, which fostered individuality, free activity, and learning through experience?

    A. Common School Period

    B. Early National Period

    C. Modern Period

    D. Progressive Period

Answers and Explanations

Case I

Cases, or "constructed responses," are graded holistically on a scale of 0–2, with 0 being the lowest score. For details on this type of question, be sure to read Chapter 5. In this section, you'll find the content categories and suggested content to include in your case study responses. For more information about the content category, you can study Chapters 7, 8, 9, and 10. The suggested content is designed to help you get a sense of the type of response required, but it may not cover all the correct options in such an open-ended question. You may also find it helpful to share your constructed responses with an education professor, adviser, or educator.

1. **Suggested content:** Strengths include real-life connections between content and learners, use of computer technology, collaboration with the English teacher, and providing modeling and direct instruction.

2. **Suggested content:** Ways to communicate with Jason include, but are not limited to, praising his success, acknowledging his interests and talents in this area, breaking task into smaller steps, and using appropriate humor.

3. **Suggested content:** Appropriate accommodations include, but are not limited to, supporting organization of the binder, probing for Jason's understanding before sending him off to do his homework, offering frequent check-ins with Jason, and communicating with guardians through the school's website or via e-mail.

Case II

4. **Suggested content:** Strengths of Ms. Brousseau's lesson include both student-centered and teacher-centered techniques to meet the needs of a wide range of learners, real-life purposes for content, and using a concrete example to open the lesson, which builds background knowledge and motivates learners.

5. **Suggested content:** Accommodation suggestions include, but are not limited to, working with a partner during application in class practice, offering more concrete examples before moving into practice, and using guided discovery methods instead of direct explanation to teach definitions.

6. **Suggested content:** Ways to assess students in this lesson include, but are not limited to, formative assessment, such as students sharing examples using the overhead; thinking aloud responses; and having a partner check problems in class. Summative assessment ideas include creating a performance assessment using the student-generated pictures of geometry-related replicas.

Discrete Multiple-Choice Questions

Answer Key			
Question	**Answer**	**Content Category**	**Where to Get More Help**
7.	B	Students as Learners	Chapter 7
8.	C	Students as Learners	Chapter 7
9.	C	Students as Learners	Chapter 7
10.	A	Students as Learners	Chapter 7
11.	D	Instruction and Assessment	Chapter 8
12.	B	Instruction and Assessment	Chapter 8
13.	C	Instruction and Assessment	Chapter 8
14.	B	Instruction and Assessment	Chapter 8
15.	A	Teacher Professionalism	Chapter 10
16.	D	Teacher Professionalism	Chapter 10
17.	B	Teacher Professionalism	Chapter 10
18.	D	Teacher Professionalism	Chapter 10

Explanations

7. B. Gilligan's theory of moral development, known as "the ethic of care," is based on Kohlberg's, Piaget's, and Freud's theories but reframes these theories for women. Like Kohlberg, she defines three stages: preconventional, conventional, and postconventional.

8. C. Kohlberg's theory of moral development suggests that the third stage, postconventional, is not always reached by all adults. At this stage, people demonstrate understanding of social mutuality and show a genuine interest in the welfare of others.

9. C. The migration of Theresa's family in pursuit of work may be affecting her sense of safety. According to Maslow's theory, safety needs relate to establishing stability and consistency in a chaotic world. Theresa may also have physiological needs that are not being met, such as food and sleep, but this was not an answer choice.

10. A. Involving parents in planning and decision-making in schools where migration is common provides greater opportunity for effectiveness of instructional methods and students' academic achievement.

11. D. Discovery learning is a student-centered approach in which students construct their own understanding of a concept. This approach is based on the work of Jerome Bruner and John Dewey.

12. B. This choice is central to Canter's assertive discipline model. The other three answer choices are all hallmarks of Kounin's classroom management plan.

13. C. There are three basic approaches to classroom management styles: authoritarian, laissez-faire, and authoritative. A teacher with a laissez-faire style of classroom management does not set rules and behavior expectations.

14. B. Test validity is related to measuring what it is meant to measure. Test reliability is related to whether the test remains consistent across testing times and settings.

15. A. A teacher who uses a student-centered approach considers students' areas of cognition, interest, and social adjustment when planning lessons.

16. D. Guided discovery learning is a student-centered approach in which the teacher "guides" students through questions and directions.

17. B. Schoen advanced the idea of reflection-in-action and reflection-on-action. Reflection-in-action is often tacit or unexpressed.

18. D. The Progressive Period (1880–1920) was based on the educational philosophy first advanced by John Dewey.

PART II

PREPARING FOR THE FORMAT OF THE PLT

This chapter will help you approach the constructed-response questions in a systematic way in order to save time on the actual test. The *CliffsTestPrep* strategies you practice here will also help you respond to these questions in a clear, accurate, and concise way. That's exactly what the ETS is looking for in your constructed responses.

How to Approach the Constructed-Response Questions

Let's look back at a case history and a sample constructed-response question based on that case history from Chapter 4.

Scenario: Jason

Jason is an eighth-grade student in Mr. Pope's health class. Jason shows great interest in the course content, actively participates in class, and responds well to Mr. Pope's enthusiastic and positive teaching style. Jason does very well with an assignment that Mr. Pope designed for a test grade and repeats once a month throughout the marking period. Below is a brief synopsis of the assignment:

> Find an article related to health and fitness on the Internet or in a magazine. Write a summary of the article that includes at least three main health-related points of the article and then make one connection between the article and your knowledge/experiences. Be sure to cite your article and its source properly.

Mr. Pope introduced this assignment by providing a model and then offering direct instruction on how to write the summary. He also gave examples of personal connections between the article and his knowledge and experiences and showed the students how to add this information to the end of the summary. Mr. Pope modeled his writing process by thinking aloud and actually demonstrating his writing using the overhead projector. Mr. Pope teamed up with his eighth-grade English teaching colleague and planned to teach how to cite Internet sources and periodicals carefully. The two devised a guide sheet that they provided to students and turned into a poster for both of their classrooms.

Jason earned a B on his first health summary because he misunderstood or did not read some of the directions carefully. In addition, the assignment was one day late. Jason was discouraged that he forgot his homework on his desk at home, which is a problem he often has with homework. Mr. Pope has noticed that Jason's health binder is usually disorganized, and Jason frequently forgets to bring a pencil to class.

Mr. Pope reviewed the second health summary assignment individually with Jason, checking with Jason to make sure that he had an appropriate article a week before the assignment was due. He also had his class work in pairs to discuss real-life connections to the topics of their articles during class time a few days before the next summaries were due. On the second assignment, Jason earned an A. He continued to earn A's on his other summary assignments, with the exception of one, which was late. Jason became an active class contributor and appeared confident in his abilities to find health-related information on the Internet and in magazines, as well as in his ability to write a summary.

Sample Constructed-Response Question

Identify TWO strengths of Mr. Pope's health assignment. Explain how each strength demonstrates aspects of effective planning. Be sure to base your response on the principles of planning instruction.

As you can see, the constructed-response questions are made up of a case history for you to read and then followed by a question that requires you to provide a short answer. In this next section, I have some suggested approaches for you to try for the constructed-response questions on your PLT test.

CliffsTestPrep Strategies for the Constructed-Response Questions

Here are some suggested *CliffsTestPrep* strategies for answering constructed-response questions:

1. **Read the questions first.** Remember, you are reading each case history in order to get the answers to the questions right. Before you spend time reading the case history, think about *why* you are reading it!
2. **Actively read each case history.** Take notes, keep your mind on the questions, and think as you read. You'll find more on this a bit later in this chapter.

3. **Reread each question and make a brief plan or sketch of your response points.** For example, a brief plan for the sample question about the strengths of Mr. Pope's lesson might look like this:

> Strength ONE
>
> Specific example
>
> Explanation
>
> Strength TWO
>
> Specific example
>
> Explanation

4. **Review the case history.** Make sure that you have referred specifically to the case history and have included two strong points (or as many points as the question requires) with examples and details.

5. **Review your response.** Were you clear, concise, specific, and accurate? Did you base your response on the principles of learning and teaching? Did you answer all parts of the question? Beware of the two-part constructed-response question! These questions ask about two points rather than just one. The length of your response will vary on the question. In general, you will write a one to two paragraph response. It is okay for you to use bulleted lists or brief examples. You do not need to have perfectly written paragraphs to earn a high score. The most important aspect of your response is the content you write and the accuracy of the examples you provide.

6. **Be mindful of your testing time.** You have 2 hours total to read four case histories, answer six constructed-response questions, and answer 24 multiple-choice questions. Each test-taker will need a different amount of time to respond to a constructed-response question accurately and completely, so I cannot give you a specific time to spend on each case history. You'll have to practice your timing before the actual test. Constructed-response questions are likely to take more of your testing time, so practice the full-length tests at the back of this book with your watch in hand. Be sure to check your watch at the start of the test and then every 30 minutes. You want to be halfway through the full-length test after 1 hour.

How to Read a Case History

Now that you better understand how to approach the constructed-response questions, you're ready to look more closely at the case history itself. All case histories on the test are approximately the same length, 800 to 850 words, and each one is followed by three constructed-response questions. None of the cases requires knowledge from specific academic areas, such as science, social studies, mathematics, or English language arts; rather, the questions seek your knowledge of the four categories on the PLT:

- Students as Learners
- Instruction and Assessment
- Communication Techniques
- Teacher Professionalism

The next important thing you need to remember is that there are two types of case histories on the PLT test:

- Teacher-based
- Student-based

Teacher-Based PLT Cases

Teacher-based case histories examine the teaching practice of one or more teachers. This type of case history will include enough information about the teaching context, lesson goals, objectives, lesson plans, teaching strategies, and interactions with students to help you identify issues of teaching and learning involved in the situation so that you can respond to the questions about the teacher's practice. It is never acceptable to respond that there is not enough information for you to respond to the question. There is always enough required information included for you to come up with an answer. You also need to be able to offer new examples or suggestions, and not just repeat an example or teaching idea presented in the case history.

You can rest assured that the teaching examples are positive, and you will not be asked to make value judgments about a teacher's practice. A case history may ask you to provide an additional teaching idea or another way of looking at the teaching and learning discussed in the case.

Student-Based PLT Cases

Student-based cases examine one student and include specific information about the student's background, strengths, or weaknesses. These cases may include examples of student work, excerpts of classroom conversations, and descriptions of the student's classroom learning. As with the teacher-based cases, the case history will provide all the information you need to respond to the question. Remember, too, that there is nothing "wrong" with the student. Teachers must demonstrate positive approaches to teaching *all* children, even those who have difficulty learning in a classroom setting.

Two Different Formats

Both teacher-based case histories and student-based case histories can be presented in one of two formats—document-based and narrative.

Document-Based

Document-based case histories consist of three or more documents that relate to the teacher or student-based case. Teacher-based cases might include lesson plans; assignments; student work; notes from a principal, parent, or mentor; or teacher journals. Student-based cases might include excerpts from class discussions, conversations between teachers and colleagues, student records, student work samples, or notes from parents, counselors, or colleagues.

Narrative-Based

Narrative-based case histories present a nonjudgmental account of a teaching or learning situation—in a school, in a set of classrooms, or in a class. This type of case history provides an excerpt of a situation. You do not know everything that is happening in this teaching or learning situation. When answering the questions, you *can* assume that the information about the teacher or student that is included is valuable.

Suggested Strategies for Reading Case Histories

Remember to read the constructed-response questions first and then:

1. Read the case history carefully, closely, and actively.

   By carefully, I mean read slowly enough to comprehend what you've read. By closely, I suggest that you keep the major content categories in mind (see Chapter 7). By actively, I mean to make margin notes, underline key points, and think about why this information is included.

2. Ask questions as you read.

   What issues about teaching and learning does this case history raise? How might the teacher help the student(s) in this situation? How else might the teacher or student resolve the issues presented?

3. Keep in mind that all information is there for a reason.

   This is why you read the constructed-response questions before reading the case history. As you read the case history, ask yourself how the information presented in the case history addresses each question.

Scoring Guide

This section of the chapter helps you focus on how to earn the highest score. It can also help you better understand what makes a less effective response. You'll see that your answers need to be *complete, relevant, appropriate, thorough,* and *specific to the principles of teaching and learning.* While an appropriate response must be legible and accurate content-wise, note that you are not required to use perfect spelling, grammar, or handwriting.

Criteria for Scoring

Constructed-response questions are scored on a 0-2-point scale. The Educational Testing Service offers the following general framework for scoring constructed responses:

A response that earns a score of 2:

- Demonstrates complete understanding of the parts of the case that are relevant to the question
- Responds appropriately to all parts of the question
- When an explanation is required, provides a thorough explanation that is well supported by relevant examples
- Demonstrates a strong knowledge of pedagogical concepts, theories, facts, procedures, or methods relevant to the question

A response that earns a score of 1:

- Demonstrates a basic understanding of the parts of the case that are relevant to the question
- Responds appropriately to one portion of the question
- When an explanation is required, provides a weak explanation supported by relevant evidence
- Demonstrates some knowledge of pedagogical concepts, theories, facts, procedures, or methods relevant to the question

A response that earns a score of 0:

- Demonstrates misunderstanding of the parts of the case that are relevant to the question
- Does not respond appropriately to the question
- Is not supported by relevant evidence
- Demonstrates little knowledge of pedagogical concepts, theories, facts, procedures, or methods relevant to the question

No credit is given for blank or off-topic responses.

How Is an "Appropriate Response" Determined?

The ETS uses the term *appropriate* in its scoring guide. It's important that you consider how the ETS scorers determine "appropriate responses":

- Two or three education experts are asked to read case histories and answer the questions.
- Benchmark papers are selected from individuals who have agreed to participate in a pilot test. In other words, your test is not used to train scorers!
- The test writer uses the experts' "model answers" to develop a specific scoring guide for each case history and its questions. These models become examples of correct answers, not *the* correct answers.
- Next, the specific scoring guide is used to select model answers that serve as "benchmark papers" for training scorers for your exam.

- During the training session and when reading benchmark papers, scorers can add new answers to the scoring guide as they see fit.

- Training sessions are designed to train scorers to use benchmark papers and the specific scoring guide, not their own opinions or preferences.

How to Use the Scoring Criteria to Assess Your Own Responses

You can share your preview test or one of the upcoming full-length practice tests with an experienced teacher or educator and ask him or her to use the scoring guide to provide feedback to you. You may also want to assess your own responses and make sure you are addressing all the important aspects of each question.

While the ETS has set up a reliable and valid way to score test-takers' written responses, you may have concerns about how your own constructed responses are scored. You can request and pay for your score to be verified. See the website www.ets.org/praxis for more information.

Apply the *CliffsTestPrep* Strategies

In this section, you'll have a chance to try out the strategies I've gone over in this chapter. It's important to practice the suggested strategies to make sure that you feel comfortable approaching the constructed-response questions in this way. If you find an approach that works better for you and you're getting the credited responses, you should use it.

Try the suggested strategies with the following case history and its three constructed-response questions. If you'd like more practice reading case histories and answering constructed-response questions, turn to any of the full-length practice tests in Part IV of this book.

Case I

Directions: Questions 1–3 require you to write short answers, or "constructed responses." You are not expected to cite specific theories or texts in your answers; however, your knowledge of specific principles of learning and teaching will be evaluated. Be sure to answer all parts of the question. Write your answers in the space provided.

Scenario: Justin

Justin is an 11-year-old boy in the fifth grade. He is taller and heavier than most children in his age group, yet socially and emotionally he appears to be less mature. He recently moved with his three older sisters, father, and mother, who is a naval officer, to a school district that largely serves a Navy community since there is a military base within walking distance of the school. Justin has moved five times in his life and is very quiet on the first days of school. After those first few days, he has more overt difficulties. Mr. Hole is concerned that Justin may not be adjusting well to his new classroom, school, and community.

Mr. Hole does not have a cumulative record for Justin since it takes the school system several days, sometimes weeks, to request and obtain records through the central administration department in this large district that serves many transient students. This is a common problem in the school system and one that Mr. Hole has learned to work around. He has planned several "get-to-know-you" activities during the first weeks of school. Based on early observations and pretesting, Mr. Hole has the following assessments to report to the Multi-Disciplinary Team (MDT) in late September:

- On the first few days of school, Justin wore his hood over his head and face and was very quiet. He seemed to observe the happenings in the classroom with interest, but did not participate in any discussions or activities. He was compliant when it came time to go to lunch, recess, and specialists' classes, such as Art, Music, and Physical Education. At lunch and recess, he sat alone.

- Justin has difficulty following class rules, especially raising his hand, taking turns, and remaining in his own personal space during work time and when walking in the hallway.

- On September 10, Justin initiated an argument in the coatroom that escalated to shouts and Justin throwing his backpack at a fellow student.

- Justin's instructional reading level is at the beginning of grade 3. His comprehension appears to be very weak, yet his vocabulary and word recognition skills are strong.

- Justin is also below grade-level expectations in mathematics. He has difficulty with multiplication and division as well as problem-solving that requires two or more steps.

- On September 15, Justin and another boy were observed taking candy from the teacher's desk. While the other boy admitted his part in the incident, Justin adamantly denied that he took the candy.

- Justin enjoys drawing and music.

- On September 23, Justin took a new set of crayons from a boy in class, broke each one in half, and left them on the student's desk.

- On the same day, Justin had a fistfight on the playground and was suspended from school.

Mr. Hole is concerned about Justin's adjustment to his new school. He knows that students who move a lot, such as those like Justin who come from military families, often have gaps in academics, low self-esteem, or difficulty behaving. Mr. Hole has thought carefully about Justin's learning situation and has tried the following strategies to support Justin's transition to his new school and classroom before requesting the MDT meeting on Justin's behalf:

- "Classroom buddy"—A student who has also moved frequently and is high-achieving and polite has been assigned to help Justin as needed.

- Individual attention—Mr. Hole has allowed Justin to do special jobs for the teacher and has spent one-to-one time with him during a special "lunch with the teacher."

- Authentic praise—Mr. Hole has made a point to recognize Justin's positive contributions to the classroom and in his individual work.

- Lower-than-grade-level tasks—Mr. Hole has given Justin mathematics problems and reading materials at his instructional level. This has led to some social difficulties, though, because Justin is the only student performing this far below grade level.

- Home/school communication—Mr. Hole has communicated with Justin's family by phone and in one parent-teacher conference. Justin's family appears to be concerned about and involved in Justin's educational progress. The parents reported that Justin has had difficulty with behavior at other schools and has frequent outbursts at home.

The Multi-Disciplinary Team reviewed this information and samples of Justin's work and determined that Justin should be evaluated by the school psychologist and an educational diagnostician to determine the cause of his behavioral difficulties and his below-grade-level performance.

1. Identify TWO additional strategies that Mr. Hole could use to support Justin's learning in his fifth-grade classroom while he waits for results from the school psychologist and the educational diagnostician. Be sure to base your response on the principles of learning and teaching.

2. Identify TWO potential reasons for Justin's behavior and academic performance in fifth grade. Be sure to base your answer on the principles of learning and teaching.

3. Suggest TWO additional ways that Mr. Hole and Justin's parents can work together to support Justin's behavior and academic performance in school. Be sure to base your response on the principles of learning and teaching.

Answers and Explanations

1. This question requires you to read carefully about Mr. Hole's attempts to help Justin and to describe two new ideas that Mr. Hole has not tried. These ideas must be grounded in principles of learning and teaching. You may have other "reasonable responses" that would be considered exemplary responses by the ETS. The points below are just examples, so you'll want to ask an experienced educator to read *your* response for specific feedback and suggestions. These ideas are not written as complete responses to the PLT; rather, this section provides suggested content. You will find sample responses at the end of each of the practice tests in Part IV of this book. Here are a couple of suggestions you could offer Mr. Hole:

   - Clearly review the classroom rules and expectations that the class as a group has determined and then start a behavior plan for Justin that includes natural consequences for his choices. Glasser's "choice theory" suggests that students must have choices, clear expectations, and natural consequences for their actions.

   - Try placing Justin in a heterogeneous cooperative group for reading or math work instead of providing individual work. Students working in effective cooperative groups develop a sense of camaraderie, and peer support often provides intrinsic motivation for students to make positive contributions to the group.

2. This question requires you to analyze and synthesize all the information presented in the case. Mr. Hole does not have access to Justin's previous student record, so he needs to hypothesize what may be the reasons behind Justin's behavior and academic performance. These ideas must be grounded in principles of learning and teaching. You may have other "reasonable responses" that would be considered exemplary responses by the ETS. These ideas are not written as complete responses to the PLT; instead, this section provides suggested content. You will find sample responses at the end of each of the practice tests in Part IV of this book. You'll want to ask an experienced educator to read *your* response for specific feedback and suggestions. Here are a couple of reasons why a student may present learning behaviors such as those in Justin's case:

   - Justin could be upset about his recent move and the many times he has had to meet new teachers and make new friends. Students whose families move a lot may experience diminished self-esteem or behavior problems.

   - Justin could have a behavior disorder. Mr. Hole has observed withdrawn behavior, acting out, stealing, difficulty with rules, and aggression toward people. These are behavioral indicators of a behavior disorder. It is the teacher's role to report behaviors and the MDT's role to determine the existence of a disorder or the need for outside medical evaluation.

3. Mr. Hole has had one parent conference and one parent phone call. In this question, you are to suggest two additional ways Mr. Hole and Justin's parents can work together to support Justin. For all students, but particularly those who move a lot, it is very important for the teacher and the student's caregivers to be involved in the student's school life. Since they know the child best, the caregivers may be in a better position to "teach" the student in each transition between schools and communities. Your suggestions must be grounded in principles of learning and teaching. You may have other "reasonable responses" that would be considered exemplary responses by the ETS. These ideas are not written as complete responses to the PLT; rather, this section provides suggested content. You will find sample responses at the end of each of the practice tests in Part IV of this book. You'll want to ask an experienced educator to read *your* response for specific feedback and suggestions. Here are a couple of ideas to help Mr. Hole and Justin's family work together to support his education:

   - Establish a home/school log between teacher and parents. Each day Mr. Hole writes a brief note to Justin and his parents about Justin's accomplishments as well as one difficulty, if there was one. He also asks for ways to help Justin at school and suggests ways to help Justin at home. Justin's parents write back to Mr. Hole, and Justin signs his name at the end of the journal entry to signify that he has read his teacher's and his parents' entries. If Justin would like to contribute to the journal, he can. Note that this log highlights the many positive contributions Justin is making and de-emphasizes his poor choices or difficulties.

   - Mr. Hole and Justin's parents can communicate via e-mail and the Internet using a school Web page that Mr. Hole creates. This page identifies each homework assignment, lists the class rules and expectations, and shows examples of student work. In addition, Mr. Hole could post suggested reading and websites to enrich or remediate the week's lessons. Mr. Hole and Justin's parents could communicate more specifically and privately about Justin's daily or weekly progress via e-mail.

Multiple-Choice Questions

In this chapter, you will learn about the format and types of multiple-choice questions on the PLT test. Multiple-choice questions require you to analyze situations, synthesize information, and apply knowledge, all of which takes time. Knowing the format of the questions will get your mind ready to recognize the patterns of these questions. This chapter also includes helpful tips to help you achieve your goal—a passing score on the PLT!

How to Approach the Multiple-Choice Questions

There are a total of 24 discrete multiple-choice questions on the PLT. These questions are unrelated to the constructed-response questions and the case histories (see Chapter 5). Multiple-choice questions require strong reading skills and knowledge of the three PLT areas tested:

- Students as Learners
- Instruction and Assessment
- Teacher Professionalism

You may have noticed that the Communication Techniques content is not tested in the multiple-choice section. This category appears only in the case history and constructed-response questions.

There are five types of multiple-choice questions: Complete the Statement, Which of the Following, Roman Numeral, LEAST/NOT/EXCEPT, and Graphs/Tables/Reading Passages. The following sections give you an example of each type of question.

Complete the Statement

Example: During oral reading, one student reads the word *cape* as *cap*. This child most likely needs help with

A. concepts about print.
B. encoding.
C. comprehension.
D. phonics.

Answer: D.

Which of the Following

With this multiple-choice question type, you read a short question that ends with the phrase "which of the following?" This is the most frequent question type on the PLT.

Example: A mathematics lesson plan that is organized with direct instruction, guided practice, and independent practice is likely to provide which of the following to students?

A. Grade-level expectations
B. Phonemic awareness
C. Scaffolding
D. Vocabulary development

Answer: C.

Roman Numeral

Roman Numeral multiple-choice questions require you to read a short passage that includes several options to consider. The answer choices are presented as a list of Roman numerals. You must use your critical reasoning to determine which of the answer choices contain all of the correct options. These questions take more time than most multiple-choice questions and appear infrequently on the PLT.

Example: Mrs. Humbyrd, the principal of Calfee Corner Middle School, wants to convene an IEP meeting for Jeffrey, a sixth-grader with learning disabilities. IDEA requires Mrs. Humbyrd to invite the following participants:

I.   Jeffrey's regular education teachers
II. Special educators who may work with Jeffrey
III. The school nurse
IV. Jeffrey's parents

A. I, II, III, IV
B. I, II, III
C. I, II, IV
D. I, II

Answer: C.

LEAST/NOT/EXCEPT

Example: Mrs. Antosh strives to make accommodations for the students in her kindergarten class who have short attention spans, have difficulty starting a task, and often appear distracted by the busy classroom. Which accommodation is LEAST likely to support these students?

A. Providing a quiet, less visual area to work
B. Providing short tasks with immediate positive feedback
C. Moving the students closer to the teacher
D. Seating the students in a group

Answer: D.

Graphs/Tables/Reading Passages

These type of multiple-choice questions present a longer passage, a graph, or a table for you to read and interpret. Be careful to read headings on the graphs and tables. Of course, the longer reading passage questions may take longer for you to answer, so be ready for this. Fortunately, this question type does not appear very frequently on the PLT.

Example: Mrs. Lahiri is a teacher assistant in Mrs. Campbell's primary grade-level resource classroom. Mrs. Campbell has provided a lesson plan for Mrs. Lahiri to implement with a small group of students who need additional support with their writing. While Mrs. Lahiri works with the small group of students drafting a story, the principal asks her to assist in the office because of an absence. Mrs. Campbell and Mrs. Lahiri are discouraged that their plans have been interrupted. Furthermore, their students will not receive the small-group instruction delineated in their Individualized Education Plans.

Which of the following is a professionally responsible and reflective way for Mrs. Campbell to approach this situation?

A. Discuss concerns with Mrs. Lahiri and encourage her to file a complaint
B. Discuss concerns with the school principal and offer alternative solutions to the problem
C. Support the change in student services in order to be a team member
D. Discuss concerns with colleagues in the teacher's room and brainstorm solutions to the problem

Answer: B.

CliffsTestPrep Strategies for the Multiple-Choice Questions

Now you know that there are 24 multiple-choice questions that are unrelated to the constructed-response questions and case histories, and you know to look for five basic types of multiple-choice questions. In this section, you will review a systematic approach to the multiple-choice questions and then practice the strategy.

1. **Read the question stem.** The bold part of the question below is the question stem:

   Mrs. Dougherty's first-grade students work in small groups at the blocks center three days a week. Which of the following provides the best rationale for blocks center work?

   A.   Direct instruction
   B.   Discovery learning
   C.   Independent practice
   D.   Visual learning

   Answer: B.

2. **Read all the answer choices.** Don't be too quick to select the answer choice you think is correct without carefully considering all the answer choices. Remember, one key thing that this test assesses is your critical reasoning skills, so each test question has at least one "distracter." This is an answer choice that appears correct in some way—either it's related to the topic, it has a similar spelling or meaning, or it is almost correct, but not as good as the credited response. The credited response is the answer choice that will get you the points on the PLT, so clearly this is the one you want!

3. **Use the process of elimination.** Cross out any answers that you know are incorrect. It's fine to write in your test booklet. Underline key phrases and words if you find it helpful. Analyze the situation and apply your knowledge to the question. If you do not clearly know the correct answer, your goal is to find the best two choices of the four. If you can use the process of elimination to get this close to the credited response, you have a one-in-two chance of choosing the right one. If you simply guess, you have a one-in-four chance. Your odds are clearly better when you use the process of elimination!

4. **Insert the answer choices into the question stem.** Try out the best two answer choices to find the credited response.

5. **Mark your bubble sheet carefully.** Because you have the ability to skip questions or start at any point on the PLT that *you* would like, it is important for you to mark your bubble sheet carefully so that each answer choice refers to the correct question. You also want to completely fill in the bubble and not make any stray marks on the sheet since a computer is scoring your multiple-choice question responses.

Apply the *CliffsTestPrep* Strategies

Now it's your chance to practice the strategies for the multiple-choice questions. Remember to read the question stem first, skim all the answer choices, and use the process of elimination to get to the credited response. In this practice section, you will work on 12 multiple-choice items made up of all five types of multiple-choice questions: Complete the Statement, Which of the Following, Roman Numeral, LEAST/NOT/EXCEPT, and Graphs/Tables/Reading Passages.

After you complete these 12 questions, review the answers and explanations, paying particular attention to the types of questions you got correct and the types that you got incorrect. If you are answering the majority of the "students as learners" questions correctly, then you may not want to spend much more test preparation time on this content review. You may find that one type of question is harder for you, in which case you'll want to spend more time practicing that type of question in the full-length tests that appear in Part IV of this book.

In addition, I have included the categories "Students as Learners," "Instruction and Assessment," and "Teacher Professionalism" to help you diagnose any strengths or weaknesses in your knowledge of the principles of teaching and learning. You will find Part III of this book particularly helpful in closing any gaps you discover. You may find it helpful to note that I've started numbering your multiple-choice questions in this section at #7. On the real PLT exam, your first six questions will always be constructed-response questions and your first 12 multiple-choice questions will always be #7–18.

Sample Multiple-Choice Questions

Directions: Questions 7–18 are not related to the previous cases. For each question, select the best answer and mark the corresponding letter space on your answer sheet.

---

7. Researchers have found patterns of learning differences between girls and boys. Girls tend to rely on

    A. self-esteem.
    B. mathematics.
    C. memorization.
    D. physical activity.

---

8. Which of the following multiple intelligences involves a student's ability to understand people and relationships between people?

    A. Intrapersonal intelligence
    B. Introspective intelligence
    C. Intergeneral intelligence
    D. Interpersonal intelligence

---

9. In your teaching career, you will create a classroom atmosphere that fosters which of the following:

    I.   Love
    II. Assistance
    III. Prior knowledge
    IV. Respect

    A. I, II, IV
    B. II, III, IV
    C. I, III
    D. II, III, IV

10. Auditory learners tend to approach learning in all of these ways EXCEPT

   A. exploration.
   B. listening.
   C. lecture.
   D. read-aloud.

Question 11 is based on the following passage:

Mr. Behr, a first-grade teacher, has an interactive, constructivist view of education based on his teacher education program and his successful experiences as a preschool teacher. He provides a variety of meaningful activities for his students, including listening to quality children's literature read aloud, opportunities for creative expression and dramatic play, and hands-on experiences with mathematics situations.

11. His principal can best describe Mr. Behr's practice as

   A. teacher-directed.
   B. emergent literacy.
   C. leader-centered.
   D. developmentally appropriate.

12. Teachers who establish the rules and expect students to follow them, as well as use a set of rewards and punishments for following or breaking the rules, are considered

   A. authoritative teachers.
   B. authoritarian teachers.
   C. Arthurian teachers.
   D. laissez-faire teachers.

13. Which of the following is an example of an informal assessment used in education settings?

   A. Metropolitan Achievement Test
   B. State licensure exam
   C. Running records
   D. Rorschach inkblot assessment

14. Bloom's taxonomy is a classification system for organizing the level of abstraction of educational objectives and questions that teachers may ask. This taxonomy is made up of three domains, including the following:

   I. Cognitive
   II. Evaluative
   III. Affective
   IV. Psychomotor

   A. I, II, IV
   B. I, III, IV
   C. II, III, IV
   D. I, II, III

15. Which of the following is NOT a provision of the Americans with Disabilities Act (ADA) (1990)?

    A. Prohibits discrimination on the basis of disability

    B. Describes the special services designed to meet the unique needs of individuals

    C. Sets clear and enforceable standards that address discrimination

    D. Invokes the power of congressional authority and the U.S. Constitution

Question 16 is based on the following table:

The History of American Education		
Time Period	*Key Contributor*	*Description*
Late 1800s	McGuffey Readers	Moralistic books
Early 1900s	Dewey	"Progressive" schooling
1908	Montessori	Multi-aged grouping
1950s	Sputnik and the space race	Essentialist schooling
1965	Johnson Administration	Elementary and Secondary Education Act
1970s	Goodman	Whole language
1980s	Reagan Administration	A Nation at Risk Report
Early 2000s	George W. Bush Administration	No Child Left Behind Act

16. Those educators in the essentialist movement have a view opposite to progressive education. Which of the following would an essentialist educator value the most?

    A. Discovery learning

    B. Observations of students

    C. Student-centered curriculum

    D. Achievement test results

17. The intent of Public Law 94-142 is to provide

    A. a free and appropriate education to all handicapped students.

    B. directions on assessing students with learning disabilities.

    C. appropriate education in the "least restrictive environment."

    D. transition services for high school students.

18. Which of the following is true about teachers' rights and responsibilities?

    A. Teachers may be dismissed for belonging to a radical religious group.

    B. Teachers may be dismissed for conduct "unbecoming to an educator."

    C. Teachers may be sued and be held liable for negligence.

    D. Teachers may be asked to provide information unrelated to employment.

Answers and Explanations

Question	Answer	Content Category	Question Type
7.	C	Students as Learners	Complete the Statement
8.	D	Students as Learners	Which of the Following
9.	A	Students as Learners	Roman Numeral
10.	A	Students as Learners	LEAST/NOT/EXCEPT
11.	D	Instruction and Assessment	Graphs/Tables/Reading Passages
12.	B	Instruction and Assessment	Complete the Statement
13.	C	Instruction and Assessment	Which of the Following
14.	B	Instruction and Assessment	Roman Numeral
15.	B	Teacher Professionalism	LEAST/NOT/EXCEPT
16.	D	Teacher Professionalism	Graphs/Tables/Reading Passages
17.	A	Teacher Professionalism	Complete the Statement
18.	C	Teacher Professionalism	Which of the Following

Answer Key

7. C. Girls tend to emphasize memorization, whereas boys tend to emphasize physical activity and hands-on learning.

8. D. In Gardner's theory of multiple intelligences, people with interpersonal intelligence are people-smart. These students tend to be the leaders on the playground and understand people and relationships to a higher degree than others. Answer choice A, intrapersonal intelligence, is the opposite of interpersonal intelligence; it serves as the "distracter" in this question. Those who possess intrapersonal intelligence have a good sense of whom they are, their inner feelings, and their moods. Answer choices B and C are made up, so I hope that you crossed them out and were able to use the process of elimination to get to the credited response.

9. A. Love, assistance, and respect are three important aspects of creating a positive classroom atmosphere. Although tapping into students' prior knowledge is important, it is not an aspect of the classroom atmosphere and therefore serves as the "distracter" in this question. Love may seem like a less important aspect of creating a positive classroom, especially as you move up the grade levels, but a teacher's love of her subject, enthusiasm about working with students, and pleasure in teaching add considerably to the classroom environment at any grade level.

10. A. Auditory learners have a learning style that emphasizes listening. Exploration is not connected to an auditory learner, although providing opportunities for exploration may be a successful approach with an auditory learner. Exploration is the "distracter" and requires you to reason critically to find the credited response, not the plausible-but-not-as-good answer.

11. D. The passage describes hallmarks of developmentally appropriate practice according to guidelines established by the National Association for the Education of Young Children (NAEYC). Answer choice A, teacher-directed, is not a part of the teaching scenario in Mr. Behr's classroom. Answer choice B, emergent literacy, is a term that may be used in a developmentally appropriate classroom, but this term is used to describe students' literacy development, not a teacher's practice. Answer choice C, leader-centered, is not a term used in education to describe a teacher's practice.

12. B. Authoritarian teachers use a teacher-centered approach to classroom management. The teacher sets the rules; the teacher monitors the breaking or following of the rules and metes out punishments or rewards as he or she sees fit.

13. C. Running records are used in reading assessment to note a student's oral reading, word recognition, fluency, comprehension, and self-correction behaviors. The state licensure exam and the Metropolitan Achievement Tests are norm-referenced or formal assessments. The Rorschach inkblot assessment is used primarily by clinical psychologists and is a projective test.

14. B. Bloom's taxonomy is made up of the cognitive, affective, and psychomotor domains. The cognitive domain involves knowledge and development of educational attitudes and skills. The affective domain involves development of emotional areas and attitudes. The psychomotor domain involves manual or physical skills. Evaluation or evaluative questions are a part of Bloom's taxonomy of the cognitive domain. This answer choice is the distracter.

15. B. Answer choice B describes the purpose of an Individualized Education Plan (IEP), not the basic tenets of the ADA. All the other choices are important features of this act, which prohibits discrimination on the basis of disability.

16. D. Those in the essentialist schooling movement would more highly value teacher-centered instruction, subject-oriented curriculum, and the results of achievement tests.

17. A. The essence of Public Law 94-142 is to provide a free and appropriate education to all handicapped students. Answer choice B is not related to any public law. Answer choice C relates to PL 99-457. Answer choice D relates to PL 98-199.

18. C. Teachers may be sued and be held liable for negligence. Successful lawsuits against teachers generally have found that the teacher reasonably could have foreseen the event, or that the teacher acted differently than a reasonable teacher would have acted in a similar situation. Answer choice A violates a teacher's right to religious or political freedom. Answer B is a distracter in that "conduct unbecoming to a teacher" is widely open to interpretation. If a teacher has broken the law, then the teacher could be dismissed after a due-process hearing. Answer choice D is also incorrect; teachers may not be asked to provide information about their age, marital status, sexual orientation, religious affiliation, political affiliation, or any other information unrelated to employment.

Final Tips for Answering the Multiple-Choice Questions

- Remember, your goal is to *pass* the PLT, not to compete with another's score or to set PLT test-taking records. Norm-referenced tests are designed for you *not* to know all the answers. Be prepared for several difficult questions.

- You can work on the multiple-choice questions in any order. In other words, you can skip the ones you're having difficulty with. If you do so, be sure to mark your bubble sheet carefully and accurately.

- Write in your test booklet if it helps you. Underline, circle key words, and make note of any items you skipped. Just be sure to mark your final choice on the bubble sheet. Your test booklet is not scored, but it is collected at the end of the test session.

- Remember that there are no patterns to the order in which questions are posed or to their credited answers.

- There is no penalty for guessing. Don't leave any multiple-choice questions blank! Remember to use the process-of-elimination strategy if you have the time to do so.

- Monitor your testing time. Don't rely on the proctor or your sense of time. Bring a watch and make sure that you are working quickly but carefully.

- Read all the answer choices before choosing the credited response.

- If time permits, check your answers. Yes, it's okay to change your answer if you have taken the time to analyze the question stem and realize that your initial thought was incorrect.

PART III

PREPARING FOR THE CONTENT OF THE PLT

Students as Learners

The Students as Learners category of questions on the PLT requires that you know the key theories, theorists, and terms in the areas of psychology of learning and student differences. You will be expected to apply your knowledge in this category to both the multiple-choice and constructed-response questions.

Student Development and the Learning Process

Theorists and Theories to Know

Students learn and develop in a variety of ways. You will recognize many of the names of the theorists and theories from your education psychology or psychology of learning coursework. If you're like my students (and me when I was in your shoes), you'll find the outline format of this content helpful as you prepare to answer questions about this information on the PLT. If you are completely unfamiliar with a term, theory, or theorist, I suggest that you review a current edition of an education psychology textbook or search the Internet for reliable sources on this topic.

Bandura, Albert

Theory: "Social (or Observational) Learning Theory"

Bandura found that children learn by observing others. In a classroom setting, this may occur through modeling or learning vicariously through others' experiences.

Bruner, Jerome

Theories: "Discovery Learning" and "Constructivism"

Bruner suggests that learning is an active process in which learners construct new ideas or concepts based on knowledge or past experiences. His constructivist theory emphasizes a student's ability to solve real-life problems and make new meaning through reflection. Discovery learning features teaching methods that enable students to discover information by themselves or in groups.

Dewey, John

Theory: "Learning through Experience"

Dewey is considered the "father" of progressive education practice that promotes individuality, free activity, and learning through experiences, such as project-based learning, cooperative learning, and arts integration activities. He theorized that school is primarily a social institution and a process of living, not an institution to prepare for future living. He believed that schools should teach children to be problem-solvers by helping them learn to think as opposed to helping them learn only the content of a lesson. He also believed that students should be active decision-makers in their education. Dewey advanced the notion that teachers have rights and must have more academic autonomy.

Erikson, Erik

Theory: "Eight Stages of Human Development"

Erik Erikson was a psychologist who suggested the following eight stages of human development, which are based on a crisis or conflict that a person resolves.

Stage	Age Range	Crisis or Conflict	Key Event
Stage 1: Infancy	0–1	Trust vs. mistrust	Feeding
Stage 2: Toddler	1–2	Autonomy vs. doubt	Toilet training
Stage 3: Early childhood	2–6	Initiative vs. guilt	Independence
Stage 4: Elementary and middle school	6–12	Competence vs. inferiority	School

Stage	Age Range	Crisis or Conflict	Key Event
Stage 5: Adolescence	12–18	Identity vs. role confusion	Sense of identity
Stage 6: Young adulthood	19–40	Intimacy vs. isolation	Intimate relationships
Stage 7: Middle adulthood	40–65	Generativity vs. stagnation	Supporting the next generation
Stage 8: Late adulthood	65–death	Integrity vs. despair	Reflection and acceptance

Gilligan, Carol

Theory: "Stages of the Ethic of Care"

Gilligan's work questions the male-centered personality psychology of Freud and Erikson, as well as Kohlberg's male-centered stages of moral development. She proposed the following stage theory of the moral development of women:

Approximate Age Range	Stage	Goal
Not listed	Preconventional	Individual survival
Transition from selfishness to responsibility to others		
Not listed	Conventional	Self-sacrifice is goodness
Transition from goodness to truth that she is a person, too		
Maybe never	Postconventional	Principle of nonviolence

Kohlberg, Lawrence

Theory: "Theory of Moral Development"

Elementary school–aged children are generally at the first level of moral development, known as "Preconventional." At this level, some authority figure's threat or application of punishment inspires obedience.

The second level, "Conventional," is found in society. Stage 3 is characterized by seeking to do what will gain the approval of peers or others. Stage 4 is characterized by abiding the law and responding to obligations.

The third level of moral development, "Post-conventional," is rarely achieved by the majority of adults, according to Kohlberg. Stage 5 shows an understanding of social mutuality and genuine interest in the welfare of others. Stage 6 is based on respect for universal principles and the requirements of individual conscience.

Level	Stage	Social Orientation
Pre-conventional	1	Obedience and punishment
Pre-conventional	2	Individualism, instrumentalism, and exchange
Conventional	3	"Good boy/good girl"
Conventional	4	Law and order
Post-conventional	5	Social contract
Post-conventional	6	Principled conscience

Maslow, Abraham

Theory: "Hierarchy of Needs"

Maslow is known for establishing a theory of a hierarchy of needs in which certain lower needs must be satisfied before higher needs can be met.

1. **Physiological needs:** These very basic needs include air, water, food, sleep, and sex.
2. **Safety needs:** These needs help us establish stability and consistency in a chaotic world, such as a secure home and family. Safety needs sometimes motivate people to be religious, ensuring the promise of safety after we die.
3. **Love and belongingness needs:** This next level of the hierarchy occurs when people need to belong to groups: churches, schools, clubs, gangs, families, and so on. People need to be needed at this level.
4. **Esteem needs:** At this level, self-esteem results from competence or the mastery of a task and the ensuing attention and recognition received from others.
5. **Self-actualization:** People who have achieved the first four levels can maximize their potential. They seek knowledge, peace, oneness with a higher power, self-fulfillment, and so on.

Montessori, Maria

Theory: "Follow the Child"

Maria Montessori was an Italian physician whose philosophy and teaching practice affects many early-childhood programs and charter schools today. She believed that childhood is divided into four stages:

- Birth–age 2
- Ages 2–5
- Ages 5 and 6
- Ages 7–12

This belief led to multi-aged groupings of students based on their period of development. Montessori also believed that adolescence can be divided into two levels:

- Ages 12–15
- Ages 16–18

She believed that there are three stages of the learning process:

- **Stage 1:** Introduce a concept by lecture, lesson, experience, book read-aloud, etc.
- **Stage 2:** Process the information and develop an understanding of the concept through work, experimentation, and creativity.
- **Stage 3:** "Knowing," which Montessori described as possessing an understanding of something that is demonstrated by the ability to pass a test with confidence, teach the concept to another, or express understanding with ease.

Montessori established her school Casa Bambini in 1908, and modified versions of her approach to education are found in some U.S. schools today.

Piaget, Jean

Theory: "Stages of Cognitive Development"

Piaget, a cognitivist theorist, suggested four stages of cognitive development:

Stage	Age(s)	Behavior
Sensorimotor	Birth–2	Explore the world through senses and motor skills.
Preoperational	2–7	Believe that others view the world as they do. Can use symbols to represent objects.
Concrete operational	7–11	Reason logically in familiar situations. Can conserve and reverse operations.
Formal operational	11 and up	Can reason in hypothetical situations and use abstract thought.

Skinner, B. F.

Theory: "Operant Conditioning"

Skinner is thought of as the "grandfather of behaviorism," as he conducted much of the experimental research that is the basis of behavioral learning theory. His theory of operant conditioning is based on the idea that learning is a function of change in observable behavior. Changes in behavior are the result of a person's response to events (stimuli). When a stimulus-response is reinforced (rewarded), the individual becomes conditioned to respond. This is known as *operant conditioning.*

Vygotsky, Lev

Theory: "Zone of Proximal Development"

Vygotsky is credited with the social development theory of learning. He suggested that social interaction influences cognitive development. His learning theory, called the zone of proximal development, suggests that students learn best in a social context in which a more able adult or peer teaches the student something he or she could not learn on his or her own. In other words, teachers must determine what a student can do independently and then provide the student with opportunities to learn with the support of an adult or a more capable peer. I think of this as finding the "just right" next lesson to teach a student and provide an appropriate level of educational support.

Terms to Know

In addition to knowing the key theories and theorists, you will need to know specific terms to both include in your constructed-response questions and identify in the multiple-choice questions. Below, you will find several common terms from this area of content, along with the definition of the term.

Constructivism

A philosophy of learning based on the premise that people construct their own understanding of the world they live in through reflection on experiences.

Discovery Learning

Teaching methods that enable students to discover information by themselves or in groups.

Extrinsic Motivation

Motivation that comes from "without," or from outside a person. Stickers, behavior charts, and incentives for learning are all examples of extrinsic motivators for students.

Intrinsic Motivation

Motivation that comes from "within," or from inside a person. Providing students time to reflect on goals and achievements or helping students see what they have learned and how it's important are examples of intrinsic motivators for students.

Learned Helplessness

A tendency for a person to be a passive learner who is dependent on others for guidance and decision-making.

Metacognition

A person's ability to think about his or her own thinking. Metacognition (*meta* = between; *cognition* = thinking) requires self-awareness and self-regulation of thinking. A student who demonstrates a high level of metacognition is able to explain his or her own thinking and describe which strategies he or she uses to read or to solve a problem.

Readiness to Learn

A context within which a student's more basic needs (such as sleep, safety, and love) are met and the student is cognitively ready for developmentally appropriate problem-solving and learning.

Scaffolding

Instructional supports provided to a student by an adult or a more capable peer in a learning situation. The more capable a student becomes with a certain skill or concept, the less instructional scaffolding the adult or peer needs to provide. Scaffolding might take the form of a teacher reading aloud a portion of the text and then asking the student to repeat the same sentence, for example.

Schema

A concept in the mind about events, scenarios, actions, or objects that have been acquired from past experience. The mind loves organization and must find previous events or experiences with which to associate the information, or the information may not be learned.

Transfer

The ability to apply a lesson learned in one situation to a new situation—for example, a student who has learned to read the word *the* in a book about cows and then goes home and reads the word *the* successfully in a note that a parent left on the counter.

Zone of Proximal Development

This is a key concept in Vygotsky's theory of learning. His learning theory, called the "zone of proximal development," suggests that students learn best in a social context in which a more able adult or peer teaches the student something he or she could not learn on his or her own.

Students as Diverse Learners

Theorists and Theories to Know

In this next section in the category of Students as Learners, we review key theorists and theories relevant to the diversity of students as learners.

Gardner, Howard

Theory: "Multiple Intelligences"

Gardner developed his theory of eight multiple intelligences in the early 1980s. These eight multiple intelligences are as follows:

- **Verbal/linguistic intelligence:** Students who have verbal/linguistic intelligence learn best by saying, hearing, and seeing words.
- **Logical/mathematical intelligence:** Students who have logical/mathematical intelligence are conceptual thinkers, compute arithmetic in their heads, and reason problems easily.
- **Visual/spatial intelligence:** Students who have visual/spatial intelligence think in mental pictures and visual images.
- **Bodily/kinesthetic intelligence:** Students who have bodily/kinesthetic intelligence are athletically gifted and acquire knowledge through bodily sensations.
- **Musical intelligence:** Students who have musical intelligence have sensitivity to pitch, sound, melody, rhythm, and tones.
- **Interpersonal intelligence:** Students who have interpersonal intelligence have the ability to engage and interact with people socially, and these students have a strength in making sense of their world through relationships.
- **Intrapersonal intelligence:** Students who have intrapersonal intelligence have the ability to make sense of their own emotional life as a way to interact with others.
- **Naturalist intelligence:** Students who have naturalist intelligence have the ability to observe nature and see patterns.

Hidalgo, Nitza

Theory: "Three Levels of Culture"

- **Concrete:** This is the most visible and tangible level of culture. It includes surface-level aspects such as clothes, music, games, and food.
- **Behavioral:** This level of culture is defined by our social roles, language, and approaches to nonverbal communication that help us situate ourselves organizationally in society (for example, gender roles, family structure, and political affiliation).
- **Symbolic:** This level of culture involves our values and beliefs. It is often abstract, yet is key to how one defines himself or herself (for example, customs, religion, and mores).

Moll, Luis

Theory: "Funds of Knowledge"

Moll's research into the lives of working-class Mexican-American students and their families revealed that many families had abundant knowledge that the schools did not know about. His view that multicultural families have "funds of knowledge" contends that these families can become social and intellectual resources for a school. Moll urges teachers to seek out and use these funds of knowledge and to gain a more positive view of these capable, but misjudged, students and their families.

Student Learning

ADD

Attention deficit disorder may be found to impact student learning. Students with ADD may have difficulty focusing, following directions, organizing, making transitions, completing tasks, and so on. The diagnosis is made by a medical professional, not by school personnel.

ADHD

Attention deficit hyperactivity disorder may be found to impact student learning. Students with ADHD may have many of the same difficulties as students with ADD (difficulty focusing, organizing, etc.) but may also have difficulty with impulsivity, sitting still, and taking turns. The diagnosis is made by a medical professional, not by school personnel.

Auditory (or Aural) Learner

Auditory learners process information through listening. They learn through lectures, discussions, listening to tapes, repeating information, and reading aloud.

Autism Spectrum Disorders

Autism spectrum disorders may include autism, Asperger syndrome, and other pervasive developmental delays (PDD). Students with these disorders have difficulty socializing and communicating.

Behavior Disorder (BD)

Behavior disorder (also known as conduct disorder) is a type of disruptive behavior disorder in children and adolescents. Students with behavior disorder may violate rules, show aggression toward people or animals, destroy property, or practice deceitfulness.

Concrete Operational Thinkers

Children approximately ages 7–11 think in logical terms, not in abstract terms. Students in this age range require hands-on experiences to learn concepts and manipulate symbols logically.

Developmental Delays

Developmental delays are identified by a medical professional in a child before the age of 22. The student may have one or more of the following difficulties: self-care, expressive or receptive language, learning, mobility, self-direction, capacity for independent living, and economic self-sufficiency.

ELL or ESL or PLNE

English language learner (ELL), English as a second language (ESL), and primary language not English (PLNE) are terms used to describe students who are learning English as a second (or third or fourth) language. Teachers of bilingual and multilingual students can support English language acquisition and learning in several important ways, including building on students' culture, supporting students' proficiency in their native language, giving students time to learn English (two years for conversational English, seven years for academic English), and offering opportunities for students to work and talk in small groups.

Formal Operational Thinkers

Children approximately ages 11–15 develop hypothetical and abstract thinking. Students at this stage can use logical operations to work abstract problems. For example, students at this stage are better able to complete algorithms when working math problems as opposed to using math manipulatives to understand the problems.

Functional Mental Retardation (MR)

Functional MR is a diagnosis determined by a medical professional for a child who exhibits difficulties with the following: age-specific activities (for example, playing), communication, daily living activities, and getting along with others.

Kinesthetic Learner

Kinesthetic learners process information through moving and doing. They learn through acting out scenes, putting on plays, moving to the beat, pacing out measurements on the sidewalk, and so on.

LD

Learning disabilities are determined by a multidisciplinary team or a physician. Students with learning disabilities are not learning to their potential in one or more areas, such as reading, writing, oral language, or mathematics. There are three main types of learning disabilities: reading, mathematics, and written. Common characteristics of students with learning disabilities include:

- Poor coordination
- Poor depth perception
- Short attention span
- Impulsivity
- Difficulty following simple directions
- Hyperactivity
- Perseveration (get stuck on one thought or idea or repeat a behavior)
- Distractibility
- Delayed speech
- Limited vocabulary
- Difficulty recalling what is heard
- Dislike of being touched or cuddled
- Inappropriate use of words
- Low or high pain threshold
- Overreaction to noise

Tactile Learner

Tactile learners process information through touching. They learn through active involvement with the physical world—hands-on experiences.

Visual Learner

Visual learners process information through seeing. They learn through visual displays, films, illustrated books, handouts, graphic organizers, bulletin boards, and so on.

Legislation to Know

ADA

The Americans with Disabilities Act is a federal law that prohibits discrimination on the basis of a person's disability for all services, programs, and activities provided or made available by state and local governments. The ADA is not dependent on the receipt of federal funds.

Due Process

Due process is a set of procedures or safeguards that give students with disabilities and their parents/guardians extensive rights. Those rights include notice of meetings, opportunities to examine relevant records, impartial hearings, and a review procedure.

IDEA

The Individuals with Disabilities Act is a federal statute made up of several grant programs to states in educating students with disabilities. The IDEA specifically lists types of disabilities and conditions that render a child entitled to special education.

IEP

An Individualized Education Plan is a written plan for a student with disabilities developed by a team of professionals (teachers, special educators, school psychologists, and so on) and the child's parents or caregivers. An IEP is based on a multidisciplinary team's evaluation (MDT) of the child and describes how the child is doing presently, what the child's learning needs are, and what services the child will need. IEPs are reviewed and updated yearly. They are required under Public Law 94-142, the Individuals with Disabilities Education Act (IDEA).

LRE

The Least Restrictive Environment is the educational setting that, to the maximum extent appropriate, students with disabilities are educated with nondisabled peers.

Section 504 of the Rehabilitation Act

Section 504 of the Rehabilitation Act of 1973 is a civil rights law prohibiting discrimination against individuals with disabilities by federally assisted programs or activities. Eligibility for protection under Section 504 is not restricted to school-age children; it covers individuals from birth to death.

Accomodations

Alternative Assessments

Alternative or authentic assessments include anecdotal records of student behavior, portfolios, checklists of student progress, and student/teacher conferences. Alternative assessments can be contrasted with traditional assessments. Alternative assessments provide a view of a student's process and product, which is closely related to the instructional activity. Traditional assessments usually provide only a view of the product of the learning, such as the score on a test, and may not be as closely related to classroom instruction.

Differentiated Instruction

According to Tomlinson (1995), differentiated instruction involves a flexible approach to teaching. A teacher plans and implements varied approaches to teaching content, process, and product in an effort to respond to student differences in readiness, interests, and learning needs.

Testing Accommodations

Common testing accommodations provided to students include, but are not limited to, longer testing times, untimed tests, having someone write or type for the student (scribe), Braille or large-print fonts, short breaks during testing, and sign-language interpretation for directions. Offering approved testing accommodations for students who qualify for those accommodations is a desirable differentiation of assessment and is especially important on higher-stakes tests and standardized assessments.

Influences on Diverse Learners

Age-Appropriate Knowledge and Behavior

Teachers must understand their students' physical, social, emotional, and cognitive development. Student progress is seen on a developmental continuum, and growth, or lack of progress toward age-appropriate growth, must be recorded and reported to parents. A student whose knowledge or behavior is outside the norm for the age group may need differentiated instruction or other supports. For example, a ten-year-old student who has a well-developed understanding of working with fractions may need more challenging work with fractions than his or her grade-level peers. Likewise, a student who is unable to form the letters of the alphabet in grade 2 may need supports for fine motor skill development.

Cognitive Patterns

Students make meaning in a variety of ways. According to Piaget's theory, children move from the preoperational to the concrete operational and then the formal operational stage during their school years. One student can make sense more easily through listening, while another prefers visual information. Successful teachers understand their students' thinking styles—especially for those with learning disabilities and those who are accelerated—and plan lessons to accommodate a wide variety of ways to make meaning.

Family Culture

Families can provide valuable funds of knowledge (Moll) for teachers to tap into and utilize for successful lessons. Communicating with families, knowing the school community, and appreciating the differences and similarities of family cultures will help teachers offer instruction that meets the needs of all children.

Linguistic Patterns

Many students' first language is not English; furthermore, students within the same school district may speak in various dialects. Students whose first language is not English or who use a dialect that is not "standard American English (SAE)" benefit when a teacher views these differences as sources of enrichment in the classroom. Students who are new to speaking English may experience a period of silence and may prefer listening in the classroom, which is to be expected and respected. Language is always used in a social context; therefore, students who have linguistically diverse language patterns may "code switch." In other words, a student may use a certain dialect on the playground and another in the classroom. One dialect, African American English Vernacular (AAEV), or Ebonics, is spoken by many African Americans. Which are the best teaching methods for children who speak AAEV became a political controversy in the 1990s. Teaching techniques similar to those used with children whose primary language is not English appear to be most successful for children who speak with dialects of standard American English.

Multicultural

Students come from a wide variety of cultures, and successful teachers help students define and understand their own cultures to deal with mutual misconceptions and to inform future lesson planning. Hidalgo's three levels of culture—concrete, behavioral, and spiritual—can be discussed to build a sense of relatedness and respect in the classroom. Sometimes a family's expectations may differ from a teacher's expectations for a student. Making positive connections between schoolwork and home life can support students' success.

Physical Issues

Successful teachers communicate with the school nurse, families, school mental health professionals, teacher assistants, and the student to understand how the student's physical issues can be supported so that the child can learn at an optimal level. Physical issues common among students include vision, hearing, and mobility problems. Some students suffer from asthma, seizures, and allergies. A teacher should be aware of any physical issues and procedures to ensure the child's safety, especially during field trips, fire drills, and other emergencies.

Social and Emotional Issues

As Maslow's theory reminds us, students whose most fundamental needs (nutrition, emotional care, and so on) are not met may experience social or emotional issues in school until those needs are met. Teachers can report observations to families, the principal, school social workers, nurses, or mental health professionals to advocate for the child's basic needs. Differences in socioeconomic status (SES) among students and between the teacher and the students can lead to misunderstandings about students' social and emotional needs. For example, a student from a low or high SES may act out or demand excessive attention. A teacher must consciously set high expectations for all students regardless of SES and modify instructional methods to help each student achieve a sense of success in the classroom. Some students have physical or mental health issues that lead to social or emotional issues in the classroom. Collaborating with families and colleagues who know the child's needs can help the teacher create a successful learning environment for the student. Students who have low self-esteem, have anxiety, or are easily distractible may also present social or emotional behavioral issues in school.

Students and School Culture

Students are affected by the school's student culture. Issues that impact student culture include bullying, teasing, cliques, threats to personal safety, freedom to take risks or make mistakes, collaborative groups, gender relationships, and the structure of the classroom environment. Students are also affected by the larger school culture. School policies, procedures, norms for dress, communication expectations, and teacher responsiveness all affect a student's experience in school.

Student Motivation and the Learning Environment

In this next part of our review of Students as Learners, we turn to the key theories, theorists, and terms related to student motivation and to setting up a classroom environment conducive to student learning.

Theorists and Theories to Know

Ausubel, David

Theory: "Advance Organizer"

Ausubel suggested a teaching technique called the advance organizer. The advance organizer is introduced before learning begins and is designed to help students link their prior knowledge to the current lesson's content—for example, semantic webs, KWL charts, and concept maps.

Bandura, Albert

Theory: "Modeling"

Observational learning, or modeling, requires several steps:

1. **Attention:** Attending to the lesson
2. **Retention:** Remembering what was learned
3. **Reproduction:** Trying out the skill or concept
4. **Motivation:** Willingness to learn and ability to self-regulate behavior

Canter, Lee

Theory: "Assertive Discipline"

Teachers clearly communicate expectations and class rules and follow through with expectations. Students have a choice to follow the class rules or face consequences. If a child chooses not to follow a rule, he or she will have to experience the consequences of that action.

Glasser, William

Theories: "Choice Theory," also known as "Control Theory"

Teachers focus on students' behavior, not students, when resolving classroom conflicts. Teachers who subscribe to control theory use class meetings to change behavior in the classroom. Students who have a say in the rules, curriculum, and environment of the classroom have greater ownership of their learning. Glasser's approach emphasizes creating a safe space to learn—"our space to learn"—and is designed to promote intrinsic motivation to learn and to behave in the classroom.

Kounin, Jacob

Theory: "With-it-ness"

Teachers must have "with-it-ness," or an awareness of what is happening in their classrooms, in order to manage their classrooms well. In addition, teachers must pace their lessons appropriately and create smooth transitions between activities.

Hunter, Madeline

Theory: "Direct Instruction"

Hunter's method of direct instruction emphasizes the following parts of an effective lesson:

- Objectives
- Standards of performance
- Anticipatory set or advance organizer
- Teaching (which includes modeling, student input, directions, and checking for understanding)
- Guided practice and monitoring
- Lesson closure
- Extended practice

Pavlov, Ivan

Theory: "Classical Conditioning"

Pavlov conducted classical conditioning experiments with dogs in the 1920s. He found that dogs naturally salivate in an unconditioned response (one that is naturally occurring) to the unconditioned stimulus (one that automatically produces an emotional or physiological response) of food. He showed that dogs also salivate in response to a conditioned stimulus (one that creates an emotional or physiological response after learning), and he called that response (salivation) a conditioned response (a learned response to something that was previously neutral). Many people credit Pavlov for the experimental basis of behaviorist learning theory.

Lesson Planning

Objectives are written to answer the question "What are students supposed to know or be able to do at the conclusion of the lesson or unit?" Be sure to write lesson objectives that include all levels of Bloom's taxonomy, not just the knowledge level.

You should be familiar with the state and national **standards** for content and student performance and know how to use them in lesson planning. In addition, you should be familiar with local curriculum guidelines and how a scope and sequence informs your lesson planning.

Learner factors inform your lesson planning. Be familiar with ways to differentiate instruction for a variety of learners, such as English language learners, students with learning disabilities, and students with attention difficulties. Also consider students' different learning styles and multiple intelligences when planning lessons.

Environmental factors must be considered in lesson planning. Will students work in small groups, as a whole group, or individually? Will students have access to learning centers, technology resources, and multimedia as part of the instruction? Is the room temperature too warm or cold for all students to concentrate? Is there too much print on the wall that might distract or overstimulate a learner?

You should know a variety of ways to effectively **open, develop, and close** a lesson. Be sure to know how to incorporate a variety of teaching strategies into your lesson plans across the content areas, such as mathematics, science, language arts, and history.

Finally, **assessing a lesson's objectives** is an important part of lesson planning. Know how to set criteria for student performance of a lesson's objectives and show how you can measure and evaluate student success. Key assessments include criterion-referenced tests, norm-referenced tests, performance assessments, and rubrics.

Principles of Effective Classroom Management

Know your students:

- **Age:** Remember that younger students need more concrete experiences, shorter lessons, less lecture, and more small-group and individual instruction. Older students need less teacher-directed structure, longer lessons, more detailed information, many opportunities to share ideas, time to talk with peers, and more time working with the whole class.

- **Strengths:** Get to know your students' interests, talents, favorite subjects, learning styles, family backgrounds, and cultural and linguistic backgrounds in order to highlight these strengths in your classroom.

- **Areas to support:** Get to know the areas in which your students may need support, such as reading (and other content knowledge) levels, learning differences, physical impairments that may impact learning, and English language background, in order to make instructional decisions and support all students' learning needs.

Know your role as a teacher:

- Set clear expectations.
- Enforce rules fairly and consistently.
- Possess positive and realistically high expectations that all students can learn.
- Highlight students' strengths and support their achievement of goals.
- Model appropriate behavior.
- Accept and understand children within the student-teacher relationship.

Set up the classroom for learning:

- Place materials for student use in easy-to-access places.
- Use wait time when questioning students.
- Create a safe and comfortable learning environment that promotes students' risk-taking and deters bullying, harassment, and disrespectful behavior.
- Seek to have student materials simultaneously available whenever possible. For example, set up four crates of student notebooks and place one crate next to each of the four worktables in your classroom. Each group of students will be able to get materials rather than wait for notebooks to be handed out individually.

Punishment vs. discipline

Understand the fine line between punishment and discipline and set clear expectations for student behavior in the classroom.

Punishment	Discipline
Is teacher-centered and authoritative	Is student-centered and is based on logical consequences
Communicates anger or disappointment	Communicates concern
Closes choices for students	Keeps choices open for modifications
Is concerned with retribution or revenge	Is concerned with changing behavior
Is negative and short-term	Is positive and long-term

Specific Classroom Management Techniques

Canter and Canter: Lee Canter and Marlene Canter suggest a model of classroom management known as "assertive discipline." The approach, suggested in the 1980s and still used today, includes teachers setting clear expectations for behavior and following through consistently and fairly with consequences. Students have a choice to follow the rules or face the natural consequences.

Kounin: Jacob Kounin's research from the 1970s shows that teacher "with-it-ness" (constant monitoring and awareness of student behavior), grouping decisions, and lesson planning are hallmarks of effective classroom management. Smooth transitions between lessons and lessons that maximize learning time are more effective.

Ginott: Haim Ginott's research from the late 1960s and 1970s promoted supportive and preventive discipline by recognizing the importance of the classroom atmosphere—socially and emotionally. He suggested that teachers use "sane messages" in which they simply describe the issue or event of concern. This approach attempts to leave students' self-esteem intact and enables students to consider the situation and develop their own solutions with respectful support from their teacher.

Glasser: Glasser's "choice theory" guides teachers who use this approach to conduct class meetings with students to co-determine class rules, guidelines, and consequences. Teachers use these class meetings to change students' behavior and focus on student behavior, not an individual student's behavior problems.

Hunter: Hunter's approach to class management centers on the strength of effective lesson planning. The teacher opens a lesson with an "anticipatory set" to help students connect new content to prior knowledge or experiences. Next, the teacher models and provides guided practice for the new content to be learned. Then the teacher provides an opportunity for individual and extended practice.

Jones: Fredric Jones studied time on task and found that 50% of instructional time is lost because students are off-task. He found two common types of misbehavior: talking (80%) and goofing off (20%). Jones found that most misbehavior occurs during independent practice times. Jones suggests three strategies to improve student time on task:

- Teacher body language (a.k.a. "the look")
- Incentive systems
- Efficient individual help for students

Instruction and Assessment

In this chapter, you will study key theorists, theories, and terms related to instruction and assessment content covered on the PLT test for both the constructed-response questions and the multiple-choice questions. I suggest that you carefully study the content of "Instruction and Assessment," as well as the other chapters in Part III of this book. As I mentioned in the last chapter, this outline is meant to help you streamline your test preparation efforts. You should not spend your time gathering several books and other sources of information. You can use this chapter to determine what you already know and what you need to learn or recall about instruction and assessment. If you need to learn this content for the first time, you then may want to refer back to one current education psychology text or perform an Internet search for a reliable source to give you fuller information about this subject.

The "Essential Nine" Instructional Strategies

An experienced teacher carries many instructional strategies in his or her teaching toolkit. First, let's examine the "essential nine" instructional strategies suggested by researchers at Mid-continent Research for Education and Learning (McREL), as those nine strategies are most likely to improve student achievement across the content areas in all grade levels.

Identifying Similarities and Differences

When students identify similarities and differences, they can see patterns and connections. Students use thinking strategies such as comparing, contrasting, and classifying information. Teachers can use discussion, inquiry, graphic organizers, and examples, such as metaphors and analogies, to help students break a concept into its similar and dissimilar characteristics.

Summarizing and Note-Taking

Summarizing information is an important comprehension strategy that can be taught and developed from the early grades through adulthood. Teachers in the upper elementary, middle school, and secondary levels must explicitly teach their students to take notes. Common approaches to note-taking include the double-entry page, graphic organizers, and SQ3R (survey, question, read, recite, review).

On a double-entry notebook page, the student draws a line down the middle of the page. On the left side of the page, she takes notes from the reading or lecture. After the reading or lecture, she rereads the notes and writes her reactions, reflections, and connections in the right-hand column next to the corresponding information on the left.

I share examples of graphic organizers in this chapter under the "graphic organizers" heading.

The SQ3R method for note-taking while reading a text is widely used in schools today. The steps are as follows:

1. **Survey:** The student previews the chapter to assess the organization of the information.
2. **Question:** The student examines the chapter's headings and subheadings and rephrases them into questions.
3. **Read:** The student reads one section of the chapter at a time selectively, primarily to answer the questions.
4. **Recite:** The student answers each question in his or her own words and writes the answers in his or her notes. The student repeats this note-taking sequence for each section of the chapter.
5. **Review:** The student immediately reviews what has been learned.

Reinforcing Effort and Providing Recognition

Students' beliefs and attitudes play a significant role in school performance. Parents and teachers must show students the connection between effort and achievement. Methods of doing so include sharing stories of people who did not give up and succeeded, personalizing recognition, and supporting students when they are struggling. Teach students the ultimate goal of effort—the harder you try, the more successful you'll be.

Assigning Homework and Practice

Homework provides an opportunity for extended practice of a lesson. Homework should vary from grade level to grade level; should require minimal, if any, parental involvement; and should merit teacher feedback. Research on homework best practice shows that homework should not be an afterthought; rather, it should be an integral part of instruction to help students acquire the content presented.

Fostering Nonlinguistic Representations

Knowledge is stored in two forms:

- Nonlinguistic (visual, kinesthetic, whole body)
- Linguistic (reading or hearing)

Students should have many opportunities to use both forms of storing knowledge to represent their learning and an opportunity to use all senses when learning. Nonlinguistic representations have been found to stimulate and increase brain activity. Teachers can foster nonlinguistic representations by using words and symbols to convey relationships and by using physical models and physical movement to represent new information. Visual representation software (programs that provide tools for making graphic organizers) offer students a way to express their understanding of content in a nonlinguistic form.

Encouraging Cooperative Learning

Cooperative learning activities require students to work together to solve a problem or achieve a goal. Key features of cooperative learning activities include:

- **Positive interdependence:** Students must work together to successfully accomplish a task.
- **Positive interaction:** Interaction that promotes face-to-face or individual interaction and relationships.
- **Individual and group accountability:** To be assessed as successful, students must contribute to the group's success and complete their portion of the task.
- **Interpersonal skills:** Students must be taught and learn to use teamwork and positive social skills when working with others.
- **Group processing:** Teachers must provide an opportunity for feedback, not only on the group's product but also on the group's process.

Examples of cooperative learning structures for lessons include the following:

- **Student Teams Achievement Divisions (STAD):** Students are assigned to heterogeneously grouped teams of four or five members who collaborate on worksheets designed to provide extended practice on instruction given by the teacher.
- **Jigsaw:** Instructional materials are divided and then studied by individuals or pairs of students. After students become "experts" on their sections of information, they share the information with the group.
- **Numbered Heads Together:** Students are heterogeneously grouped into a "home team." Then each student is assigned a number so that he or she can join all the students with the same number to become an "expert" on assigned materials. For example, all the students who were assigned the number five read about and discuss music during the Harlem Renaissance. Once each of the numbered group has had time to learn the assigned materials, the students return to their home team and teach their peers the content they have learned.
- **Think-Pair-Share:** The teacher poses a problem or situation and asks students to think individually. The teacher then suggests that each student pair with a peer and share his or her thinking on this problem or situation. Sometimes students then share their ideas as a whole group; other times, the students share only in pairs.

Setting Objectives and Providing Feedback

Teachers must set clear expectations for a lesson and unit of study. It's important to help students see what they are learning, why they are learning it, and how this learning connects to other experiences and events. Student ownership of the lesson goals makes a difference in student achievement. Setting goals and objectives for a lesson must be focused, yet not so narrow as to diminish the content's importance. Using advance organizers is one effective method to introduce goals to students.

Generating and Testing Hypotheses

Generating questions and testing hypotheses taps into students' natural curiosity to each student's advantage. This practice helps students more deeply understand the concepts being taught. In this inquiry-type approach, students must clearly explain their hypotheses and conclusions, which deepens their understanding of key concepts and helps them apply their new knowledge in new settings.

Using Cues, Questions, and Advance Organizers

Cues, questions, and advance organizers help prepare students' minds for instruction. Advance organizers are structures, either visual or verbal, that provide a general idea of the new information to be learned, building knowledge of the key concepts to be learned in the lesson. Ausubel introduced advance organizers in the 1960s and suggested that new information is more easily acquired when it can be linked to previously learned experiences or knowledge. Researchers have found that learning increases when teachers focus on what is most important, not on what students might think is the most interesting.

Additional Instructional Strategies

While the "essential nine" instructional strategies are foremost in educators' minds because of the recent emphasis on research-based practices, the instructional approaches reviewed in this section have been proven in the classroom (and seen on the PLT test!).

Anchored Instruction

This instructional approach ties information to an "anchor." In other words, the student uses concrete applications of the concept being taught (the anchor) to connect what he or she is learning to a concrete experience.

For example, students learning about the Civil Rights Movement might simulate walking over the Edmund Pettus Bridge at a local river bridge. Doing so teaches students through hands-on and experiential learning and provides a concrete experience for the students to build on. The teacher (in this real-life example, my colleague Mrs. Wildman) can then anchor the students to this experience as they read and discuss the Civil Rights Movement during their social studies lessons.

Differentiated Instruction

When a teacher differentiates instruction, he or she is responding to the wide range of abilities present in the classroom. Carol Ann Tomlinson is a foremost expert in this area. Teachers can differentiate content, learning processes, or products. Content encompasses the concepts, principles, skills, and strategies we want our students to learn. Teachers strive to teach the same core content to all students; to do so successfully, they must differentiate. Learning processes are the methods teachers use to present content. Products are the culminating events that demonstrate what the students have learned.

There are a variety of methods to differentiate instruction, including:

- **Tiered instruction:** The teacher offers the same core content to each student but provides varying levels of support for students.
- **Curriculum compacting:** The teacher finds the key content that must be learned and reduces the number of examples, activities, or lessons so that a student, usually one who is advanced, can demonstrate the content and move on to another level.
- **Curriculum chunking:** The teacher breaks down a unit's content into smaller units or chunks and provides support and frequent feedback to the student as he or she demonstrates understanding of each chunk of information.
- **Flexible grouping:** Flexible groups are groups that change as the students' learning needs change. For example, students who need to better understand how to make inferences in a book work together until they are proficient, and then the group disbands.

Direct Instruction

Direct instruction is an overarching method for teaching students that includes carefully planned lessons presented in small, attainable increments with clearly defined goals and objectives. Direct instruction often includes lecture, demonstration, review of student performance, and student examination.

Demonstrations

Teacher demonstrations involve explicitly showing students what something is or how to do something. For example, a science teacher might demonstrate the proper use of a Bunsen burner in a lab.

Graphic Organizers

Graphic organizers are visuals that show relationships between concepts, terms, facts, or ideas in a learning activity. Other terms related to graphic organizers that you may encounter are visual, visual structures, concept maps, cognitive organizers, advance organizers, and concept diagrams. There are several types of graphic organizers.

Story Maps

Story maps are used with narrative texts to help students identify and recall key story elements, such as characters, setting, plot, and conclusion.

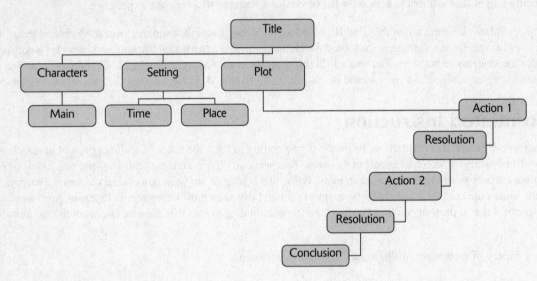

Cause-and-Effect Maps

Visuals, such as this cause-and-effect map, help students identify causes and effects in narrative or expository texts.

Cause and Effect

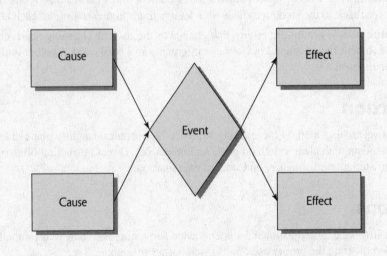

Sequence Diagrams

Students can use a sequence diagram, with the teacher's modeling and guidance, to remember the sequence of events in a factual or fictional text.

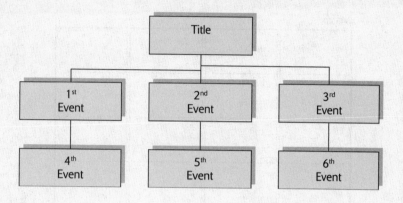

Continuums

A continuum graphic organizer can be used to help students learn key vocabulary or concepts. For example, the teacher can label the sample continuum "feelings" and ask students to generate a list of words that represent feelings along a positive-to-negative continuum. The teacher or students chart the terms on a graphic organizer, which provides an opportunity for students to activate and develop prior knowledge of the feeling words that will be discussed in an upcoming health lesson on interpersonal relationships.

Continuum

Cycle Maps

A cycle map is beneficial when a teacher wants students to understand the cyclical nature of a text. For example, the graphic organizer shown here can be used to chart events at the beginning, middle, and end of a butterfly's life cycle.

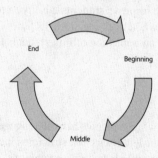

Matrixes

A matrix graphic organizer can be used for a variety of purposes to help students recall information. For example, a teacher might list categories along the first row and ask students to provide examples from the lesson for each category.

Matrix

Hunter's Model

Madeline Hunter's "effective teaching model" emphasizes the following parts of an effective lesson: objectives, standards of performance, anticipatory set or advance organizer, teaching (which includes modeling, student input, directions, and checking for understanding), guided practice and monitoring, and lesson closure and practice.

Mastery Learning

When a teacher uses a mastery learning approach, he or she uses a group-based teacher-centered instructional approach to provide learning conditions for all students to achieve mastery of assigned information.

Mnemonics

Using mnemonics is an instructional strategy often suggested for students with memory difficulties or learning disabilities. Mnemonic instruction is designed to help improve students' ability to remember key information. For example, teachers commonly use mnemonic strategies when teaching students letter identification and sounds. The teacher may introduce the letter A by showing a picture of an apple and telling students that the sound of A is like the beginning of the word *apple*.

Discussion

Discussion is a key instructional technique in which students actively engage in discourse about course content. Discussions can be teacher-led or peer-led. Peer-led discussion structures include literature circles and cooperative learning activities. Teacher-led discussion structures include lectures, recitations, reciprocal teaching, and Socratic seminars.

Field Trips

Field trips are excursions off the main campus of a school that provide students with an opportunity to gain deeper, real-life, hands-on knowledge about a concept of study. Field trips are commonly used after the culmination of a unit, but field trips used at the beginning of a unit can build students' background knowledge and provide an anchor for future lessons.

Independent Study

Independent study sessions or units give students a chance to work at their own pace under the teacher's leadership or guidance. Independent study units can be particularly beneficial for students who need course material modified to be more challenging or simplified.

Interdisciplinary Instruction

Interdisciplinary instruction incorporates information from two or more content areas (for instance, science, mathematics, physical education, technology, and literacy) to help students see the connections and real-life links across the disciplines. An interdisciplinary unit on the Harlem Renaissance, for example, might include lessons on jazz music and the literary works of Zora Neale Hurston and Langston Hughes, as well as social studies lessons about Greenwich Village, Harlem, and the 1920s and 1930s.

Learning Centers

Learning centers are designed to enable individuals or small groups of students to interact with course content after the teacher has taught the focus lesson or while the teacher is leading small-group sessions. The success of learning centers in the classroom depends on several factors: the teacher's planning, management, and supervision, as well as the student's ability to work independently and with others. Purposes of learning centers vary:

- To provide an alternative to seatwork
- To reward students
- To provide enrichment or remediation
- To foster collaboration
- To accommodate individual learning styles

Common learning centers in an elementary classroom are blocks, computers, writing, reading, math games, listening, and creative play. Though they're used less frequently at the middle-school and secondary levels, learning centers at these levels include writing, conferencing, independent reading, and computers.

Primary Sources/Documents

Primary source materials or documents are statements or records of law, government, science, mathematics, or history in their original, unaltered form. Public documents such as census records and law reports, as well as private records like personal journals and letters, are examples of primary sources. Teachers use primary sources from libraries, local collections, and the Internet to help their content come alive with real people's everyday actions and interactions in society.

Questioning

Teachers use questioning strategies to help students make meaning of their content. Many teachers use Bloom's taxonomy to guide their questioning of students at a variety of levels. A common structure for classroom questioning is IRE—Initiate, Respond, and Evaluate. In this pattern of discourse, the teacher begins the discussion with a question, the student(s) respond, and the teacher evaluates the quality of the student response. Sample question categories along Bloom's taxonomy include:

- **Knowledge:** Remember; recognize; recall who, what, where...
- **Comprehension:** Interpret, retell, organize, and select facts
- **Application:** Subdivide information and show how it can be put back together; how is this an example of that?
- **Analysis:** What are the features of...? How does this compare with...?
- **Synthesis:** Create a unique product that combines ideas from the lesson; what would you infer from...?
- **Evaluation:** Make a value decision about an issue in the lesson; what criteria would you use to assess...?

Reciprocal Teaching

The teacher and the student engage in a discussion of the text. Both the student and the teacher question and respond to the text in an effort to improve the student's comprehension of the material.

School-to-Work

School-to-work programs offer students opportunities to transition successfully from the classroom to the workforce.

Service Learning

Service learning is an instructional approach that combines service to the community with learning inside and outside of the classroom.

Critical Thinking

Critical thinking is rationally deciding what to believe or what to do. When one rationally decides something, he or she evaluates information to see if it makes sense, whether it's coherent, and whether the argument is well founded on evidence.

Discovery Learning

Discovery learning fosters inquiry rather than didactic (e.g., lecture) methods for learning. Students are encouraged to ask questions and to hypothesize as they deduce the concepts and principles of the lesson experience.

Inquiry Model

An inquiry approach to teaching involves students in the process of exploring the natural and/or material world in an effort to help them discover meaning. In social studies, a teacher might have students listen to the music of the Civil War to examine the themes and issues raised in the lyrics. In science, a teacher might have students experiment with a variety of soil types to see which absorb more water. In mathematics, a teacher might have students use tiles to create tessellations to discover patterns and relationships among the geometric shapes.

Play

Play is a child's work. Quality early-childhood programs provide opportunities for student play in an effort to provide stimulating, rewarding, and purposeful work. During play, children observe, explore, model, hypothesize, and discover. Play fosters students' learning and development in a fun, soothing, and motivating way.

Project-Based Learning

Project-based learning includes an in-depth investigation of a real-world, authentic topic or problem that is meaningful to students. The students work in small groups or pairs to solve a problem or learn more about the topic. The teacher facilitates student projects and supports students' inquiries and discoveries.

Simulations

Teachers use simulations to help students become immersed in the content being studied. For example, in an interdisciplinary unit of study on the Westward Movement in the United States, students are grouped into wagons and wagon trains and provided with realistic scenarios to consider during each day of the simulation. Computer and video technology offers teachers many opportunities for simulations.

Technology

Instructional technology (for example, computers, CD-ROMs, video, and the Internet) serves as a tool for learning in schools today. Teachers must become proficient in their use of technology to teach and must also help their students skillfully and critically use technology to support learning.

Planning Instruction

Now that we've reviewed instructional strategies, it's time to turn to planning instruction effectively. In this section, we review common aspects of planning a great lesson.

Anticipatory Set

Also known as *set induction,* creating an anticipatory set is an activity at the start of a lesson used to set the stage for learning in order to help motivate students and activate prior knowledge. For example, an English lesson on *To Kill a Mockingbird* might begin with primary source documents of trials set during the Civil Rights Movement.

Behavioral and Cognitive Objectives

Behavioral objectives are lesson objectives that focus on observable student behaviors (define, describe, re-create, and so on). Cognitive objectives focus on students' cognitive behaviors (reflect, recognize, comprehend).

Curriculum Frameworks

Curriculum frameworks list the broad goals of a school district, state, or school and provide subject-specific outlines of course content, standards, and performance expectations.

Emergent Curriculum

An emergent curriculum is based primarily on the interests of children. The teacher works together with family and other community members to set possible direction for a project and then determine the actual curriculum based on student interest. An emergent curriculum is most often used in early-childhood settings, although examples can be found in alternative-model secondary schools that emphasize personalization of student learning and community involvement in education.

Grouping Practices

Teachers must offer a wide variety of grouping practices to meet the needs of all learners. Types of groups include:

- **Partner check:** Individual students complete work and then pair with an assigned student to check work and discuss content.
- **Group investigation:** Students are assigned a topic and prepare a report or summary to share with the whole class.
- **Whole-group instruction:** Students work as a class to read, discuss, or solve a problem. This method is desirable when teacher modeling or direct instruction is necessary. Teachers should use whole-group methods only for short amounts of time because this grouping structure can allow some students to become less active or passive learners.

Lesson Planning

There are a variety of frameworks for lesson planning. Here is one failsafe model to use on the PLT (and in your own classroom!), but you should feel free to use more familiar frameworks for lesson planning from your teacher education institution or teaching experiences.

Lesson Plan Component	Planning Notes
Instructional objectives	The student will...
National, state, and/or local standards addressed	Cite standards here
Materials	List all the materials you'll need for the lesson so you're well prepared.
Learner and environment factors	Learner factors include the target grade level for this lesson, as well as any specific learning styles or modalities the lesson addresses. Environment factors include the room arrangement, arrangement of materials, need for student movement, noise-level expectations, etc.
Opening Set induction Connection to previous lesson Share lesson objectives (in student-friendly terms) and let students know why this lesson is relevant or purposeful	The teacher lets the students know what they'll be learning and why it is important. It is important that the teacher activates, assesses, and/or develops prior knowledge during the opening of the lesson.
Middle Model strategy or content to be learned Provide guided practice of strategy or content Teacher monitors student progress	This is where a lesson varies greatly depending on the instructional method chosen—student-centered—teacher-centered.
Closing Lesson closure Assign independent practice or homework	Summarize, connect to prior knowledge, discuss process or products of the lesson, review key concepts, preview tomorrow's lesson, etc.
Assessment Either formal or informal	See the assessment section of this chapter for further information

Standards

Standards are specific expectations of what a student must know and be able to do. National, state, and local standards guide curriculum and instruction in the United States. There are two types of standards:

- **Performance standards** set the level of performance expectation for student groups (for example, first-graders or five- to seven-year-olds). Performance standards are generally set at the state and local level and can generally be found on your state's department of education website or your local school district's website.

- **Content standards** provide expectations for the knowledge students must demonstrate. You should be familiar with the content standards for your discipline, which you can find on the websites for the following national specialized professional associations.

For more specific information on the standards in your content area, go to the websites that follow.

English Language Arts

National Council of Teachers of English: www.ncte.org

International Reading Association: www.reading.org

Foreign Languages

American Council on the Teaching of Foreign Language: www.actfl.org

Mathematics

National Council of Teachers of Mathematics: www.nctm.org

Science

National Science Teachers Association: www.nsta.org

Social Studies

National Council for the Social Studies: www.ncss.org

Thematic Instruction

Thematic instruction is a way to organize curriculum around large themes. Thematic units are integrated across several content areas, such as reading, social studies, math, and science. Thematic units might include such topics as dinosaurs, friendship, justice, civil rights, or patterns.

Transfer

Students are able to use previously learned material in a new situation or context. Teachers can promote students' ability to transfer learning experiences to new situations by developing "conditional knowledge" or helping students know when and how they might use the learned information in a new setting. Transfer of learning is often supported in the closing of the lesson and during extended practice opportunities.

Assessment Strategies

Along with planning a great lesson, you will need to assess what your students have learned in order to plan future instruction and to inform others of your students' progress. Next, we'll review assessment types and key aspects of educational measurement.

Assessment Types

There are several ways to assess student learning. Below, you'll find a helpful list of the many types of assessments and each of their primary purpose.

- **Achievement tests** are written for a variety of subjects and levels designed to measure a student's knowledge or proficiency in something that has been learned or taught. Examples of achievement tests include the Stanford Achievement Tests (SAT), the Metropolitan Achievement Test (MAT), and the California Achievement Test (CAT).

- **Anecdotal records** are the written notes teachers maintain based on their observations of individual children. Teachers use a variety of methods to organize anecdotal records, such as file folders, mailing labels, index cards, and Post-It notes.

- **Aptitude tests** are standardized (or norm-referenced) tests that are designed to measure a student's ability to develop or acquire skills and knowledge.

- **Authentic assessments** measure student understanding of the learning process and product, rather than just the product. For example, student understanding of patterns can be assessed by using teddy bear counters. Students actually create patterns using the counters, identify the patterns, and explain how they know this pattern to the teacher, who actively observes the student at work. In authentic assessments, students develop the responses rather than select from predetermined options. Clear criteria of success are established, which relate closely to classroom learning opportunities.

- **Criterion-referenced tests** determine how well a student performs on an explicit objective relative to a predetermined performance level, such as grade-level expectations or mastery. Criterion-referenced tests do not help teachers compare student results to those of other test-takers. An example of a criterion-referenced test is a teacher-made or publisher-made exam at the end of a social studies text chapter.

- **Diagnostic evaluations** are usually standardized or norm-references and are given before instruction begins to help teachers understand students' learning needs. These tests help teachers learn about students' areas of difficulties, but not the cause of those difficulties.

- **Essay** questions require students to make connections between new and previously learned content, to apply information to new situations, and to demonstrate that they have learned the new information.

- **Formative evaluations** provide information about learning in progress and offer the teacher and the student an opportunity to monitor and regulate learning.

- **Journals** can be used as an authentic assessment of a student's understanding of key concepts or his or her ability to communicate ideas in writing. Generally, journals are used as places to draft, and the teacher assesses the process, not the product, informally. In other words, a teacher rarely corrects spelling and grammar in a journal entry; rather, the teacher reads the journal entry to understand the student's thought process on a topic of study.

- **Norm-referenced tests** are also known as standardized tests. These tests are used to determine a student's performance in relation to the performance of a group of peers who have taken the same test. Norm-referenced tests are most often used by school personnel to make decisions about curriculum and school performance levels.

- **Observation** of students is arguably the most important assessment tool in your teaching toolkit. Also known as *kidwatching,* a term suggested by Ken Goodman in the 1960s, observing student interactions and learning behaviors is important to any classroom assessment plan. Teachers can take notes on their observations, called anecdotal records, or reflect on student observations after a lesson. It is important for teachers to observe students in other settings besides the classroom environment to gain a deeper understanding of a student's performance in school.

- **Performance assessments** require a student to perform a task or generate his or her own response during the assessment. For example, a performance assessment for a composition class would require a student to write something rather than answer multiple-choice questions or match test question items.

- A **portfolio** is a carefully selected collection of student products, and sometimes teacher observations, collected over time, that reflect a student's progress in a content area. Well-prepared student portfolios include student decision-making in the portfolio contents, demonstration of instructional outcomes, and multiple measures of student performance, and multiple products created over time.

- **Responses** can take many forms across the content areas. Students can respond orally, in writing, or through the visual and performance arts. Responses can be used as authentic assessments and are often assessed by using a set of criteria and a scoring rubric.

- **Self-evaluation** is a not-to-be-forgotten assessment. Students' monitoring and regulation of learning is important in the transfer of learning to new experiences. A student self-evaluation can provide "a window into the student's mind" that can let a teacher know how the student sees his or her progress and how the teacher might improve instruction for that student. Self-evaluations can be freeform in a discussion or in writing or can be more structured tasks, such as a self-evaluation in the form of a Likert scale. Teachers should be mindful to ask for student evaluation on the course content as well as the student's learning process.

- **Standards-based assessments** measure student progress toward meeting goals based on local, state, and/or national goals. Standards-based assessments can be based on content or performance standards and can be criterion-referenced or norm-referenced.

- **Summative evaluations** provide information about learning to be used to make judgments about a student's achievement and the teacher's instruction.

Educational Measurement

Next, we'll review the important aspects of educational measurement that may be on the PLT and will definitely impact your teaching once you begin your career.

Analytical Scoring

Analytical scoring is typically used to assess constructed-response test questions (essays, short-answer) and includes detailed descriptions of the criteria. For example, a teacher might ask for two reasons why the United States engaged in the Civil War. The teacher would construct an analytical scoring guide that includes all the possible correct responses to the prompt before reading the student responses. If a student included two of the causes listed on the analytical scoring guide, then the student would earn full credit. Analytical scoring guides are particularly useful when a teacher is new to an assessment or when a teacher has many items to score.

Grade-Level Equivalent Scores

Grade-level equivalents demonstrate the grade and month of the school year to which a student score can be compared. For example, a score of 5.1 would indicate that a student is performing at a fifth-grade, first-month level.

Holistic Scoring

Holistic scoring is typically used for constructed-response test questions (essays, journals, short-answer). It uses general descriptions of the criteria for success on each question. Holistic scoring can be more efficient than analytical scoring if the teacher has fewer test items to score.

Mean, Median, and Mode

The *mean* is the average of a set of scores. The *median* is defined as the midpoint of a set of numbers. The *mode* is the most common number in a set of numbers.

Percentile Rank

Percentile ranks show the percentage of students in a group (either a national or a local norm) whose scores fall above or below the given student's scores. The score range is between 1 and 99. If a student scored in the 50th percentile, 50 percent of the scores in the norm group fell below on this same test.

Quartiles

When you divide a normal distribution of scores into four equal parts, you can describe student data as it falls into one of the three quartiles.

- Q1 = The first quartile cuts off the lowest 25% of the data set = 25th percentile (lower quartile)
- Q2 = The second quartile cuts the data set in half = 50th percentile (median)
- Q3 = The third quartile cuts off the highest 25% or the lowest 75% of the data set = 75th percentile (upper quartile)

Quartiles enable school personnel to see the distribution of student scores and can help define student achievement patterns over time.

Raw Score

A student's raw score is equivalent to the number of questions he or she answered correctly on an assessment. Raw scores are helpful in determining the number of items actually answered correctly or incorrectly.

Reliability

Reliability is the extent to which an assessment is consistent with its measures.

Rubrics

A rubric is a scoring guide used in assessments. Rubrics can be subject-specific, task-specific, or generic.

Samples

A sample is a smaller number of participants drawn from a total "population." Sometimes it is not feasible for researchers to collect or analyze all the scores of a given population; therefore, a sample of scores is selected.

Scaled Scores

Scaled scores are based on a mathematical transformation of a raw score. Scaled scores can be helpful when determining averages and to study change over time.

Standard Deviation

Standard deviation is a measure of variability that indicates the typical distance between a set of scores of a distribution and the mean, or average score. For example, students' motivation level was rated on a scale of 1 to 4, with 4 being the highest and 1 being the lowest. For one class set of scores, the average score was 2.5, and the distribution of scores was uneven with scores primarily at the 1 or the 4 level. The standard deviation was determined to be 2, meaning that the amount of variability between scores on the distribution was two points. If the classroom teacher had used only the average student score on the motivation measure (a 2.5), he or she might have determined that students' motivation was moderate. Standard deviation becomes very helpful in this situation because it helps the teacher see that overall student motivation is very high or very low, not moderate at all for this class (distribution of scores).

Standard Error of Measurement

The standard error of measurement is the standard deviation of test scores you would have obtained from a single student who took the same test multiple times.

Stanines

Stanines (derived from STAndard NINE) are based on a nine-point standard scale with a mean of five and a standard deviation of two. Rarely do classroom teachers (with the exception of all of you math teachers out there) actually use the formula to calculate a stanine, but all of us will have to read score reports that often contain stanine scores. Stanines enable school personnel to see the distribution of scores for any grade level or group of students and may help schools see patterns of change in student achievement over time.

Validity

A test is found to be valid if it measures what it was designed to measure.

Communication Techniques

In this chapter, you will study key theories and terms covered on the PLT test sections with the constructed-response questions. You should carefully read and study this content on communication techniques, as it will help you respond to the case histories and create your constructed-response answers. Specifically, this chapter offers ideas for effective communication with students, colleagues, parents, and others you'll interact with when you are a teacher. As you'll recall, the Communication Techniques Content is not found in the multiple-choice format questions.

Environmental Factors to Promote Communication

Promoting Respect and Caring

Effective communication is fostered in an environment that promotes caring and respect. The teacher continually acts as a role model for effective communication and plays a key role in setting up a classroom conducive to open discourse. Teachers who are empathetic, patient, resourceful, and consistent provide an exemplary model of the kinds of behaviors that promote good communication. Active listening, valuing differences, highlighting student strengths, and turn-taking help promote caring and respect between teacher and student, as well as among students. Teachers should be mindful to use appropriate humor to diminish tension if it builds in the classroom, but they should be cautious in the use of sarcasm, especially when it is at the expense of a student. "Saving face" is very important in many cultures, and it is especially important to students in their teenage years. Use of sarcasm can diminish trust and respect in a classroom. Students must also have responsibilities in the classroom, which helps the student develop a sense of shared ownership in the work of school. One of the key responsibilities students can experience is the requirement that they care for others, themselves, and school property.

Goal-Setting

Early in the school year, the teacher can help students to articulate long-term and short-term learning goals. Parents can also provide direction and support for a student's goal-setting. Once goals have been established, the teacher can show respect and support for each student's goals and share student successes with the class. This practice fosters a sense of teamwork and camaraderie among students, and it helps the students to see individual goals and differences as strengths.

Effective Class Management

Whichever style you choose for your classroom management, the following suggestions will help your classroom become a place where students can learn and communicate openly:

- Move around the classroom and maintain eye contact with your students
- Pace and structure your lessons
- Establish a quiet signal or routine
- Maintain an interruption-free place to work
- Offer positive reinforcement for each student's efforts
- Allow students to interact and talk with one another during collaborative work times. Of course, there are times when quiet or independent work is necessary, but this should not be the majority of the class period or day.

In addition, it is important for teachers to establish daily routines and schedules and to establish classroom rules and consequences. Teachers must also use effective communication skills when working with colleagues and the students' caregivers. It is important for the teacher to maintain two-way communication with parents and guardians, keep accurate records, provide timely feedback, respond to student behavior, and offer objective descriptions of student behavior while maintaining student confidentiality.

Problem-Solving

In a classroom environment that promotes problem-solving, students see challenges as problems to be solved, rather than negative or frustrating events. Students who are problem-solvers consider their goals, the current situation, and the means to achieve the goal. Teachers play an important role in problem-solving discussions by asking probing questions and encouraging students to articulate their goals and situations, and then consider possible ways of achieving these goals. Also, teachers can model their thinking process in a variety of situations throughout the school day.

There are two main ways teachers aid students in resolving problems or conflicts in the classroom—behavior modification techniques and conflict resolution techniques. Conflict resolution helps students who have had a conflict to work together to arrive at a mutually beneficial solution. The goal is for students to resolve conflicts peacefully and cooperatively without using the traditional school discipline plans or structures. Behavior modification techniques are used to change observed behavior. The steps include:

1. Identify the problem behavior
2. Plan a method for changing the behavior
3. Offer a positive reinforcement when the student's behavior is positive
4. Use positive reinforcement consistently to shape and change the problem behavior

Curbing School Violence

If students do not feel safe, they will struggle to do well in school. School violence not only involves guns, knives, drugs, and gangs, but also includes bullying, harassment, intolerance, and insults. One way schools are working to curb violence is to create a more personalized school environment. Smaller class sizes, advisories, and schools within a school are models for creating a personalized environment. Research shows that when children feel a strong sense of belonging in school, they engage in fewer violent acts and do not allow their peers to engage in violence. Two-way communication between home and school can also diminish school violence.

Risk-Taking

In order for students to take risks—to ask a "silly question" or to offer an incorrect response—the teacher must ensure that the classroom environment promotes risk-taking. Such an environment does not allow sarcasm, interruption, ridicule, or harassment. The teacher can reframe "incorrect" responses as positive steps toward achieving deeper understanding and achieving a learning goal.

Stimulating Curiosity

There are many ways a teacher can stimulate student curiosity to promote student discussion and engagement—music, thought-provoking questions, mystery, film clips, etc. One example that comes immediately to mind is the "Mission Impossible" opening of a lesson conducted by one of my student teachers in an urban high school English classroom. Prior to the arrival of his students, Mr. Wynkoop set up their desks in a circle and put one desk in the center of the classroom. On the center desk, he placed a cassette tape player. As the students arrived, Mr. Wynkoop encouraged the students to play the tape and learn what they would do in English class today. The tape began with the theme from "Mission Impossible," which segued to Mr. Wynkoop's mysterious voice telling the students that they were about to begin a mission that would be impossible to complete without the teamwork of the class. His narration directed the students to an envelope under the center desk. A letter inside the envelope provided further directions for the mission—to read a new piece of literature collaboratively. Clearly, Mr. Wynkoop stimulated the students' and *my* curiosity, which promoted lots of student discussion to open the lesson!

Positive Interdependence

Positive interdependence is built when students must work well together to successfully complete a task. The previous example of Mr. Wynkoop's "Mission Impossible" also built positive interdependence. Once the students opened the envelope in the center of the classroom, they learned that they would be working in groups of four and that each group had tasks assigned to help the whole class achieve their "mission." Within each group, individual students had responsibility for a part of the assignment. For example, one student had to define three key vocabulary words; another had to learn more about the author. The students were able to help each other achieve the task and had to work together responsibly and effectively. Each student had to make a contribution, and each received an individual grade for his or her contribution.

Techniques to Foster Verbal and Nonverbal Communication

Setting Clear Expectations

Clear expectations can be conveyed in several important ways. First, the teacher can tell the students what they are going to learn in a lesson and why it is important. At the close of the lesson, the teacher can help students see when they can and cannot use this new information in new contexts. Clear expectations for student performance and behavior can be set in mutually agreed upon rules and criteria for excellence in student work. Setting up routines, procedures, and schedules help students become more responsible for their own learning and provide necessary structure to the school day. For students, parents, and administrators, teachers can provide clear expectations about units of study, goals, and standards the unit addresses.

Providing Clear Directions

Beginning teachers must take time to plan for clear directions. Clear and focused directions require no more than three student actions in one statement: state the type and quality of performance expected, describe each step of the task, and provide visual as well as oral representation of more complex directions. Beginning teachers often plan a narrative script ahead of time and demonstrate or model a task before asking students to perform the activity on their own.

Break Down Complex Tasks

Breaking down more complex tasks, such as long-term projects or group projects, is important for students, especially those with learning differences and attention difficulties. The teacher should provide clear directions, as stated in the previous section of this chapter, and should offer frequent "check-ins" to encourage students when they are making progress and to re-teach students when they are having difficulties.

Signal Transitions

Having a classroom routine and a posted schedule implicitly signals transitions from one activity to the next, but teachers often need to explicitly signal transitions for the wide variety of learners in the classroom. The elementary teacher often uses a clapping pattern, a song, or a bell to signal 5 minutes of work time left or time's up. The secondary teacher often lets the students know more verbally when transitions will occur, although I have worked with several teachers who use music or timers to signal transitions in the upper grades. For example, students work for a set amount of time and then when time is up they will share the work.

Explicit Teaching

Rosenshine (1987) suggests ten basic principles for the development of an explicit teaching session:

1. Short statement of lesson purpose
2. Short review of previous, prerequisite learning
3. Present new material in small steps, with student practice
4. Provide clear, detailed explanations and instructions
5. Provide active practice for all students
6. Ask effective questions, check for student understanding, and encourage all pupil response
7. Guide students during practice
8. Offer feedback and corrections
9. Provide practice for independent work and monitor students
10. Continue practice until students are ready to use new information confidently and independently

Highlight Key Information

Effective communicators highlight the key points to remember. You can literally highlight key points on the chalkboard, overhead projector or Power Point presentation. Other ways to "highlight" important information include opening and closing a lesson with the key points to remember, preparing study guides for students, and signaling students when they have learned something important.

Gestures

Nonverbal communication, such as gestures, also plays an important role in effective classroom communication. Positive gestures include nodding, the thumbs-up sign, and smiling. Gestures may also communicate negative messages, so teachers must be mindful of their nonverbal messages, such as turning away from a student to attend to something else, pointing, and tapping a foot. Teachers often videotape lessons to reflect on lesson strengths and areas to improve, and video can help teachers see the gestures they use and student reactions. Many of us have gestures that are part of a habit of communication (using my hands to gesture when I talk is one of mine!), so video or peer observations can help teachers know which communications are perceived positively and which are perceived in a less desirable way.

Eye Contact

Some students believe their teachers really *do* have eyes in the back of their head! This, of course, is not a prerequisite to good teaching, but keeping your eyes on your students, making eye communication, and fully attending to your students' communication are all signs of a teacher who communicates effectively. One should be mindful that not all students will be comfortable making eye contact with the teacher, though. This could be for cultural reasons, or it could be because of a timid personality or difficulties with social skills.

"With-it-ness"

Kounin describes teacher "with-it-ness" as an ability to know what is going on in the classroom at all times. For example, the teacher must have an ability to attend to a group, and also be aware of the actions of the remainder of the class. One lesson beginning teachers learn early is to not keep your back to the class for too long a period of time!

Personal Space

Teachers can communicate respect for students by understanding their students' need for personal space. Some children need lots of personal space, while others do not seem to know where their space ends and a classmate's begins. For example, a first-grader may need redirection or structure when she wants to always sit next to the teacher or to brush her friend's hair. One fourth-grade student I observed appeared to cringe when the student teacher knelt at a reasonable distance beside him to explain something. I later learned from the classroom teacher that this student was diagnosed with a mild level of autism and that the student needed an exceptional amount of space when working with others. In addition, a simple gesture such as patting a student on the back can be misunderstood or upsetting to the student. It's important to know and respect your students' needs for personal space. Of course, you will also want to teach your students to respect each other's needs for personal space, as well as your own.

Noise Level

Too much noise and too little noise can hamper classroom communication. Teachers must determine the "just right" noise level they can tolerate and clearly communicate with students when they are approaching too much noise. Nonverbal cues, such as red, yellow, and green index cards can signal when students can freely talk, when they are at a warning noise level, and when they must stop talking. Conversely, teachers must not require so little noise in the classroom that students have little to no opportunity to talk with one another. Borrowing from James Britton's quote, "Talk is the sea upon which all else floats." Classroom communication clearly requires a certain amount of noise.

Questioning Techniques

Room Arrangement

To promote active discussion, your room arrangement must facilitate face-to-face communication. Horseshoe table arrangements, semi circles, or clusters of tables are more effective than arrangements where students' backs are to one another, such as rows.

Getting the Discussion Started

Methods to start a discussion include opening with a shared experience, a concrete experience (such as showing an object that symbolizes a key concept), reading aloud a passage of the text, showing a film clip, or playing a music clip. Students can also complete a quick-write (a free recall writing) based on the experience or the reading assignment. It's also helpful to set out the parameters of the discussion, such as guidelines for turn-taking and for ending the discussion.

Factual Recall

Questions on the knowledge level of Bloom's taxonomy require factual recall. For example, who, what, when, why, and how questions. Other ways to promote factual recall include flash cards, games that require memory and immediate recall, and computer drill programs. Approaches to improving memory may include:

- Mnemonic devices (described in Chapter 8)
- Mental imagery—suggesting students form pictures in their mind
- Patterns of organization—present material to students in a logical and organized manner and help students see the pattern to the content
- Recitation—the student reads and repeats important content out loud.

Higher-Level Thinking

Higher-level thinking can be promoted in a variety of ways in the classroom. Questions based on Bloom's taxonomy at the evaluation, synthesis, and analysis levels promote higher-level thinking. Higher-level thinkers ask pertinent questions, make inferences, assess arguments, and are able to suspend judgment until all facts are gathered and considered. Teachers must be mindful to promote higher-level thinking in the classroom, and not just factual recall. Open-ended questions require higher-level thinking and probe for student understanding. Open-ended questions have no right or wrong answers.

Probing for Student Understanding

When following up on a student's initial response, teachers offer an opportunity to help the student think more deeply. Teachers can ask probing questions, ask other students to respond to the student's initial response, or ask higher-level questions. In addition, following up on a student's response shows the student that the teacher recognizes, appreciates, and values the student's ideas. Teachers might probe for student understanding by asking the following questions:

- How do you know?
- Can you tell me more?
- Please explain your thinking.
- Convince us of your strategy or argument.
- Why did you make this conclusion?

Student Question Generating

Good questions make great hypotheses. When students ask good questions, they are demonstrating a higher level of understanding of concepts. Teaching students to generate good questions is important to their higher-level thinking. Best practices for teaching students to generate questions include:

- Probing for understanding
- Modeling higher-level questioning
- Highlighting patterns and connections
- Provide a framework for the questioning
- Provide scaffolding of instruction and watch for misconceptions (correct, as needed)

All Pupil Response

There are several techniques teachers can use to ensure that more than one student responds to a teacher's inquiry. For example, you can give each of your students a set of letters to practice spelling the words you are teaching in a word study lesson.

Wait Time

Wait time is a purposeful pause of time that a teacher uses to give a student and the remainder of the class a chance to think and more deeply formulate a response. Research studies have shown that teachers usually wait less than 1 second between asking a question and moving to a response. Be sure to give students time to think. Effective discussion leaders use wait time and refrain from interrupting the thinking process with a prompt or another question.

Helpful Roles in a Discussion

You can teach your students several roles they can enact during a discussion, such as:

- **Summarizer:** This person listens to the discussion carefully and either summarizes one person's point or the entire discussion.
- **Note-taker or illustrator:** This role requires active listening and good note taking or drawing skills. The notes can be read at the close of the discussion or to open the discussion another day. A visual representation of the discussion can be shared to further the understanding of the group.
- **Quotable quotes:** In this role, the student finds a meaningful line or passage from the text and reads it to the group to trigger deeper understanding in the discussion.
- **Gatekeeper:** This person watches the time for the overall discussion as well as the equitable chances for people to speak.
- **Question generator:** This person asks probing questions or asks for clarification.
- **Facilitator:** The facilitator manages the overall discussion to keep students actively moving toward deeper understanding.
- **Evaluator:** The evaluator offers a critical, constructive view of the discussion's process and content.

Diversity in Classrooms Today

Cultural and Linguistic Diversity

The demographics of our communities are rapidly shifting. This rapid change suggests that the enrollment of school-children from linguistically and culturally different populations (from the so-called "mainstream" U.S. culture) is expected to increase. To improve the achievement of all children, teachers must be responsive, sensitive, and informed about the variety of cultures in the U.S. and particularly in their school community. By linguistic diversity, I refer to the many students whose first language is not English, as well as the variants of English that are spoken in American schools. By cultural diversity, I refer to Sonya Nieto's (1999) definition of culture, which describes it as a multidimensional constellation of ever-changing values, traditions, relationships, and worldview that binds a people together. People can come together by a combination of factors, such as shared history, geographic location, language, social class, and religion. Researchers have found that teachers' expectations, when communicated both verbally and nonverbally, influence children's behavior and performance. Therefore, teachers must treat all students as competent and expect high standard work from all children. To do so, teachers must not only know their content, but also know their students.

Abt-Perkins and Rosen (2000) suggest five important knowledge bases for teachers of culturally and linguistically diverse students:

- **Self knowledge:** Teachers must first understand the influence of their own cultures before they can meet the diverse cultural and linguistic needs of their own students. Teachers must critique their own values to ensure that these values are not inadvertently creating barriers to teaching all children.

- **Cultural knowledge:** A teacher with cultural knowledge shows an understanding of the importance of culture and how culture affects student views of the world. Teachers can meet the diverse needs of their students by knowing their students' families, languages, literacy practices, communities, and values.

- **Linguistic knowledge:** Teachers must understand the patterns of communication and dialects of the students they teach. Even though Standard American English (SAE) is the language of instruction in a majority of public schools, it is not always the language in the classroom. Delpit (1993) suggests that teachers must acknowledge and validate a student's home language. Teachers can foster a student's classroom communication by building on the student's home language and linguistic strengths.

- **Culturally informed teaching knowledge:** Teachers who have culturally informed teaching knowledge create a collaborative and culturally sensitive classroom environment. Teachers must learn to support the learning needs of each individual student, be sensitive to and respectful of a student's culture, and see the students' differences as "funds of knowledge" (Moll, 1992).

- **Knowledge of multicultural materials and methods:** Multicultural literature and texts that present balanced global views of historical events offer powerful ways for teachers to show respect for their students' cultures, as well as promote cross-cultural understanding.

Communication is a key aspect of culture. Differences between cultures can be perceived as threatening, so a teacher must be mindful of these differences in the classroom. The best way to learn about another's language and culture is, quite simply, to experience that language and culture. I am reluctant to share specific patterns of cultural and linguistic communication in this book because many misconceptions and stereotypes exist. I will leave this to anthropologists, linguists, sociologists, and you, the future classroom teacher. Nonetheless, I strongly suggest that, as a role model for your students, you learn as much as possible about the diverse languages and cultures in your community.

Next, we'll examine four general elements of communication that will help you to consider your own cultural and linguistic communication style and compare and contrast your style to that of your students. These four elements of communication are as follows:

- Directness
- Context
- The importance of "saving face"
- The difference between the task and the person

Degree of Directness

First, we'll consider the level of directness in communication. On the most direct side of a communication continuum, people say what they mean and mean what they say. There is little subtlety, and it's important to tell it like it is. A person with a direct communication style believes honesty is the best policy and that the truth is more important than sparing a person's feelings.

On the other end of this communication continuum, people with an indirect communication style imply or suggest what they are saying. You must be a good interpreter of the person's meaning and use inference to gather the person's true message. Those with an indirect communication style believe that, if the truth hurts, it should be tempered.

The Role of Context

The second pattern involves context—a continuum of low context to high context communication. Context means the amount of instinctive understanding a person is expected to bring to the communication setting.

Low context communication cultures tend to be heterogeneous and individualist. In this culture, little is believed to be known, so there is a high emphasis on verbal communication.

High context communication cultures tend to be homogeneous and collectivist (emphasis is placed on the group, not the individual). In a high context culture much is already known by the members, so the spoken word is not the primary means of communicating. Nonverbal cues and the communication setting are central in the communication.

The Importance of "Saving Face"

Another important communication continuum to consider is where the importance of "saving face" falls in a culture. By saving face, I refer to an act that avoids the loss of a person's dignity or prestige. In a culture where saving face is highly valued, people tend to maintain harmony, avoid confrontation, and have a difficult time saying no. The overall goal in such a culture is harmony. Often, what one says and what one feels is not the same.

In a culture where saving face is less important, a person's dignity is less important. Facts and getting something done efficiently are more highly valued. Criticism and feedback are straightforward, and it is fine to confront people or to say no.

The Task and the Person

The last pattern of communication we'll consider is the importance of the task compared to the importance of the person. In a culture where the task is foremost, the task is separated from the person. People do business first and socialize or engage in a bit of small talk. Building relationships is not central to getting the job done well. In a culture where the person is foremost, the goal is to build relationships first. The task and the person cannot be separated. The people in this culture often begin with small talk and then move to business. Personal relationships are central to getting the job done well.

Other Areas of Diversity in Classrooms Today

In addition to being knowledgeable and appreciative of cultural and linguistic diversity in your classroom, teachers must also be understanding and aware of other areas of diversity in classrooms today.

Socioeconomic Background

Socioeconomic status (SES) and school achievement are highly correlated. Teachers must consider similar aspects of understanding differences in SES cultural and linguistic diversity as they do for students from cultural and linguistically diverse backgrounds. You may experience teaching students from a much higher SES or much lower SES than your own. The key here is to have high expectations for all of your students and to communicate these expectations positively and supportively.

Social Styles

Are you the type of person who loves a big gathering with lots of friends, or would you prefer a smaller get-together with a close friend or a few couples? Your students also have social styles that impact their learning in the group setting of your classroom; therefore, students need opportunities to work in the whole group, small groups, and individually in the course of the school day, in the case of younger learners, and in the course of the school week, in the case of older students.

Learning Styles

As discussed in Chapter 7, people have a variety of ways of making sense of what they are learning, such as visual, auditory, kinesthetic, or tactile learning styles. Teachers strive to communicate with their students in a way that is most beneficial to each student's learning style. For example, after I explained a three-step task to my juniors, I wrote a brief, bulleted list of the directions on the chalkboard and then asked students to visualize each step and ask questions, as needed.

Scholastic Abilities and Challenges

You may teach students who have been identified as possessing giftedness, a learning disability, a musical or athletic talent, a physical handicap, an attention deficit, a bipolar disorder, Tourette's syndrome, or an addiction to alcohol. Each of these students brings abilities to the classroom that you, the teacher, can identify and can capitalize on when teaching your lesson. Each student brings abilities and challenges; therefore, a teacher must assume responsibility for teaching each student in his or her classroom and must persevere to find the right instructional strategies for each child. Sometimes, you will need to confer with colleagues who have more experience or expertise with students possessing scholastic abilities and challenges.

Lifestyles

There are many configurations to our students' families, all of which require us, as teachers, to suspend judgment and to keep an open mind, even when a child's family structure is very different than the teacher's perception of a "good" family. Children live in the homes of happy and healthy single-parents, grandparents, foster-parents, step-parents, same-sex parents, married parents, and more. Of course, not all children live in families that are happy and healthy. As a teacher, it is your responsibility to strive to teach all of your students well. In addition, some children live in several homes in the course of a school year or do not live in a permanent home at all. While working with the diverse lifestyles of our students' families can be a challenge, teachers are responsible for professionally communicating with all children and for communicating with students' caregivers no matter their living situation. Again, focusing on student *strengths* and valuing what their caregivers *can* teach us about their child are important strategies for teachers. Support personnel, mentors, and colleagues—such as social workers, psychologists, school nurses, and principals—can provide professional expertise and experience to you as you strive to teach *all* children well.

Stimulating Discussion and Responses in the Classroom

Planning for Discussions

Teachers should be mindful of the following points when preparing for classroom discussions:

1. Determine goals of the discussion
2. Assess prior knowledge and experiences of the students
3. Assess and build your background knowledge on the topic
4. Provide a supportive environment for discussion
5. Offer your viewpoint, when necessary, to build knowledge or correct misinformation
6. Allow for alternative viewpoints—to agree to disagree
7. Plan for meaningful connections between the discussion, other course content, and real-life experience

Discussion Methods

Whole-Class

The entire group is taught in whole-class discussion. Teachers often use whole-class discussion for lectures, demonstrations, explanations, questioning, recitations (oral practice), and work on a set of problems, or use of the same materials, such as a science text or a piece of literature. Whole-class discussions are helpful when the information to be covered requires a common understanding for all, but it should not be the only or primary method of discussion because differentiated instruction cannot occur in this configuration. Also, students have fewer opportunities for active participation during whole-class discussions, which can lead to disruptive classroom behaviors.

Small-Group

Effective small groups are made up of between four and six students. Small groups can be comprised of heterogeneous (different level or style) learners or homogenous (similar) learners. Common types of small groups include ability groups, peer tutors, and cooperative learning groups. Ability groups are groups of students who have been judged to be performing on a similar academic level in a particular content area. Peer tutoring involves peers teaching peers. Teachers can set up peer tutors within the same classroom or might partner with another classroom or grade level of students. Cooperative learning groups are discussed in Chapter 8.

Literature Circles

Literature circles are small groups of students who read and discuss the same materials together. The teacher talks to all of the students about their responsibilities, key roles, and necessary new content, and then they break into small groups, each group working independently to discuss and understand the text. Common literature circle roles include facilitator, connector, summarizer, vocabulary master, and illustrator. Literature circles offer students an opportunity to actively participate in discussions and to take responsibility for learning.

Panels and Debates

A panel is a formal discussion structure in which four to eight participants discuss a topic while the rest of the class listens. After the panel discussions, the class is able to question the panel members and discuss the topic further.

A debate is another formal discussion structure made up of a set of speeches by students from two opposing views. Debate groups present their views, followed by rebuttals of the opposing side's views.

Reports

Students can prepare reports to present and discuss with the class or a wider audience. In doing so, students can employ a variety of creative formats. For example, students might use Power Point or artwork to present report information to the school community in an effort to inform others about a topic of interest.

Reader Response

Readers can respond to text in two main ways:

1. With an efferent stance
2. With an aesthetic stance

When students discuss the text with an efferent stance, they make sense of the content, the meaning of the text, or the factual points of the text. When students discuss the text with an aesthetic stance, they connect personal experiences to the text, discussing thoughts and feelings about the text. Reader response is grounded in the theory that readers bring prior knowledge and experiences to reading and attempt to make meaning from text. The following formula provides a visual representation of a current view of making meaning with texts:

Reader + Text = Meaning

A teacher with this view of student response strives to question students in order to help them come to their own interpretations of the text, not necessarily the teacher's or the author's view. Reader response is a way of communicating with students about *their* interpretation of texts.

Teacher Professionalism

In this chapter, we will review the last of the four categories of content on the PLT: Teacher Professionalism. This content is found on both the multiple-choice and the constructed-response questions. While there tend to be fewer questions from the teacher professionalism category (22% of the test, as you may recall from Chapter 1), this content is important to review. My pre-service teachers report that they appreciate this outline review, which includes information about teachers as reflective practitioners, the rights of teachers and students, key historical information about U.S. schools, and other legal aspects of teaching in the United States.

The Reflective Practitioner

The School and Society

Public schools in the United States play a key role in society. Public schools represent the greater public interest by promoting democratic principles, teaching common values, and educating about the diverse cultures of global society. Schools also offer parents and citizens a variety of ways to have a voice in the direction of public education. Parents and citizens alike have an interest in the ability of our nation's students to acquire the knowledge, skills, and dispositions to lead productive, healthy, responsible, and successful lives. The ways students are educated today will affect the quality of American life for years to come. U.S. citizens living in a free and democratic nation must value and practice a common set of principles, such as equality and freedom for all, equal opportunity, self-governance, civic responsibility, respect for the laws of the nation, and social mobility. Decisions about content standards, performance standards, curriculum, and texts, as well as lessons in content areas and activities in school governance provide opportunities for students and citizens to practice working effectively in a democratic society. Public education offers an opportunity for students and citizens to learn about the diverse members of our global society and to practice tolerance, respect, and understanding for people of different cultures and backgrounds. Teachers must become reflective practitioners in order to be most effective. Reflective practice is grounded in John Dewey's Progressive Education movement. Dewey emphasized the need for teachers' reflective action to facilitate the knowledge of their students. Reflective practitioners display such characteristics as:

1. Not be afraid to say they do not know or understand something.
2. A desire to be caring educators.
3. Show a willingness to collaborate and to discuss experiences.
4. Have an ability to critically analyze their practices.
5. View teaching and student behaviors through a reflective lens.
6. Demonstrate rational, careful thought to improve practices.
7. Possess an awareness of their own culture, values, and beliefs.
8. View diversity as a positive, enriching aspect of teaching.
9. Show persistence.
10. Possess effective interpersonal communication skills.
11. Value the importance of empowering learners.

Advocacy for Learners

Teachers must advocate for the educational needs of *all* learners. Ways in which teachers advocate for learners include, but are not limited to, the following:

1. Attending professional development training.
2. Staying abreast of latest education findings and practices.
3. Actively participating in meetings about their students.
4. Fostering open communication with caregivers, colleagues, and other personnel who work with their students.
5. Modifying instructional practice to meet unique learning needs.

Teachers must understand the awesome responsibility placed upon one in the teaching profession. Your local school district may have a stated code of ethics for teachers. In addition, professional associations like the National Education Association provide guidance on ethical standards for teachers. Teachers must demonstrate, for example, the highest commitment to students and to the teaching profession through actions such as the following:

1. Nurturing each student's academic, social, emotional, physical, and civic growth.
2. Creating and sustaining a positive, challenging, and safe school environment.
3. Committing to lifelong learning for all, including the teacher's own learning.

4. Collaborating with colleagues, students' caregivers, and other professionals.

5. Advancing the intellectual foundation of the school community and education profession.

6. Following U.S. laws, including those that pertain specifically to schools, such as:

   • Discrimination against students, teachers, parents, or others based on race, sex, ethnicity, or religion.

   • Prayer in public schools.

   • Using books that have been removed from the school library or curriculum by a decision of the school board.

   • Withholding school records from parents or guardians.

Teachers' Rights

You may be asked questions about the rights of teachers in the United States. It is important for you to know that teachers have several rights, guided by school and civic law, including:

1. The right to withhold information unrelated to employment, such as age, marital status, sexual orientation, etc.

2. Pregnant teachers cannot be required to take maternity leave.

3. Teachers cannot be fired for behavior that does not interfere with teaching effectiveness. While teachers have a right to a personal life and behaviors associated with a personal life beyond school, the teacher may be fired for personal behavior that impacts teaching effectiveness both during the school day and beyond.

4. Teachers can be sued and may be found liable for negligence. For example, if a teacher could have reasonably foreseen a situation, or if the teacher acted differently than a reasonable teacher placed in the same situation would have acted, the teacher may be found liable.

5. Teachers have freedom of speech, as well as all other freedoms guaranteed in the U.S. Constitution.

6. While corporal punishment is not unconstitutional, it may be illegal and can only be administered according to the laws of the state.

7. Teachers have a right to freely associate on and off school hours with whomever they choose, such as any political party, religious group, or community group, even those not seen favorably by the school committee or local administration.

8. Teachers can be suspended or dismissed for not doing their jobs, but such administrative actions must include due process.

Students' Rights

Several court cases have helped to form the basis of students' rights in American schools today. In the *Tinker v. Des Moines Independent Community School District* case of 1969, the court established that students do not lose their constitutional rights of freedom of speech or expression in school. In the *Goss v. Lopez* case of 1971, the court established that students facing suspension must be afforded a hearing and notice before being denied their right to an education. This became known as due process. Students' rights are more frequently infringed in the areas of search and seizure, freedom of speech and expression (e.g., censorship, school dress codes, and privacy invasion), zero tolerance, and corporal punishment. Students have a limited freedom of press and a limited freedom of speech in schools. For example, student newspapers supported by the school system may be edited by school personnel. School periodicals supported solely by student groups may not be censored or edited by school officials. A student's freedom of speech may be withheld if it causes a major disruption in the school. A student may not use speech considered vulgar or offensive. School records must be made available to students and their parents upon request. Handicapped students between the ages of 3 to 21 have a right to a free and appropriate public education. This education must take place in the least restrictive environment.

Resources

Professional Associations

Each content area has a national professional association, and many professional associations have local chapters. By joining a professional association you show your willingness to become a lifelong learner and good colleague. Inevitably you will benefit from the many publications, website resources, conferences, and people you will interact with while a member of the association. Below is a list of major professional associations, but remember that there are more available to you!

English Language Arts

National Council of Teachers of English: http://www.ncte.org

International Reading Association: http://www.reading.org

Mathematics

National Council of Teachers of Mathematics: http://www.nctm.org

Science

National Science Teachers Association: http://www.nsta.org

Foreign Languages

American Council on the Teaching of Foreign Language: http://www.actfl.org

Social Studies

National Council for the Social Studies: http://www.ncss.org

Colleagues

Your colleagues, both new and experienced, are valuable resources in your teaching toolkit. Teaching with excellence is a complex and demanding task. By networking with colleagues, you develop a mutually beneficial relationship to ease the demands of teaching, as well as model the type of cooperative behavior you expect of your students.

Conferences

Reflective practitioners are lifelong learners. Attending conferences is one great way to learn more about teaching. There are many conference opportunities, both locally and nationally, of which you should take advantage. Besides the important information you will gain, conferences offer an opportunity to network with colleagues outside of your school building. They also provide time to reflect upon your teaching practice.

Professional Literature

When you join a national professional association, you usually will receive a professional journal or newsletter as a membership benefit. Professional journals and newsletters are available in many libraries, perhaps even the one at your school. Professional magazines are available by subscription. Many professional literature resources can be accessed online. Professional literature provides the opportunity for you to stay current in your field and to read about the best, research-based practices.

Professional Development

Professional development, or in-service education, is an opportunity for you to learn and grow as an educator. You may attend a small discussion group, a large conference, or an individual session with a coach. You could also register for a college course. Whatever the format, professional development provides a chance for you to reflect, refine your teaching skills, and add to your teaching knowledge base.

The Larger Community

Educational Law

Americans with Disabilities Act (ADA), Title II

Americans with Disabilities Act is a federal law that prohibits discrimination on the basis of a person's disability for all services, programs, and activities provided or made available by local and state governments. The ADA is not dependent on the receipt of federal funds.

Individuals with Disabilities Act (IDEA)

The Individuals with Disabilities Act is a federal statute made up of several grant programs targeted at helping the states to educate students with disabilities. The IDEA specifically lists types of disabilities conditions that render a child entitled to special education.

Individualized Education Plan (IEP)

An Individualized Education Plan is a written education plan for a student with disabilities developed by a team of professionals (teachers, special educators, school psychologists) and the child's parents or caregivers. An IEP is based on a multidisciplinary evaluation (MDT) of the child, describing how the child is presently doing, what the child's learning needs are, and what services the child will need. Each IEP is reviewed and updated yearly. IEPs are required under Public Law 94-142, the Individuals with Disabilities Education Act (IDEA).

Section 504

Section 504 is a civil rights law. Enacted in 1973, the law forbids organizations and employers from preventing individuals with disabilities an equal opportunity to receive program benefits and services.

Public Law 94-142

Public Law 94-142 was passed into legislation during the Ford administration in 1975. This law was created to ensure a free and appropriate education is provided to handicapped children and adults ages 3–21. The term "least restrictive environment" originated with this law; it states that handicapped persons must be educated, to the maximum extent possible, with their regular education peers. Special education programs and meetings to determine special education eligibility and placement are regulated by the original Public Law 94-142 and more recent iterations of the law. One important aspect of the law requires a school to provide written permission from the parent or guardian before conducting any evaluation of a child.

Massachusetts Laws of Education 1642 and 1647

The Law of 1642 established that parents (or "masters") were responsible for instilling the principles of religion and the capital laws of the Commonwealth of Massachusetts. All children and servants were required to demonstrate competency in reading and writing as outlined by the government. Not all children attended formal schools; therefore, it was the responsibility of parents to teach children basic literacy skills so they could abide by the governing laws of the land.

The Law of 1647 was established to combat parental negligence in educating the child or servant according to the Law of 1642. This law required that towns of 50 families or more hire a schoolmaster who could teach the children to read and write. Education became more of a social responsibility with the enactment of the Massachusetts Law of 1647.

Land Ordinance of 1785

By 1785, the separation of church and state were evident in American education. The Land Ordinance of 1785 helped to establish a way to fund public education. The sixteenth section in each township was reserved for the maintenance of public schools.

Northwest Ordinance of 1787

The Northwest Ordinance of 1787 provided land in the Great Lakes and Ohio Valley regions for settlement. One part of the ordiance stated that religion, morality, and knowledge are necessary for a strong government. The federal government began to create a public school system offered to all children.

Plessy v. Ferguson

After the Civil War ended, many Southern states were driven to limit the rights of former slaves. A group of New Orleans black businessmen decided to test the laws limiting their rights to use the railroads freely, laws supported in the South but not by the railroad owners. A man named Home Plessy volunteered to break the law by taking a seat in a "white-car only." Plessy was arrested and at his trial he argued that the laws violated his civil rights. Judge Ferguson found Plessy guilty and charged him a $25 fine. The Supreme Court reviewed the case of *Plessy v. Ferguson* and found the law of separate railroad cars consitutional. The Supreme Court ruled that "separate but equal facilities" was allowable by law. In 1896, Brown wrote the majority opinion; Harlan was the lone dissent vote. Brown wrote that a state law providing separate but equal facilities for black and white passengers does not infringe upon the 13th or 14th Amendments of the U.S. Constitution. The "separate but equal" view prevailed in the U.S. until the Supreme Court ruled that separate is "inherently unequal" in the *Brown v. Board of Education* case.

Oregon School Case of 1925

This case is also known as *Pierce v. Society of Sisters*. The Oregon school system participated in a decision to "Americanize" schools by requiring all children ages 8 to 16 to attend public schools. Exceptions were offered in a few instances, such as for those with physical handicaps and those who had completed the 8th grade successfully. The Society of Sisters of the Holy Names of Jesus and Mary and a group of educators from a nearby private military school disputed the constitutionality of this Oregon state law. In 1925, the court ruled that the state of Oregon could not require all students to attend public schools, as this violates a student's 14th Amendment right of "personal liberty." Students *can* be required to attend public *or* private schools.

Brown v. Board of Education

On May 17, 1954, the United States Supreme Court announced its decision in the *Brown v. Board of Education* case that "separate educational facilities are inherently unequal," thereby changing the face of American education forever. The decision effectively denied the legal basis for segregation in Kansas and 20 other states with segregated classrooms. *Brown v. Board of Education* was an important first step toward providing equal rights for all children in U.S. schools. For many years, several schools in the South continued to challenge "separate is unequal." In 1957, nine black students from Little Rock, Arkansas, nonviolently and bravely decided to challenge their right to attend the all-white Rock Central High. The students were met with racial slurs, and rocks and bottles were thrown at them. Federal soldiers had to escort the children through the doors of the school. The courageous students who advanced the civil rights movement became known as "The Little Rock Nine."

History of U.S. Education

Colonial Period (1600–1776)

The Puritan Influence

The Puritans were a group of people who worked toward religious, moral, and societal reforms. They grew unhappy with the Church of England, escaped persecution from church leaders and the King of England, and fled to America. Free schooling was offered to all children, and the Puritans formed the first formal American school in 1635, called the Roxbury Latin School. In 1638, the first printing press was used. The Puritans were the first to write books for children. Schools during this time were strongly influenced by religion. In 1642, a law was passed stating that all children should learn to read. It was the Puritans' belief that an inability to read was Satan working to keep people from reading the Bible.

Latin Grammar School

The Roxbury Latin School was the first Latin Grammar School, established in 1635. Originally, these schools were designed for the sons of upper social classes who were destined to become leaders in the church, state, or judicial system. Girls were not considered for these schools. The schools taught reading, writing, and arithmetic. Besides preparing the boys for leadership positions, the more practical purpose of the Latin Grammar School was to prepare the boys for the entrance examination for Harvard College. These schools can be compared to the American Secondary Schools, which prepare today's students for higher education.

Establishment of Harvard College

Harvard College was established in 1636 by vote of the Great and General Court of the Massachusetts Bay Colony. The initial mission of the College was to ensure that the leaders of the church, state government, and judicial system were well-prepared and learned. During these early years, the College offered a classic academic course of study, not only based on the English university model, but also consistent with the Puritans' philosophy of education.

Hornbooks

Hornbooks were used by children for several centuries starting in the mid-15th century in Europe. A hornbook consisted of a wooden paddle, parchment with the lesson, and a cover for the lesson made of a piece of transparent horn. Lessons included such things as the alphabet, the Lord's Prayer, vowels, and consonant patterns.

New England Primer

The Primer was a textbook used by students. First printed in 1690, over 5 million copies of the book were sold. The New England Primer combined alphabet study with Bible verses.

Early National Period (1776–1840)

Benjamin Franklin (1706–1790)

Among his many contributions, Ben Franklin advanced formal education in America. He established a plan for the English-language grammar school in Philadelphia in 1749. The school would teach English, rather than Latin, and enact a curriculum focused on scientific and practical skills. The English grammar schools would educate a wider range of students who could make contributions to politics, government, society, as well as a variety of occupations and professions. Franklin's plan, which was never instituted, called for schools equipped with laboratories, books, maps, and globes so that students could connect practical knowledge with the world around them. The English grammar schools did not succeed, but Franklin's proposal led the way to the future American education institutions, which offered a comprehensive curriculum designed for the growing needs of the growing nation.

Thomas Jefferson

The third U.S. President, Thomas Jefferson, worked for several years after his presidency to create the University of Virginia at Charlottesville, which was established in 1825. His vision for the school was to introduce American students to new ideas about government and equality. He understood that different students had different educational needs, so he allowed for electives in the curriculum. Jefferson conceived of every aspect of the university—surveying the site, planning for the buildings, supervising the construction, and establishing the curriculum.

Noah Webster

Webster established the first uniquely American dictionary, published in 1828 and called the *American Dictionary of the English Language*. His dictionary was adopted by Congress in 1831 and was considered the national standard for English in the U.S. Webster also influenced American education by opposing the British texts used in schools and suggesting the need for American textbooks that included our language and experiences. He also established a grammar book, a reader, and *The American Spelling Book*.

Yale Report of 1828

This report demonstrated the strength of the conservative view of education—the need for a classical curriculum—which was centered at Yale University. The following issues at the time were causing controversy in higher education:

- Church vs. state control of higher education
- The value of a college vs. a university education
- The importance of the classical curriculum vs. the curriculum that allows for electives

Common School Period (1840–1880)

Common School

The common school was a school that would be available to all people, a part of the birthright of every American child, and founded on the principle of "social harmony." The common school movement contained elements of oppression and emancipation. Common schools attempted to respond to the needs of expanding capitalist industries and the realities of growing cities, such as the training of immigrants, so that these individuals could become productive workers. The common school movement also provided educational opportunity for children who had previously been excluded.

Horace Mann

Horace Mann believed that a "common school" would be the great equalizer. Horace Mann is considered the father of American education, and, as Secretary of Education in 1839, he presided over the establishment of the first normal school in the United States. Normal schools were established for the primary purpose of training teachers.

Henry Barnard

Henry Barnard was a great education reformer of the 19th century. He was a lifelong advocate for common schools—a design for a universal system of public education. Barnard also strongly believed in the importance of the education of women. Barnard created the first board of education in Connecticut and became the first secretary of education in this state in 1838. Barnard faced resistance of his progressive ideas for education from the conservative political forces, parochial schools, and some parents. The conservative political forces were concerned that common schools would mean that children were less available to work and that taxes would be higher. Parochial schools felt that public education threatened their religious values. Some parents were concerned with the concept of a universal education, fearing that schools would become charitable organizations, more concerned with equality in education than excellence for their children.

Normal School

The first normal school in the United States was established in 1839 in Lexington, Massachusetts, for the purpose of training teachers. This first normal school is today known as Framingham State College. The normal schools were developed to support the growing need for teachers in the common schools.

McGuffey Readers

The first McGuffey Readers were published in 1836. These texts had a great influence on public education in the U.S. The books had graded, or "leveled," readers, which upheld the values, beliefs, and way of life for Americans during this time. The first editions sold 7 million copies; by 1879, more than 60 million had been sold. There were several readers—The Eclectic First and Second Readers (1836), the Third and Fourth Readers (1837), the Fifth Reader (1844), the Sixth Reader (1857), and the Eclectic Spelling Book (1846). The readers passed through several publishers and were revised in 1879 by Van Nostrand Reinhold to include a collection of eight revised editions.

Compulsory Education

The Massachusetts Compulsory Attendance Act of 1852 required compulsory school attendance for children between the ages of 8 and 14 for at least three months of the calendar year; it also mandated that at least six weeks of each child's school attendance be consecutive. The penalty for not sending a child to school was a maximum fine of $20. The compulsory attendance law was revised in 1873, with the age limit lowered to 12 and the required length of attendance increased to 20 weeks each calendar year. By 1918, a compulsory education attendance law had been enacted in all U.S. states.

Morrill Act of 1862

Also known as the Land Grant College Act, the Morrill Act of 1862 established institutions in each state to provide an education in agriculture, home economics, mechanical arts, and other practical professions. The goal was to assure that education would be available to people in all social classes.

National Education Association

The National Education Association (NEA) began in 1857 as the National Teachers Association and was founded by 43 educators in Philadelphia. The NEA is currently the largest educational association in the world. It was founded to advance the teaching profession, increase interest in teaching, and promote the cause of public education in the U.S. The NEA allowed women to become members in 1866.

Establishment of Kindergartens

The first kindergarten in the world was established by Friedrich Froebel in 1837 and became known as the "father of kindergarten." In the U.S. early kindergarten programs were established in 1856 in Wisconsin and in 1873 in Boston. Kindergartens were first created to support children living in poverty and those with special needs. The curriculum emphasized the importance of play. In 1872, kindergartens won the support of the National Education Association (NEA).

Progressive Period (1880–1920)

Impact of Business and Industry on American Education

Our present American Education system was heavily influenced by the Industrial Revolution. During this period in history, the U.S. had to prepare people trained in agriculture to work in factories. The importance of mass production influenced the design of schools during this time, and vestiges of this system still influence American secondary schools today. The "mass production" mentality created a school system that was efficient and produced measurable gains. Successful graduates were ready to meet the increasing demands of industry and business. In the Southern Black schools at the turn of the century, the goal was to ensure blacks remained agricultural and domestic workers. The General Education Board (GEB) established three key programs: State Supervisors for Negro Rural Schools, County Supervising Teachers, and County Training Schools. The discriminatory practices of these programs continued at least until *Brown v. the Board of Education,* but vestiges of these discriminatory educational policies are still seen in U.S. schools today, such as inadequate funding for poor, urban schools, which educate a majority of minority students.

The Superintendent

Horace Mann was an education reformer concerned with school policy and leadership. He suggested that a senior teacher provide leadership in the school. To free the teacher for administrative duties, teacher aides and advanced students taught groups of the senior teacher's students. This practice became known as monitorial education, and it did not prove practical in many parts of the U.S. but served as a model for future schools. The term "Superintendent of Schools" came from the Industrial Revolution terminology of the times, with similar leaders in Superintendent of Railroads, Superintendent of the Factory. The first training program for administrators began at Teachers College at Columbia University at the turn of the century.

The Principal

As with the role of the superintendent, the role of the principal is rooted in Horace Mann's concept of the principal teacher and dates back to the turn of the century. The principal served as a middle manager and acted as teacher, as well as many other roles in the community, such as town clerk, store clerk, and church secretary. The role of principal started in the secondary schools and eventually spread into the primary schools.

Division of Schools into Grades

As noted in this text's section on the Colonial period of education, American education was founded to prepare the elite for leadership positions and for Harvard College. As a result of the Land Ordinance of 1785 and the Northwest Ordinance of 1787, towns had to set aside land for the building and operation of schools. This provided the context for the one-room schoolhouse. In these schools, one teacher usually taught between 30 and 40 students from all ages and ability levels. As more and more children began to attend schools, the one-room schoolhouse design no longer met the needs of the children and their teachers. More buildings were erected and school buildings became larger, creating the need for effective ways to group the children. At first, most schools grouped their students by age, with children ages 6–8 in one room and children ages 9–14 in another. If a child moved beyond the upper-level room, he or she would either attend college or join the work force. Over time, the U.S. education system established a 12 grade-level system with an initial kindergarten year.

The Cardinal Principles of Secondary Education

There were seven cardinal principles of secondary education issued in a report by the Commission on the Reorganization of Secondary Education in 1918. The principles were:

1. Health (secondary schools should promote good health habits)
2. Command of fundamental processes (writing, reading, oral and written expression, and mathematics)
3. Worthy home membership (schools should promote good relationships)
4. Vocation (know the variety of career options)
5. Civic education (develop awareness and concern for one's community)
6. Worthy use of leisure (advance skills to enrich a student's mind, body, spirit, and personality during leisure time)
7. Ethical behavior (instilling personal responsibility and initiative)

NEA Committee of Ten

In 1982, the National Education Association appointed a committee, known as the Committee of Ten, that wrote a report calling for changes to liberalize the American high school. This report recommended the standardization of curricula for American high schools and elementary schools. The committee recommended eight years of elementary education, four years of secondary education and the following four curriculum strands:

1. Classical
2. Latin-scientific
3. Modern language
4. English

American Federation of Teachers

The American Federation of Teachers (AFT) was formed in 1916. The AFT is a teachers' union associated with the American Federation of Labor and Congress of Industrial Organization (AFL-CIO). AFT's motto is "Democracy in Education and Education for Democracy."

Manual Training Movement

The Manual Training movement in American education provided the foundation for the vocational education programs in schools today. A Manual Training education offered wood and metal working, and it was seen as an enhancement to the traditional high-school curriculum.

Modern Period (1920–Present)

John Dewey (1859–1952)

John Dewey made contributions to many areas during his life's work—philosophy, politics, social thought, psychology, and education. He is considered a foremost voice of American education philosophy. His philosophy of education is known as "progressive education." Dewey's core beliefs included the following:

- There is a close connection between education and social action in a democracy.
- Students should be taught to become problem-solvers.
- Students should participate in decisions about what they learn.

Dewey wrote several influential texts on educational philosophy, including *Experience and Education* and *The School and Society*. Dewey founded the American Association of University Professors in 1915 upon the principle of "academic freedom."

Adult Education

While U.S. adult education's roots can be traced back over the last 200-plus years to events like Ben Franklin's establishment of the public library and his first adult education organization, adult education programs made several advances during the modern period. The Smith-Lever Act of 1914 helped to create cooperative extensions through the Land Grant University (Morrill Acts of 1860 and 1892), which offered adult education in agriculture, rural energy, and home economics. In the 1960s, the efforts of Presidents Kennedy and Johnson led to the Economic Opportunity Act of 1964, which created the first Adult Basic Education program grant program.

Testing Movement

Lewis Terman (1877–1956) introduced the Stanford-Binet intelligence test in 1916. Terman next provided consulting services to the U.S. military and initiated a testing program to sort and categorize recruits in an effort to match each soldier with the most appropriate military occupation. He also created the Stanford Achievement Test and coined the term intelligence quotient, or IQ. Terman used a scientific approach to determine and classify student ability; this was received with overwhelming support from the Progressive educators of the early 1900s. This method of scientifically proving immigrants and minorities scored lower than whites on these tests seemingly "proved" the prevalent discriminatory views that these people were mentally inferior.

Sputnik

U.S. education dramatically changed after October 4, 1957, when the Soviet Union successfully launched the world's first satellite. The Sputnik launch led to the creation of the National Aeronautics and Space Act (NASA), as well as the American outcry for advanced coursework in mathematics and science in our schools.

ESEA

The Elementary and Secondary Education Act (ESEA) of 1965 was a federal program enacted to respond to the inequity in schools for the educationally disadvantaged. ESEA was related to President Lyndon Johnson's "War on Poverty," which created a wide range of programs, including early childhood and others targeted for the education of economically disadvantaged children. ESEA has evolved over the years and has introduced programs such as Title I, Chapter I, Reading Excellence, Reading First, and No Child Left Behind.

A Nation at Risk

A Nation at Risk was an important report written by the National Commission on Excellence in Education in 1983. The report provided evidence that American education, particularly secondary schools, was falling behind that of other countries. The connection between the United States economic health and education was emphasized. The report called for the creation of teaching, teacher education, and education standards, and it suggested that current education majors and those in the teaching force were not all highly academically qualified to teach, particularly in the content areas.

Goals 2000: The National Education Goals

Goals 2000: The National Education Goals were established during the Clinton administration and continued in the Bush administration as "America 2000." Key goals under the plan include:

By the year 2000:

1. All students will start school ready to learn.
2. High school graduation rates will meet or exceed 90%.
3. Students will leave grades 4, 8, and 12 having demonstrated competency in challenging curricula in English, mathematics, foreign language, civics, history, geography, economics, and art.
4. Teachers will have access to high-quality professional development.
5. Students in the U.S. will be first in the world in science and mathematics achievement.
6. Every adult in the United States will be literate and possess the skills and knowledge necessary to be a good U.S. citizen and to compete in the global economy.
7. Schools will be free of drugs and violence.
8. Schools will promote partnerships to increase parental involvement in education.

No Child Left Behind

No Child Left Behind (NCLB) is an historic, bipartisan education reform effort spearheaded by President Bush. The No Child Left Behind Act of 2001 reauthorized the Elementary and Secondary Education Act (ESEA)—the main federal law affecting education from kindergarten through high school. NCLB is based on four principles:

1. Accountability for results
2. More choices for parents
3. Greater local control and flexibility
4. An emphasis on doing what works based on scientific research

Promoting Partnerships

Respectful Communication

Listening, frequent and positive communication, as well as understanding all contribute to respectful communication with caregivers. Too often, school personnel contact families only when there is a problem. Special consideration must be given to families whose primary language is not English or who have other issues (e.g., financial, physical, emotional) that make communicating with teachers a challenge. Teachers must be aware of the ways culture affects communication. Some families may prefer face-to-face communication, home visits, or parent conferences. Others may prefer phone calls, e-mails, or notes.

Shared Decision-making

It is very important to give caregivers a voice in their child's education. Family members can serve on action research teams, multidisciplinary teams, or *ad hoc* committees. During parent-teacher conferences, teachers can ask parents for their suggestions, ask what their goals are for their child, and ask about ways the family has met success when working with the child.

School as Resource

Parent resource centers are places where caregivers can go to gather information, network with school personnel or other parents, and work with school personnel on issues related to education. Some schools choose to extend the school library hours to offer this service to the child's family. Many schools offer childcare, homework clubs, or enrichment activities prior to and after school hours. Some schools offer adult education classes, such as adult literacy, computer, or exercise classes.

Teacher as Resource

There are many ways a teacher can serve as a resource to students' parents and other community members. School newsletters, bulletin boards, interactive homework assignments, and reading lists are just a few examples of ways a teacher can provide resources to a caregiver. The teacher can also offer expertise to the community by leading a club, serving on a search committee, or leading a book drive to benefit a charity.

PART IV

FULL-LENGTH PRACTICE TESTS

PLT Early Childhood Practice Tests

This chapter includes two full-length PLT Early Childhood practice tests. These tests will give you an overall sense of the format of the test and help you self-diagnose content areas you need to study. You also may want to practice your pacing while taking the full-length practice tests. Remember, you will have a total of 2 hours to complete the PLT test.

When you complete the practice test, score your answers and use the explanations to help assess content areas to study in Part III of this guide. You may want to complete the full-length practice tests located in Chapters 12, 13, and 14 to help you determine further content areas to study. Even though these additional practice tests are written for other PLT test grade levels, the topics of the questions—Students as Learners, Instruction and Assessment, Communication Techniques, and Teacher Professionalism—remain the same.

------------------------------ **CUT HERE** ------------------------------

(Remove these sheets and use them to mark your answers to the multiple-choice questions.)

ANSWER SHEET FOR TEST 1

7 Ⓐ Ⓑ Ⓒ Ⓓ	25 Ⓐ Ⓑ Ⓒ Ⓓ
8 Ⓐ Ⓑ Ⓒ Ⓓ	26 Ⓐ Ⓑ Ⓒ Ⓓ
9 Ⓐ Ⓑ Ⓒ Ⓓ	27 Ⓐ Ⓑ Ⓒ Ⓓ
10 Ⓐ Ⓑ Ⓒ Ⓓ	28 Ⓐ Ⓑ Ⓒ Ⓓ
11 Ⓐ Ⓑ Ⓒ Ⓓ	29 Ⓐ Ⓑ Ⓒ Ⓓ
12 Ⓐ Ⓑ Ⓒ Ⓓ	30 Ⓐ Ⓑ Ⓒ Ⓓ
13 Ⓐ Ⓑ Ⓒ Ⓓ	31 Ⓐ Ⓑ Ⓒ Ⓓ
14 Ⓐ Ⓑ Ⓒ Ⓓ	32 Ⓐ Ⓑ Ⓒ Ⓓ
15 Ⓐ Ⓑ Ⓒ Ⓓ	33 Ⓐ Ⓑ Ⓒ Ⓓ
16 Ⓐ Ⓑ Ⓒ Ⓓ	34 Ⓐ Ⓑ Ⓒ Ⓓ
17 Ⓐ Ⓑ Ⓒ Ⓓ	35 Ⓐ Ⓑ Ⓒ Ⓓ
18 Ⓐ Ⓑ Ⓒ Ⓓ	36 Ⓐ Ⓑ Ⓒ Ⓓ

ANSWER SHEET FOR TEST 2

7 Ⓐ Ⓑ Ⓒ Ⓓ	25 Ⓐ Ⓑ Ⓒ Ⓓ
8 Ⓐ Ⓑ Ⓒ Ⓓ	26 Ⓐ Ⓑ Ⓒ Ⓓ
9 Ⓐ Ⓑ Ⓒ Ⓓ	27 Ⓐ Ⓑ Ⓒ Ⓓ
10 Ⓐ Ⓑ Ⓒ Ⓓ	28 Ⓐ Ⓑ Ⓒ Ⓓ
11 Ⓐ Ⓑ Ⓒ Ⓓ	29 Ⓐ Ⓑ Ⓒ Ⓓ
12 Ⓐ Ⓑ Ⓒ Ⓓ	30 Ⓐ Ⓑ Ⓒ Ⓓ
13 Ⓐ Ⓑ Ⓒ Ⓓ	31 Ⓐ Ⓑ Ⓒ Ⓓ
14 Ⓐ Ⓑ Ⓒ Ⓓ	32 Ⓐ Ⓑ Ⓒ Ⓓ
15 Ⓐ Ⓑ Ⓒ Ⓓ	33 Ⓐ Ⓑ Ⓒ Ⓓ
16 Ⓐ Ⓑ Ⓒ Ⓓ	34 Ⓐ Ⓑ Ⓒ Ⓓ
17 Ⓐ Ⓑ Ⓒ Ⓓ	35 Ⓐ Ⓑ Ⓒ Ⓓ
18 Ⓐ Ⓑ Ⓒ Ⓓ	36 Ⓐ Ⓑ Ⓒ Ⓓ

Practice Test I

Case I

Directions: Questions 1–3 require you to write short answers, or "constructed responses." You are not expected to cite specific theories or texts in your answers; however, your knowledge of specific principles of learning and teaching will be evaluated. Be sure to answer all parts of the question. Write your answers in the space provided.

Scenario: Miss Cindy

Miss Cindy is a beginning kindergarten teacher at South School. Her principal, Mrs. Galligan, is planning a formal observation as required by the school district's teacher contract. Miss Cindy is planning to be observed during an integrated language arts block in which she'll use poems from the book *Chicken Soup with Rice* by Maurice Sendak. Miss Cindy is required to submit a lesson plan to Mrs. Galligan in advance of the observation. Her lesson plan is provided below as Document 1.

Document 1

Objectives

- The student will identify the letter and the sound *O* in the poem for October.
- The student will repeat the poem after the teacher.
- The student will point to words in the poem.
- The student will be able to discuss the poem for October; specifically the fall season, Halloween, and the months before and after October.
- NAEYC Standard: 4b Teaching and Learning: Using Developmentally Effective Approaches

Resources

- *Chicken Soup with Rice* by Maurice Sendak—big book format
- Audiotape of "October" poem sung by Carole King
- "October" poem on chart paper
- Pointer
- Letter Person "O"—Ollie the Ghost
- Oaktag O shapes prepared by teacher
- Pre-cut magazine pictures of fall images and objects with the *O* sound

Motivation

Play the song version of the "October" poem in *Chicken Soup with Rice*. Encourage the children to sing along the second and any other times the song is played. Discuss October, Halloween, and the fall images in the song/poem.

Procedures

1. Play and sing the song
2. Read big book
3. Teach sounds of *O*
4. Read "October" poem
5. Identify letter *O*, sounds of *O*, and words with *O* in the poem

GO ON TO THE NEXT PAGE

Warm-up

Sing along to *Chicken Soup with Rice* CD sung by Carole King.

Preview

Read aloud the Big Book version of *Chicken Soup with Rice,* paying careful attention to the months of the year, the illustrations, and the four seasons. Have a general discussion about the book to help students make personal connections and to check for understanding. Discuss which months come before and after October.

Teach

Introduce Letter Person "Ollie the Ghost," who will help us to read the "October" poem from *Chicken Soup with Rice.* Discuss the sounds *O* makes and ask children to make the sounds and hear the sounds.

Read the "October" poem on the chart. The teacher points to each word as she reads. Reread and encourage children to echo read or sing read. Continue discussion about October, fall season, months before and after October.

Assessment

Ask the children to find *O*'s in the "October" poem by coming up to the chart and using the pointer. Ask children which words have an *O*.

Independent Work

On a cut out of a large *O* prepared by the teacher, each student will draw or cut out pictures of objects from October, Halloween, or with the sound of *O*. The teacher or her assistant will talk with students in small groups about their *O* independent work to reinforce the sounds of long and short *O* and to be sure each student can correctly identify the sound as well as know the names of the months before and after October.

Miss Cindy and Mrs. Galligan meet to discuss the lesson plan and to discuss particular areas she would like Mrs. Galligan to observe. Miss Cindy asks Mrs. Galligan to provide specific feedback on assessment of student performance on the objectives.

The next day, Miss Cindy teaches the lesson with great success in some parts and areas of concern in others. Document 2 is an excerpt from Mrs. Galligan's observation feedback to Miss Cindy.

Document 2

Miss Cindy asked me to observe her lesson on October from the book *Chicken Soup with Rice* with particular emphasis on her assessment of each student's achievement of the lesson objectives. The lesson opening appeared to be motivating to all students. The children sang the song and learned the melody and most of the words to the October poem quickly. This provided appropriate support for students to listen to the printed poem "October" and for all students to identify the letter *O* in the poem. Several students appeared to have difficulty identifying the sound of the letter *O*. In addition, several students could not differentiate between a letter and a word when working with the chart after reading the poem.

1. Identify ONE change Miss Cindy could make to her lesson plan to improve it. Base your response on Documents 1 and 2 as well as principles of reflective practice of teaching professionals.

2. Suggest TWO ways Miss Cindy could strengthen the assessment for this lesson plan. Be certain to base your suggestions on your careful reading of the case history as well as principles of assessment.

3. Identify ONE strength of Miss Cindy's lesson plan and discuss the principles of student learning behind her good instructional practice. Be sure to cite the specific theories or standards that support this practice.

Case II

Directions: Questions 4–6 require you to write short answers, or "constructed responses." You are not expected to cite specific theories or texts in your answers; however, your knowledge of specific principles of learning and teaching will be evaluated. Be sure to answer all parts of the question. Write your answers on paper provided in your response book.

Scenario: Annie

Annie is a first-grader who brings many strengths to her learning at school. She has numerous interests, such as animals (especially her cat Raja and dog Jasmine), crafts, dance, and mathematics. Annie likes to count things, to make collections, and to know how much money things cost. She stands out as a leader among her peers, most often providing positive leadership in the classroom; but from time to time she can lead others to silly, talkative behavior. Annie is exuberant in her approach to life—she loves learning, field trips, science experiments, and listening to the teacher read aloud. She does not prefer to read to herself and often avoids this in the classroom. She has many friends, both boys and girls, and is able to work with a wide variety of students because of her excellent social and communication skills. Annie is a kinesthetic learner who is achieving at a second-grade level or higher, especially in the areas of mathematics and science.

At a recent parent/teacher conference, Annie's teacher, Miss Lisa, shared Annie's progress with her parents and suggested ways that they can help Annie at home. Two ideas Miss Lisa suggested were: 1. setting up a behavior plan for "positive leadership" in which the teacher and the parent communicate via a home/school communication notebook, and 2. establishing a home reading program to help Annie practice her school reading.

4. Suggest ONE additional way for Miss Lisa to build a parent/school partnership with Annie's family and provide a rationale based on the principles of teacher professionalism.

5. Identify ONE strength of Annie's and suggest TWO instructional activities that would meet Annie's learning style and needs. Be sure to state why these activities are best for learners like Annie.

6. Suggest TWO effective classroom management techniques that will support Miss Lisa's instructional goals and Annie's learning style. Be sure to base your response on principles of communication techniques and instruction.

Discrete Multiple-Choice Questions

Directions: Questions 7–18 are not related to the previous cases. For each question, select the best answer and mark the corresponding letter space on your answer sheet.

7. Miss Rachel, a first-grade teacher, rarely teaches her students as a whole group; rather, she works individually with students. She carefully observes the students in their environment and plans lessons around each individual student's needs and interests. One could best describe Miss Rachel's teaching style as which method?

   A. Direct Instruction
   B. Montessori
   C. Hunter
   D. Advance Organizer

8. Zach is a five-year-old boy who used to love to play alone with his action figures in the sand box, but now often asks to play with his friend Harry. The boys enjoy figuring out how to build castles in the sandbox and like to experiment with a variety of tools to make the best castles. According to Piaget, one can best describe Zach's level of development as which of the following?

   A. Pre-conditional
   B. Post-operational
   C. Sensorimotor
   D. Pre-operational

Questions 9–10 are based on the following passage.

Pete is a student with a learning disability who has had many unsuccessful school experiences, especially in the area of mathematics. He appears unmotivated and disengaged in his second-grade classroom. Pete often avoids the task by asking to use the boys' room or by playing in the blocks area.

9. Based on the information provided, the best explanation for Pete's apparent lack of motivation is

   A. psychomotor development.
   B. low socioeconomic status.
   C. learned helplessness.
   D. multiple intelligence.

10. A student whose IQ range is between 50 and 75, is able to learn skills up to the sixth-grade level, and who is able to become fairly self-sufficient most likely has

   A. developmentally appropriate delays.
   B. formal operational thinking.
   C. functional or mild mental retardation.
   D. auditory discrimination.

11. An activity found to stimulate brain activity and requires students to use visual, kinesthetic, or whole body movement is known as

   A. non-linguistic representation.
   B. verbal representation.
   C. linguistic representation.
   D. musical representation.

GO ON TO THE NEXT PAGE

12. As part of a science unit on plants, Miss Webb brought her first-graders to a greenhouse at the local university. The children then returned to the classroom for hands-on learning experiences about plants. Miss Webb can explain the value of this field trip to her principal by saying she is using which instructional approach?

    A. Anchored instruction

    B. Tiered instruction

    C. Cooperative learning

    D. Advance organizers

13. Mr. Moore is a kindergarten teacher who uses the following centers in his early childhood classroom:

- Art easel
- Sand and water table
- Dress up
- Community (A center with changing themes such as post office, library, and grocery store)

One can say that Mr. Moore values which aspect of early childhood education in his choice of center activities?

    A. Reading

    B. Playing

    C. Writing

    D. Rote memory

14. Mrs. Foster plans her first-grade curriculum based on her students' interests. She works with the children's families and other community partners to enrich her lessons and to establish learning goals for her students. Miss Foster's approach to curriculum is called which of the following?

    A. Cognitive

    B. Behavioral

    C. Standards-based

    D. Emergent

15. Teachers who are lifelong learners and professionals need to attend _____ to stay current in their teaching areas.

    A. binding arbitration

    B. professional journals

    C. reflective practitioners

    D. professional development

16. Teachers who foster open communication with parents or caregivers, colleagues, and administrators show their ability to

    A. withhold school records.

    B. advocate for all learners.

    C. stay current in the latest research.

    D. freedom of speech.

17. Which of the following is NOT a teacher's right?

    A. Sharing information unrelated to school employment, such as age and marital status.

    B. Being fired for behavior that does not interfere with teaching effectiveness.

    C. Being permitted to take maternity leave.

    D. Using books which have been removed from the school library by decision of the School Committee.

18. Which of the following books was used during the Colonial period to support lessons on the alphabet, the Lord's Prayer, vowel and consonant patterns, and reading?

    A.   The Dick and Jane series

    B.   *Webster's Dictionary*

    C.   The Hornbook

    D.   The McGuffey Reader

Case III

Directions: Questions 19–21 require you to write short answers, or "constructed responses." You are not expected to cite specific theories or texts in your answers; however, your knowledge of specific principles of learning and teaching will be evaluated. Be sure to answer all parts of the question. Write your answers in the space provided.

Scenario: Mrs. Sevey

Mrs. Sevey is a kindergarten teacher who is planning for a math lesson on number concepts for her class made up of 16 five- and six-year-olds. Mrs. Sevey has been striving to meet the developmental needs of all of her students, but there is such a wide range of readiness for this lesson on number concepts that she has asked her mentor, Mrs. Manninen, to observe the math lesson and offer feedback on her classroom management during the lesson. Mrs. Sevey has particular concerns about meeting the needs of three students:

Jennifer is a student whose family speaks both English and Spanish at home. Jennifer was born in the U.S., but her siblings were not. Jennifer appears to have a good sense of number concepts when the lesson is discussed in Spanish, but she lags behind the other students when the directions are given in English and when she discusses the lesson with her peers. Jennifer is able to document her thinking with drawings and diagrams.

Chucky is a student of African-American descent who loves math, counting objects, and discussing patterns. He works quickly, rarely making mistakes, but then appears bored and eager to be challenged when his peers are still completing the mathematics work. Chucky loves to work with his peers, especially boys. He also loves recess, particularly baseball.

Veronica is one of the youngest children in the class who receives resource support for her speech and language disability. She also spends 30 minutes a week with the occupational therapist to help her with her gross-motor and fine-motor skill development. Veronica does not particularly like mathematics and tends to avoid working with math manipulatives. In addition, she rarely talks with her peers when working in small groups. She prefers to work alone.

Document 1

Objectives

The student will identify number and numeral 5 in multiple contexts

NAEYC Standard: 4b Teaching and Learning: Using Developmentally Effective Approaches

Resources

- Dinosaur counters
- Straws and rubber bands
- Pennies
- Whiteboard and markers

GO ON TO THE NEXT PAGE

Motivation

Students sit in a circle and play a version of the Duck, Duck, Goose game in which the student chosen is the fifth one in the circle. Students call out numbers 1, 2, 3, 4, and 5 instead of saying duck, duck, goose.

Procedures

1. Duck, Duck, Goose counting game
2. Discuss numeral and number 5
3. Teach counting to 5 and counting by 5s
4. Identify number 5 in various contexts
5. Homework: collect five objects

Warm-up

Duck, Duck, Goose game of 5s (described in motivation section)

Preview

Using whiteboard and markers, teacher draws a numeral 5 and demonstrates counting 5 objects using variety of manipulatives.

Teach

Teach counting to 5, writing numeral 5, and counting by 5s through chanting and writing on construction paper.

Identify the number 5 in various contexts, such as with counters, pennies, and bundles of straws. Also look for groups of 5 around the classroom.

Assessment

Observe students working in small groups and individually.

Independent Work

Assign family/student involvement to count 5 objects at home and bring these objects to school in a brown paper bag.

After the observation of the lesson, Mrs. Sevey and Mrs. Manninen meet to discuss the lesson's success and Mrs. Sevey's classroom management. Document 2 is an excerpt of the conversation between the two teachers.

Document 2

Mrs. Sevey: I think the lesson went pretty well overall, but I was disappointed with the Duck, Duck, Goose game. Several students got silly and began to roll on the floor. The point of counting to five was lost on many.

Mrs. Manninen: I agree, so what will you do next time to help with classroom management?

Mrs. Sevey: I'm really not sure. I think maybe the students are just too immature to handle this and I just won't let them play this kind of game.

Mrs. Manninen: They are young, I agree, but I think with a bit more direction from you and practice they can be successful in this game format. It's a good idea to have gross-motor activities for children this age. Can you think of ways to adapt or modify the game to make it more successful?

19. Identify ONE change Mrs. Sevey could make to the motivator game in her lesson. Base your response on Documents 1 and 2 as well as principles of reflective practice of teaching professionals.

20. Suggest TWO ways Mrs. Sevey could strengthen the instruction for this lesson plan. Be certain to base your suggestions on your careful reading of the case history as well as principles of instruction.

21. Identify ONE classroom management routine that would support Mrs. Sevey's goals as a teacher of kindergartners. Be sure to base your response on principles of student learning and communication techniques.

GO ON TO THE NEXT PAGE

Case IV

Directions: Questions 22–24 require you to write short answers, or "constructed responses." You are not expected to cite specific theories or texts in your answers; however, your knowledge of specific principles of learning and teaching will be evaluated. Be sure to answer all parts of the question. Write your answers in the space provided.

Scenario: Liz

Liz is a second-grader who has been diagnosed with a learning disability in reading. An excerpt from her IEP is provided in Document 1.

Document 1

Name: Liz Smith

Date of Birth: 1998

Page 4 of 8

I.   PRESENT LEVELS OF PERFORMANCE

Liz is reading at the Early-K level, which is equivalent to DRA Level 1. She knows 10 of the 26 letters of the alphabet. She has scored a 2 out of 24 on the District Test of Phonemic Awareness. She knows 3 sight words out of 52 presented on the district's high-frequency word list.

II.   ANNUAL GOALS

   a. Liz will recognize all letters of the alphabet in upper-case and lower-case format.

   b. Liz will recognize and produce the sounds of all consonant phonemes.

   c. Liz will read and comprehend at DRA Level 6.

III.   SHORT-TERM OBJECTIVES

   a. Liz will successfully complete letter lesson.

   b. Liz will segment phonemes.

   c. Liz will participate in guided reading.

IV.   EVALUATION

   a. District Letter ID

   b. Test of Phonemic Awareness

   c. DRA Kit

V   PROVIDER/LOCATION

   a. Classroom Teacher/Reg. Ed. Classroom

   b. Resource Teacher/Reg. Ed. Classroom

   c. Reading Specialist/Group lessons beginning at DRA Level 1 in the Reg. Ed. Classroom

Liz's parents request a meeting to discuss Liz's reading program and her achievement of her reading goals to date. The school convenes a meeting with the parents, the resource teacher, the reading specialist, Liz's classroom teacher, and the school's assistant principal. While Liz is making good progress, the school would like more parent involvement in reading at home. In addition, the regular classroom teacher reports that Liz is having difficulty with her peers. Liz tends to play with the first-graders at recess and has shown increasing frustration with her reading abilities and progress compared to her peers.

22. Suggest ONE way Liz's parents could be more actively involved in Liz's education plan. Be sure to base your response on principles of teacher professionalism and communication techniques.

23. Suggest ONE additional instructional goal to improve Liz's social and emotional needs in the classroom. Be sure to base your answer on principles of student learning and instruction.

24. Suggest ONE additional instructional goal to improve Liz's reading achievement in the classroom. Be sure to base your answer on principles of student learning and instruction.

GO ON TO THE NEXT PAGE

Discrete Multiple-Choice Questions

Directions: Questions 25–36 are not related to the previous cases. For each question, select the best answer and mark the corresponding letter space on your answer sheet.

25. Mrs. LaPlante believes that her students should be problem-solvers and active decision-makers in education. She also believes students should be presented with real-life problem situations and that a project-based approach to learning is best. Mrs. LaPlante's teaching philosophy is most influenced by:

    A. Gilligan.
    B. Erikson.
    C. Dewey.
    D. Smith.

26. Ricky has a difficult time following basic rules in his second-grade classroom. His parents report that he has similar difficulty at home and cannot be trusted alone with his baby brother or the family pets. He has shown unusual anger toward his baby brother and has become violent when playing with the family cat. Ricky may need further evaluation by a professional for what type of disorder?

    A. Autism Spectrum Disorder
    B. Behavior Disorder
    C. Multiple Disciplinary Disorder
    D. Mental Retardation Disorder

Questions 27–28 are based on the following passage.

Dee is a new student in Mrs. Baris' first grade. Mrs. Baris learns from Dee's school records that she has recently moved to the United States from Cambodia and that her family speaks Vietnamese in their home. Dee has been nearly silent in the classroom this first month of school, and Mrs. Baris would like to get to know Dee's literacy and educational needs better. Mrs. Baris has three other students who speak both Vietnamese and English in her class-room this year.

27. Which of the following best describes Dee's current language/literacy status?

    A. Alliterate
    B. Primary Language Not English
    C. Beginning Reader
    D. Developmentally Delayed

28. Mrs. Baris can better understand and teach her students by understanding the following three levels of Cambodian culture:

    A. Concrete, Formal, Religious.
    B. Concrete, Operational, Formal.
    C. Concrete, Sequential, Symbolic.
    D. Concrete, Behavioral, and Symbolic.

29. Which of the following are specific expectations of what a student must know and be able to do?

    A. Goals

    B. Benchmarks

    C. Standards

    D. Frameworks

30. Mr. Addison often closes his lessons with time for students to discuss how their work went, what areas students need help in, and what they learned. Mr. Addison most likely values which type of assessment for his students?

    A. Standardized testing

    B. Self-evaluation

    C. Portfolios

    D. Analytical scoring

31. Miss Burton is a new teacher at East Elementary School. She has been asked by district administrators to give an end-of-the-school-year test to her second-graders. This math test has been created by a district assessment committee and requires short-answer responses that can be time-consuming and difficult to score. The district assessment committee has created a scoring guide to support the second-grade teachers and to ensure valid and reliable assessment. What type of scoring guide has the committee created?

    A. Analytical

    B. Equivalent

    C. Holistic

    D. Raw

32. Miss Burton's school district has also started to assess their students' achievements each fall using a standardized test. Student scores are reported to the teacher by _____ to show where a student falls compared to those students who took the test nationally.

    A. raw score

    B. rubric rank

    C. mean

    D. percentile rank

33. In the *Goss v. Lopes* case of 1971, the court established that students facing school suspension must be afforded a hearing and notice before being denied their right to an education. This became known as _____ process.

    A. suspension

    B. detention

    C. IEP

    D. due

34. Which of the following laws was passed into legislation in 1975 to ensure that a free and appropriate education is provided to handicapped children and adults ages 3–21?

    A. P.L. IDEA

    B. No Child Left Behind

    C. P.L. 94-142

    D. Elementary and Secondary Education Act

35. In 1837, to support children from poverty and those with special needs, Freidrich Froebel established which of the following?

    A. Multi-aged classrooms

    B. Kindergartens

    C. Normal schools

    D. Common schools

36. Common schools, established during the 1840s to 1880s in the U.S., were designed to be available to all people and were founded on the principle of social harmony. This supporter of the common school, _____, is known as "the father of American education."

    A. Horace Mann

    B. Henry Barnard

    C. Thomas Jefferson

    D. Benjamin Franklin

Answers and Explanations, Test I

Case I

1. **Suggested content:** Miss Cindy has a strong lesson plan to teach letter identification and phonemes using *Chicken Soup with Rice*. One change she could make to improve the lesson is to place Post-It notes over the letter *O* and color index cards over sight words such as *in* and *once*. This would reinforce the concept of a letter and a word, which some students struggled with according to Mrs. Galligan's observation. On the back of the index card, she could write the word and ask students to repeat the word once it is uncovered. When students unveil a letter *O* they could make the sound of the *O,* either short *O* or long *O.* Students who struggled with her original lesson may not have enough experience or schema with the letter *O* and the concept of a word. In addition, covering up the words and letters provides a chance for students to discover the words or letter, which will be motivational and interesting.

   Content categories: Students as Learners, Instruction and Assessment, Teacher Professionalism

2. **Suggested content:** Miss Cindy's assessment plan includes asking the children to find *O*'s in the October poem by coming up to the chart and asking the children which words have an *O.* One way she could strengthen her assessment plan is to work one on one with each student. She could create a checklist for each student in her effort to individually assess each student's ability to recognize words and the sounds of *O.* This is called an authentic assessment because she is assessing each student's performance within the instructional setting. A second way Miss Cindy could assess her objectives is to work with small groups of children. She could read the "October" poem out loud and listen more carefully to individual students as they repeat the lines after the teacher. Echo reading is an excellent strategy to improve student fluency. In addition, repeat reading of predictable texts, such as *Chicken Soup with Rice*, supports phonemic awareness.

   Content categories: Instruction and Assessment

3. **Suggested content:** One key strength of Miss Cindy's lesson is her use of a quality text to teach reading. *Chicken Soup with Rice* is a predictable but engaging book that invites young readers to read and reread. The repetition and rhyme makes reading fun and also helps to develop phonemic awareness. Children can listen for the rhyme and identify the words that have the /o/ sound. The specific poem she uses for this lesson, "October," provides additional content information about seasons and months of the year.

   Content categories: Students as Learners, Instruction and Assessment

Case II

4. **Suggested content:** Annie is a bright, talented first-grader who would benefit from a stronger home/school partnership. One way Miss Lisa can build a parent/school partnership with Annie's family is to initiate a parent volunteer program in which the parents are invited in to help students with their reading. Annie's area in most need of improvement is her reading. Having one of Annie's parents in the classroom to observe firsthand the achievement of other students as well as the instruction of the teacher will directly benefit Annie and her family. Annie's parents will be better able to choose books to read with Annie and Miss Lisa will be able to offer more advice to her parents on helping Annie achieve in reading.

   Content categories: Teacher Professionalism, Communication Techniques

5. **Suggested content:** While Annie has many strengths, such as her interest in animals and in counting objects, her leadership strength is the one that I will discuss in this response. Annie is well-liked by her peers and has a strong ability to lead her peers. Miss Lisa can capitalize on Annie's strength as a leader by assigning Annie as the leader of the work group during a group project, such as a literature circle. Miss Lisa could teach Annie positive strategies for leading the group, asking questions, and checking on the progress of the group. Annie benefits from leading a literature circle because she has to stay on task herself, ask higher-level questions, and know the directions. Another instructional activity that would meet Annie's learning style is the field trip. Annie could be her group leader in this

setting also. Field trips also offer Annie the opportunity to learn by doing—meeting the needs of her preference for kinesthetic activities. Both of these activities lead Annie to be intrinsically motivated to learn and to use her leadership abilities in positive ways.

Content categories: Students as Learners, Instruction and Assessment

6. **Suggested content:** Annie is an active student who can be a positive or a negative class leader. Miss Lisa must plan her classroom management strategies to set Annie up for success, not power struggles. One strategy that Miss Lisa can use is to choose Annie as a special helper. This affords Annie the chance to lead, satisfying her attention needs, and gives her the chance to move about the room or school building more frequently, satisfying her need to move to learn. A second strategy that Miss Lisa can use is to offer positive reinforcement for Annie's efforts and successes. Both of these strategies offer Annie recognition for her successes and provide her an opportunity to lead in the classroom in positive ways.

Content categories: Students as Learners, Instruction and Assessment, Teacher Professionalism, Communication Techniques

Discrete Multiple-Choice Questions

Answer Key, Test I, Questions 7–18			
Question	*Answer*	*Content Category*	*Where to Get More Help*
7.	B	Students as Learners	Chapter 7
8.	D	Students as Learners	Chapter 7
9.	C	Students as Learners	Chapter 7
10.	C	Students as Learners	Chapter 7
11.	A	Instruction and Assessment	Chapter 8
12.	A	Instruction and Assessment	Chapter 8
13.	B	Instruction and Assessment	Chapter 8
14.	D	Instruction and Assessment	Chapter 8
15.	D	Teacher Professionalism	Chapter 10
16.	B	Teacher Professionalism	Chapter 10
17.	D	Teacher Professionalism	Chapter 10
18.	C	Teacher Professionalism	Chapter 10

Explanations

7. **B.** Maria Montessori's method was developed in the early 1900s. This method is widely used with preschool children, but it is used by many teachers of older children, as well. There are no textbooks and rarely are students working on the same thing at the same time. Students learn directly from their environment or from other students. Students gather in large groups from time to time at the beginning of class or for special events. The teacher scientifically observes students and uses these observations to inform instruction.

8. **D.** Piaget's Pre-operational Stage is distinguished by children typically ages 2–7 whose language and behavior become less egocentric and more social. Children at this stage become problem-solvers and enjoy social interaction with peers and caregivers. At this stage, the child makes progress in understanding logical concepts, but understanding is still quite concrete and limited.

9. **C.** Studies of learning disabled students have shown that some children show a learned helplessness after repeated school failures and lack of success.

10. **C.** Children with functional or mild mental retardation have an IQ between 50 and 75, are usually able to learn information generally up to a sixth-grade level, and often possess the life skills to live independently as an adult with social and community supports.

11. **A.** Activities that involve non-linguistic representations help students to store knowledge using visual, kinesthetic, or whole-body movement. Teachers are encouraged to include both linguistic (involving reading or hearing) and non-linguistic representations for students to make meaning from the lesson.

12. **A.** Anchored instruction involves a concrete learning activity for students to tie information to. The teacher uses the "anchor" to help students make connections and learn important concepts.

13. **B.** Based on the centers listed, one can infer that Mr. Moore believes that play is a child's work. These centers provide opportunities for students to learn both academic and social lessons through play.

14. **D.** An emergent curriculum is most typically found in early childhood classrooms, but can be noted in high grade levels that emphasize personalization of learning and community involvement. This approach to curriculum places the student at the center of planning, and it values family and community involvement in education.

15. **D.** Professional development provides teachers with the opportunity to learn. Professional development can take place in many forms—small groups after school, large group in-service, college coursework, or one-to-one work with a school coach.

16. **B.** Early childhood professionals understand the importance of advocating for all learners. In order to be effective at advocacy for children, teachers must effectively communicate and collaborate with parents/caregivers, colleagues, administrators, and other stakeholders.

17. **D.** Teachers have several rights that are guided by school and civic law. A teacher does *not* have the right to use a text that has been removed from the school library by a vote of a group, such as the school committee. If a book is objectionable to an individual, but it has not been banned by the school committee, the teacher may choose to use such a text, but he or she may want to discuss this issue and the text with the school librarian and the principal.

18. **C.** The Hornbook was used by children for several centuries starting in the mid-15th century in Europe. It continued to be used in U.S. schools during the Colonial Period (1600–1776). Hornbooks were made of a wooden paddle, parchment with the lesson, and a cover for the lesson, which was made of transparent horn. The McGuffey Readers, the distractor in this question, were used during the Common School Period (1840–1880) of U.S. education.

Case III

19. **Suggested content:** Mrs. Sevey has her students play a variation of the game of Duck, Duck, Goose by counting to five instead of saying "duck, duck, goose." One change Mrs. Sevey could make is to clearly set the guidelines and purpose for this game. She could explain the rules of the game and appropriate behavior when counting and running during the game. She could take the time to demonstrate this behavior by asking two or three students to take turns showing the class how to play appropriately. Bandura's social learning theory supports this practice by suggesting that students learn by observing others.

   Content Categories: Instruction and Assessment, Teacher Professionalism

20. **Suggested content:** Mrs. Sevey's goal is to teach students to identify the number five and the numeral five. Another way that she could teach this objective is create a center in which the students must count to five and write five frequently, such as a store or restaurant center. Using a real-life center such as these supports Dewey's theory that learning should be an authentic experience for children. A second suggestion is to design a project for the students. The students could work in pairs to count sets of five and arrange them in an artistic or interesting display. Dewey also supported project-based learning as an optimal educational experience for children.

   Content Categories: Instruction and Assessment, Communication Techniques

21. **Suggested content:** Mrs. Sevey could strengthen her classroom management and instructional routine by allowing students to interact and talk more while working on their lesson on the number and numeral five. Her student Jennifer would benefit from interactions with peers, as she is still learning to become proficient in spoken and written English. Veronica would benefit from working with her peers so that she could observe others work with manipulatives and solve the task. If needed, Veronica could also ask for help since working with manipulatives can be difficult for her. Chucky would also benefit from an opportunity to work with peers. He can be challenged to explain something he knows in a different way so that peers can understand. He can serve as a leader and role model to his peers.

    Content Categories: Students as Learners, Instruction and Assessment, Communication Techniques

Case IV

22. **Suggested content:** Based on Liz's parents requesting a meeting to discuss their child's progress, Liz's parents clearly want to be informed and involved in her education. Liz's teachers can welcome this interest by setting up a home/school reading program. After Liz reads a book to the teacher, a friend, and herself, she could bring the book home to read with her parents. In addition, the teacher could provide an activity to support the phonemic awareness or letter identification lesson that Liz was working on that week. If the parents need more guidance on how to read books successfully with Liz, the school could offer parent/child workshops to offer suggestions and supports to parents of children with learning disabilities. Building partnerships between home and school have proven to improve student motivation and achievement.

    Content Categories: Teacher Professionalism, Communication Techniques

23. **Suggested content:** Liz tends to play with children a year younger than her and is having difficulty working with her peers. Erikson would suggest that Liz is struggling to overcome a typical conflict—competence versus inferiority. To increase Liz's feeling of inferiority and increase her sense of competence, Liz's teacher could find out more about her strengths and highlight them during a lesson with her peers. While Liz may not be strong in reading, she is likely to have strengths in other areas, such as the arts, mathematics, science, or leisure activities involving games, puzzles, or the computer. Liz's teacher could design a lesson in which she gives Liz a leadership role in something she enjoys doing.

    Content Categories: Students as Learners, Instruction and Assessment

24. **Suggested content:** Liz is reading at least two grade levels below her peers, so increased attention to Liz's reading achievement is necessary for her success. One additional instructional strategy that her teacher could implement is systematic phonics instruction. Liz is at the beginning level of understanding the relationship between sounds and letters. A systematic phonics program with explicit lessons in sound/symbol relationships can benefit Liz. For example, in addition to learning about sounds and letters, a systematic phonics program offers multimodal ways for Liz to learn the sound/symbol code.

    Content Categories: Students as Learners, Instruction and Assessment

Discrete Multiple-Choice Questions

Answer Key, Test I, Questions 25–36			
Question	**Answer**	**Content Category**	**Where to Get More Help**
25.	C	Students as Learners	Chapter 7
26.	B	Students as Learners	Chapter 7
27.	B	Students as Learners	Chapter 7
28.	D	Students as Learners	Chapter 7
29.	C	Instruction and Assessment	Chapter 8
30.	B	Instruction and Assessment	Chapter 8

Question	Answer	Content Category	Where to Get More Help
31.	A	Instruction and Assessment	Chapter 8
32.	D	Instruction and Assessment	Chapter 8
33.	D	Teacher Professionalism	Chapter 10
34.	C	Teacher Professionalism	Chapter 10
35.	B	Teacher Professionalism	Chapter 10
36.	A	Teacher Professionalism	Chapter 10

Explanations

25. C. John Dewey is considered the father of progressive education. He promoted individuality, project-based learning, and school as a social institution. Dewey believed that real-life problem-solving was a valuable experience for learners.

26. B. Children with behavior disorders show some of the following behaviors—violate rules, aggression toward people and/or animals, destruction of property, deceitfulness, and other inappropriate behaviors typical of a child.

27. B. Based on the passage, Dee's language/literacy status is best described as Primary Language is Not English (PLNE). Mrs. Baris can support Dee by building on her culture, supporting Dee's language/literacy proficiency in her primary language (Vietnamese), and offering opportunities for Dee to work in small groups. It is common for PLNE students to remain near silent in the classroom for several months until they gain proficiency in English.

28. D. Hidalgo's three levels of culture are as follows: concrete, behavioral, and symbolic. Mrs. Baris can understand the concrete level of Dee's culture by learning more about the foods, music, games, and clothing in Cambodia. At the behavioral level of culture, Mrs. Baris must strive to understand the gender roles, nonverbal communication, and family structure of Dee's home. At the symbolic level of culture, Mrs. Baris must learn more about Dee's family's value structures, customs, and beliefs.

29. C. There are national, state, and local standards to guide expectations of what a student must know and be able to do. There are two types of standards: content-based and performance-based.

30. B. Self-evaluation is an important assessment strategy in which students monitor and regulate their learning. Self-evaluation can be in free-form discussion, as Mr. Addison does in this scenario, or in written form. Choice C, Portfolios, is the distractor here. While Mr. Addison may use portfolios, this choice is too broad and not the best answer choice based on the information provided in the question.

31. A. Analytical scoring guides are typically used to assess essays and short-answer responses, which can be difficult to score with reliability and validity. Analytical scoring guides are particularly helpful when a teacher is new to the assessment and when there are many items for the teacher to score.

32. D. Percentile ranks show the percentage of students in a group (either a national or a local norm) whose scores fall above or below the norm group scores. For example, if a student scored in the 50th percentile rank, this would mean that 50 percent of the scores in the norm group fell below this student score on this same test.

33. D. Due process is the procedure that must be followed before a student's rights to an education are denied or before a student's education programming is changed, specifically in the area of special education services.

34. C. Public Law 94-142 was passed into law during the Ford administration in 1975. This law was established to ensure that a free and appropriate education is provided to handicapped children and adults ages 3–21.

35. B. Froebel established the first kindergarten in 1837, and he became known as "the father of kindergarten." Kindergarten curriculum emphasized the importance of play and was recognized by the National Education Association (NEA) in 1872.

36. A. Horace Mann was known as "the father of American education" and supported the Common School concept of education. Mann also served as the Secretary of Education in 1839 and established the first normal school in the U.S.

Full-Length Practice Test II

Case I

Directions: Questions 1–3 require you to write short answers, or "constructed responses." You are not expected to cite specific theories or texts in your answers; however, your knowledge of specific principles of learning and teaching will be evaluated. Be sure to answer all parts of the question. Write your answers in the space provided.

Scenario: Miss Phyllis

Miss Phyllis is a first-grade teacher at Eastern Elementary School. She has concerns about meeting the needs of two of her students—Paulo and Leslie—who quickly grasp the concepts in a lesson on comprehension strategies during small group reading time.

Paulo is a six-year-old who loves sports, reading, and drawing. He often shares that his parents read aloud to him and that he likes sharing books and playing games with his little brother. Paulo provides high-level responses to discussions about his reading. He tends to work well with his peers, especially those who need extra help in reading.

Leslie, on the other hand, loves to read but rarely plays with other children at recess. She is about to turn seven. She prefers to talk with the adults on the playground about her reading and other interests, including drawing and writing. Leslie writes imaginative stories and draws detailed illustrations to accompany her writing. Leslie's parents know that she is a strong reader, so they rarely read aloud to her, although they did regularly when she was a preschooler.

Miss Phyllis shares her concern about meeting Paulo and Leslie's needs with a colleague, Miss Erin, during a teacher room conversation. Miss Phyllis explains that Paulo and Leslie are completing work accurately and quickly, which has been a challenge. She also mentions her concerns about Leslie's social development and sense of isolation on the playground. Miss Erin listens carefully and shares a few of her experiences and strategies to support students who are high achieving and perhaps gifted. Miss Erin also suggests that her colleague set up an appointment with the school psychologist to get professional advice from her.

1. Identify ONE way that the school psychologist could support Miss Phyllis in her efforts to teach Leslie and Paulo. Be sure to ground your answer in the principles of teaching and learning.

2. Suggest TWO ways Miss Phyllis could involve Leslie's family in helping their child be challenged and grow academically or socially in the classroom. Be sure to base your response on principles of students as learners and teacher professionalism.

3. Suggest ONE instructional grouping method that could help Paulo to improve his reading as well as his engagement in lessons. Be sure to base your response on principles of teaching and learning.

_____

_____

_____

_____

_____

_____

_____

_____

_____

_____

_____

_____

_____

_____

_____

_____

_____

_____

_____

_____

Case II

Directions: Questions 4–6 require you to write short answers, or "constructed responses." You are not expected to cite specific theories or texts in your answers; however, your knowledge of specific principles of learning and teaching will be evaluated. Be sure to answer all parts of the question. Write your answers in the space provided.

Scenario: Joseph

Joseph is a kindergartener in Mrs. Anderson's classroom. Joseph is a curious and active boy who loves action figures, animals, and sports. Joseph rarely sits still during group meeting time on the carpet, so Mrs. Anderson has moved him to a spot on the carpet where he can move more frequently, while not infringing upon other children's needs for space. He has shown impulsivity in his work behaviors as well as in his communication. Joseph rarely cleans up after himself and has blurted out inappropriate questions or responses to peers. He once threw a rock at a parked car in the school lot, seemingly without foreseeing the consequences of his action.

Joseph lives with his father during the school year and with his mother, who lives in a distant city, during the summer and on occasional weekends during the school year. He has been absent or late to school a total of 20 days, especially on Mondays and Fridays. Joseph is eligible for free lunch at school and also attends the before school breakfast program. His father reads to him at home most nights, although paperwork for school programs, such as fieldtrips and emergency contact cards, is rarely returned on time. Academically, Joseph appears ready to read, but he is having great difficulty with writing, mathematics, and social development.

GO ON TO THE NEXT PAGE

Joseph has made one friend in the classroom, but most children avoid him because of his impulsive and aggressive behaviors. Mrs. Anderson has talked with her kindergarten teaching colleague about ways to support Joseph, but she feels as though she is not doing enough.

4. Suggest ONE resource Mrs. Anderson can turn to for more support for Joseph. Be sure to base your answer in the principles of teaching professionalism and student learning.

5. Suggest ONE way that Mrs. Anderson can develop a parent/school partnership with Joseph's parents. Be sure to base your response in principles of communication techniques and teacher professionalism.

6. Suggest ONE instructional strategy that would benefit Joseph based on your careful reading of the case history and the principles of instruction.

Discrete Multiple-Choice Questions

Directions: Questions 7–18 are not related to the previous cases. For each question, select the best answer and mark the corresponding letter space on your answer sheet.

7. Based on Jones' time-on-task studies, which of the following is the most likely classroom management problem you will face as a beginning teacher?

    A. Talking
    B. Tardiness
    C. Goofing off
    D. School violence

8. Which of the following is an important learner factor to be aware of before teaching a lesson?

    A. Anticipatory set
    B. Attention difficulties
    C. Bloom's taxonomy
    D. Classroom set-up (tables, individual desks, size)

Questions 9-10 are based on the following passage.

Mrs. Dougherty's school district has just implemented yearly grade-level testing for all children in Grades 1–8. These tests are standardized and are nationally-normed to provide district administrators with data to inform curriculum decisions. Mrs. Dougherty is concerned about five of her students' ability to take these tests since they are nonreaders and receive special education or Reading Recovery support.

9. Which one of the following questions would you advise Mrs. Dougherty to ask her administration?

    A. Do my first-graders need to take these tests?
    B. What is the purpose of a first-grader taking a norm-referenced test?
    C. What testing accommodations are available to my students?
    D. What other tests are available?

10. In addition to testing accommodations, students with documented learning differences may also be eligible for

    A. short breaks.
    B. a criterion referenced assessment.
    C. testing in the resource room.
    D. an alternative assessment.

11. A test such as the SDRT4 offers teachers a _____ of a student; this provides the teacher with information about the student's areas of strength and weakness, which can be used to inform instructional planning for that child.

    A. criterion evaluation
    B. hearing evaluation
    C. diagnostic evaluation
    D. placement evaluation

GO ON TO THE NEXT PAGE

12. Which of the following cooperative learning grouping practices involves individual students completing their work and then teaming with another student to assess their work and discuss content?

    A. Group investigation
    B. Partner check
    C. Whole group instruction
    D. Student-Team-Achievement-Discussion

13. Mr. Manning prepares his second-grade students for a lesson on animal habitats by taking the children on a walking fieldtrip through the woods near the schoolyard. He engages the children in discussion about all of the places woodland animals might live. When Mr. Manning and his students return to the classroom, he asks the children to contribute to a chart all about woodland animal habitats. Which of the following best describes Mr. Manning's rationale for the walking fieldtrip?

    A. Creating an anticipatory set for the lesson
    B. Creating the mood for the lesson
    C. Monitoring student achievement in science
    D. Providing an authentic culminating assessment of his science objectives

14. Mrs. Horton tells her students that there is A RAT in the word *separate* to help her students remember how to spell this challenging word. What principle of learning is she using to help her students improve their spelling?

    A. Phonics
    B. Inquiry
    C. Play
    D. Mnemonics

15. Prout School offers its primary grade students and their families several services during and after school hours, such as a parent resource library, homework clubs, enrichment activities, and adult education programs in the evening. Which of the following best describes the principles of teaching that this school values?

    A. Parents as shared decision-makers
    B. Schools as a resource
    C. No Child Left Behind
    D. Teachers as a resource

16. Miss Nelson sends a weekly newsletter to her students' families and also invites families into her classroom to assist her while she's teaching. She has received feedback from the families of children who have been promoted from her classroom that working in the classroom helped the parents become better teachers of their children in the home. Miss Nelson most likely values which principle of teaching and learning?

    A. National Education Association (NEA)
    B. Parent Teacher Associations (PTAs)
    C. Respectful communication
    D. Teacher as a resource

17. During the Progressive Period in the history of U.S. education, most schools moved from being organized as a one room schoolhouse to

    A. groups of children by age, ages 6–10 and 11–16.
    B. groups of children by grade, K–12.
    C. groups of children by age, ages 6–8 and 9–14.
    D. groups of children by grade, 1–6, 7–8, and 9–12.

18. This professional association for teachers began in 1857 in Philadelphia. It was founded to advance the teaching profession, stimulate interest in teaching, and promote public education in the U.S.

    A. National Education Association
    B. National Reading Association
    C. American Federation of Teachers
    D. United Education Association of Teachers

Case III

Directions: Questions 19–21 require you to write short answers, or "constructed responses." You are not expected to cite specific theories or texts in your answers; however, your knowledge of specific principles of learning and teaching will be evaluated. Be sure to answer all parts of the question. Write your answers in the space provided.

Scenario: Ms. Horm

Ms. Horm is a kindergarten teacher who plans to teach a lesson on animals and their colors. She has prepared the following lesson plan, presented here as Document 1, to guide her teaching.

Document 1

Objectives

- The student will identify the colors and names of animals.
- The student will describe the purposes of color in the animal world.

Resources

- Images of animals from media and print resources
- Poster with colors and names for colors
- Butcher block roll of paper—white
- Crayons
- Video of Disney's *The Lion King*
- VCR or DVD player

Motivation

Show the opening 10 minutes of Disney's *The Lion King,* which includes a stampede of a wide variety of animals of many colors.

Procedures

1. Show film clip
2. Discuss animals and their colors
3. Teach colors, animals, and purpose of each animal's color
4. Draw animal and color/label

Warm-up

Review color poster and names for colors.

GO ON TO THE NEXT PAGE

Preview

Show the opening 10 minutes of Disney's *The Lion King,* which includes a stampede of a wide variety of animals of many colors.

Teach

1. Discuss the animals of *The Lion King* and their colors.
2. Teach colors, animals, and purpose of each animal's color. Use print and media sources as educational tools as needed.
3. Using large butcher block paper roll of white paper, have students simultaneously draw an animal in an appropriate color for that animal and then ask the student to label the animal and its main color(s).

Assessment

Assess each student's picture of the animal, its color, and the label.

Independent Work

Individual work on the animal drawing, coloring, and labeling.

After teaching the lesson, Ms. Horm reflects on what went well and what she could do differently the next time she teaches this lesson. Document 2 is an excerpt from her professional journal.

Document 2

Use of *The Lion King* film to open this lesson worked very well. Students were motivated and excited about the upcoming lesson. Next time I teach this lesson, I might more clearly provide a purpose for viewing the film and create visuals of specific animals in the film to preview. Several students did not know the name of several jungle animals featured in this scene.

I think the connection between animals, colors, and purpose was made clear during the lesson, but the independent work could have gone more smoothly. Several students had a difficult time working side by side with peers and several students bickered over sharing crayons.

19. Identify ONE reason why the use of the film to open this lesson may have been motivating for Ms. Horm's kindergarteners. Be sure to describe the principles of student learning that ground this practice.

20. Suggest ONE way Ms. Horm could provide independent practice for this lesson. Be sure that your suggestions are based on the case history and principles of instruction and assessment.

21. Suggest ONE classroom management strategy that would improve the students' performance during this lesson. Be sure to base your response on principles of communication techniques and instruction.

_____

_____

_____

_____

_____

_____

_____

_____

_____

_____

_____

_____

_____

_____

_____

_____

_____

_____

_____

_____

_____

Case IV

Directions: Questions 22–24 require you to write short answers, or "constructed responses." You are not expected to cite specific theories or texts in your answers; however, your knowledge of specific principles of learning and teaching will be evaluated. Be sure to answer all parts of the question. Write your answers in the space provided.

Scenario: Jessica

Jessica is a second-grader who has difficulty with spelling and visual perception. She receives resource support in the regular classroom setting from the inclusion of a special educator, Mrs. Duffy, and from her classroom teacher, Mrs. Kent.

Jessica is also distractible and has difficulty sustaining attention to tasks, especially those related to spelling and writing. She blurts out answers and frequently needs reminders to take turns. She does not appear to have a strong working memory and frequently needs reminders to use the word wall in the classroom to help her to spell words that have already been taught and tested.

Mrs. Duffy and Mrs. Kent have set Jessica up with a more able student (in the areas of spelling and writing) and are allowing them to work together on "buddy stories." Jessica seems to enjoy this activity, and the partner student is also benefiting from this experience. Mrs. Kent has planned the class schedule to include structured and organized time for spelling and writing. Mrs. Duffy has analyzed Jessica's errors with encoding and provides one-to-one instruction with Jessica in these areas of difficulty.

GO ON TO THE NEXT PAGE

Document 1

Document 1, below, shows a sample of Jessica's writing and spelling.

Mi mom and dad mad brikfst fr me. We had pancks and sossij.

(My mom and dad made breakfast for me. We had pancakes and sausage.)

22. Identify ONE strength in Jessica's writing and/or spelling development and discuss this in terms of the principles of learning addressed.

23. Identify ONE area of weakness in Jessica's writing and/or spelling and suggest ONE instructional strategy to support this weakness.

24. Suggest ONE way that Mrs. Kent and Mrs. Duffy could involve Jessica's family in her writing and/or spelling development. Be sure to base your response in principles of communication techniques and teacher professionalism.

Discrete Multiple-Choice Questions

Directions: Questions 25–36 are not related to the previous cases. For each question, select the best answer and mark the corresponding letter space on your answer sheet.

---

25. Kinesthetic, visual, and auditory are all

    A. learning modalities.

    B. learning centers.

    C. brain-based learning.

    D. multiple intelligences.

26. Students who are not learning to their potential in one or more areas, such as reading, writing, or mathematics, may be found to have _____ by a multi-disciplinary team or physician.

    A. a behavioral objective

    B. a short attention span

    C. a learning disability

    D. a personal literacy plan

Questions 27-28 are based on the following passage.

Brandon and his twin sister, Mary, are kindergarten students in Mrs. Rose's classroom. Mrs. Rose has noticed learning and developmental differences for each child. Rose often clings to her mother at drop-off time and once in the classroom doesn't engage with the other children. She prefers to sit off to the side of the class and observe others or to sit right next to the teacher. Brandon, on the other hand, cooperates well with his peers, is active in all sorts of play activities, especially imaginative games, and gives his mom a cheerful goodbye and kiss at drop-off time.

27. Erikson would describe Brandon as a child who has healthily developed through childhood's psychosocial crisis called

    A. Learning Initiative vs. Guilt.

    B. Industry vs. Inferiority.

    C. Knowledge vs. Cooperation.

    D. Trust vs. Mistrust.

28. Rose, on the other hand, is having difficulty with a stage of development for children ages 2–6. The theorist Erikson might suggest that she needs to have social experiences to help her experience which of the following stages?

    A. The Elementary & Middle Grades Stage: Competency vs. Inferiority

    B. The Early Childhood Stage: Initiative vs. Guilt

    C. The Toddler Stage: Autonomy vs. Doubt

    D. The Pre-School Stage: Individuality vs. Cooperation

GO ON TO THE NEXT PAGE

29. Mrs. Bergman often shares stories of previous first-grader's successes, or she highlights an individual student when he or she shows effort toward a learning goal. For example, yesterday Mrs. Bergman asked the class to listen to Julie explain how she solved her math problem. Julie needed to try several different ways to solve the problem before she was successful. After Julie shared her story, Mrs. Bergman let the class know that she appreciates Julie's hard work and she can see that Julie has learned a lot today. Mrs. Bergman then wrote a quick note to Julie's parents that emphasized how important Julie's efforts were to her success today. Which of the following principles of instruction are guiding Mrs. Bergman's practice in this situation?

   A. Reinforcing and providing recognition
   B. Numbered heads together
   C. Homework and practice
   D. Identifying strengths and weaknesses

30. Mr. Christie, a kindergarten teacher at East Elementary School, has just begun a unit on the author Eric Carle. Besides introducing his students to this popular and prolific children's author, Mr. Christie's goals include teaching the students about science using books such as *A House for a Hermit Crab* and *The Very Hungry Caterpillar*. He also hopes to teach the students a social emotional goal about how small things can lead to great success using additional Carle texts such as *The Mountain that Loved a Bird*, *The Honeybee and the Robber,* and *The Very Busy Spider*. Which of the following is the best way to describe Mr. Christie's unit plans?

   A. Interdisciplinary study
   B. Thematic unit
   C. Literature unit
   D. Inquiry-based

31. During a study of patterns, Mr. Forte's second-grade students participated in the following activities:

   ■ Exploration of patterns in the classroom and around the school.

   ■ Examination of patterns in children's literature texts *El Caminando* (*Taking a Walk*) and *A Pair of Socks*.

   ■ Hands-on study of patterns using teddy bear counters and pattern blocks.

   The children worked in small groups to learn more about patterns and the teacher facilitated student projects by providing resources, guidance, and ideas for further study. Which of the following best describes the principles of teaching and learning used in this lesson?

   A. Basal text unit plan
   B. Mathematics instruction
   C. Simulation learning
   D. Project-based learning

32. Miss Britton, a first-grade teacher at Curtis School, makes a point of taking notes on her students' interactions with each other and their achievements during learning center time and independent work time. She writes what she observes, and later she adds her notes in an ongoing notebook for each student. This helps Miss Britton reflect on her students' progress and to plan for her lessons in the future. Which of the following best describes this authentic assessment practice?

   A. Anecdotal records
   B. Portfolio assessment
   C. Personal assessment plan
   D. Aptitude records

33. During the Colonial period of U. S. education, this type of school was originally designed for the sons of upper social classes who were destined to be leaders of the church, state, or judicial system. Girls were not considered for these schools. Besides preparing the students for leadership positions, the practical purpose of these schools was to prepare the boys for the entrance examination for Harvard College.

   A. Hornbook School
   B. Latin Grammar School
   C. Early elementary school
   D. Common School

34. This school employee position was first suggested by Horace Mann and is derived from Industrial Revolution terminology.

   A. Teacher
   B. Teacher assistant
   C. Business manager
   D. Superintendent

35. Teachers must demonstrate the highest commitment to students and the teaching profession by creating and sustaining a positive, challenging, and safe school environment. This statement is an example of a teacher's

   A. mission.
   B. code of ethics.
   C. vision.
   D. action plan.

36. During a job interview for a first-grade position at Coventry Oaks School, Mr. Mathews showed his willingness to collaborate with colleagues, discuss teaching practices, and critically analyze his own practice. The school principal, Mrs. Daisy, assessed that Mr. Mathews showed which of the following teaching characteristics?

   A. Reflective practitioner
   B. Instructional practitioner
   C. Advocate for learners
   D. Instructional leader

GO ON TO THE NEXT PAGE

Answers and Explanations, Test II

Case I

1. **Suggested content:** The school psychologist could support Miss Phyllis in determining if Leslie and Paulo have a high IQ and/or high achievement. She could administer tests such as the Stanford-Binet IQ test or the Stanford Achievement Test. These measures, in addition to an observation of each student in the classroom setting, will help the psychologist to give advice to Miss Phyllis so she can best help these two students. The school psychologist could also meet with both students' parents to learn more about the students' interests, hobbies, background knowledge, and enrichment experiences to better inform classroom lessons.

   Content Categories: Students as Learners, Instruction and Assessment, Teacher Professionalism

2. **Suggested content:** Leslie's family can support their child by reading aloud to her and by offering her more play opportunities with peers. Miss Phyllis could meet with Leslie's parents to share the research that supports reading aloud to children, even those who are reading at grade level. Miss Phyllis can offer suggestions for books that are a year or two above Leslie's reading level to motivate her and to increase her vocabulary and comprehension. Miss Phyllis could also meet with Leslie's parents to suggest appropriate playmates for Leslie. Leslie would benefit from more support setting up play dates with peers and negotiating the play process with her classmates.

   Content Categories: Teacher Professionalism, Communication Techniques, Students as Learners

3. **Suggested content:** Paulo would most likely benefit from working in a literature circle group. This method involves a small group of children reading the same text and taking an active role in the discussion of the text. Students are assigned roles by the teacher—such as coordinator, time keeper, illustrator, word finder—and then the students "play" these roles while reading and discussing the book. Literature circles are most often used in grades higher than first grade because so many first-graders are still just learning to read. To meet Paulo's needs, the teacher might choose to have Paulo participate in a literature circle discussion with second-grade students involved in this type of reading group.

   Content categories: Students as Learners, Instruction and Assessment

Case II

4. **Suggested content:** Mrs. Anderson may want to ask for the advice of the school social worker to better understand how to help a student with Joseph's home life experiences, behaviors, and interests. The school social worker may be able to help or offer advice on how to improve Joseph's attendance, school behavior, and homework routines. The school social worker may also know of community resources that could support Joseph and his family.

   Content categories: Students as Learners, Teacher Professionalism, Communication Techniques

5. **Suggested content:** Because Joseph lives in two homes over the year, Mrs. Anderson could build a stronger school/parent partnership by sending materials to both of his parents. Day-to-day notices would not be as helpful to the mother in a distant city, but school report cards, progress reports, and notices about open houses and curriculum nights may be. Also, any parent workshops might be of interest to Joseph's family. Before she initiates sending information to both homes, Mrs. Anderson should check school registration paperwork to be certain that the parents have joint custody.

   Content categories: Teacher Professionalism, Communication Techniques

6. **Suggested content:** Joseph is an active kindergartner who may need more kinesthetic activities to learn to his potential. Mrs. Anderson might plan movement activities to support her letter identification instruction, or she might plan manipulation of large blocks to help Joseph build and identify patterns. Mrs. Anderson could also plan movement for Joseph in the course of the day, such as having Joseph pick up the teacher's mail, clean up the carpet after activities, or offering Joseph short breaks from work time. As part of a behavior modification plan, movement could be incorporated into rewards such as playing basketball with the principal or delivering school notices with the school secretary. The key here is helping Joseph feel successful while meeting his learning style needs.

   Content categories: Students as Learners, Instruction and Assessment

Discrete Multiple-Choice Questions

Question	Answer	Content Category	Where to Get More Help
	Answer Key, Test II, Questions 7–18		
7.	A	Students as Learners	Chapter 7
8.	B	Students as Learners	Chapter 7
9.	C	Students as Learners	Chapter 7
10.	D	Students as Learners	Chapter 7
11.	C	Instruction and Assessment	Chapter 8
12.	B	Instruction and Assessment	Chapter 8
13.	A	Instruction and Assessment	Chapter 8
14.	D	Instruction and Assessment	Chapter 8
15.	B	Teacher Professionalism	Chapter 10
16.	D	Teacher Professionalism	Chapter 10
17.	C	Teacher Professionalism	Chapter 10
18.	A	Teacher Professionalism	Chapter 10

Explanations

7. A. Frederic Jones studied time-on-task and found that one half of all instructional time was lost because students were talking (80%) or goofing off (20%). Teachers can improve this problem by carefully planning for and managing independent practice time. Three strategies to improve time-on-task include: 1. using teacher body language (such as the "look" or walking nearby the student); 2. implementing incentive systems; and 3. providing timely individual help for students.

8. B. Learner factors are key when lesson planning. These may include, but are not limited to, students with attention difficulties, learning differences, giftedness, learning modalities, gross and fine motor skills, and multiple intelligences.

9. C. While Mrs. Dougherty may have concerns about the rationale for testing first-graders and would prefer her students take other assessments (answer choices A, B, and D), she would not be wise to raise them now that the assessments have been selected. In the future, she might raise these questions as a committee member or when the decisions about testing are being made. The most important question at this point is to find out what, if any, accommodations are available to her students, such as shorter sessions, having a scribe (someone to write student responses), or having more time for testing.

10. D. An alternative assessment that has been agreed upon by a multi-disciplinary team, including the child's parents, may be available to students with documented disabilities. Answer choices A and C are testing accommodations; therefore, these cannot be the correct choice since the question stem asks for a response "in addition to testing accommodations." Answer choice B, a criterion-referenced assessment, would not be plausible as this type of test does not provide comparisons with other groups.

11. C. Diagnostic evaluations offer teachers a view of each student's strengths and weaknesses based on grade-level expectations. This type of evaluation is meant to provide immediate feedback to teachers and parents to better inform each student's instructional program.

12. B. Partner check is a cooperative learning grouping strategy in which students work individually to complete their work and then partner with a peer to check the assigned work and review the content. Choices A and C are cooperative learning grouping approaches. Choice D is a distractor based on another cooperative learning approach STAD, which is actually Student-Team-Achievement-Divisions.

13. **A.** When a teacher creates an anticipatory set for a lesson, as Mr. Manning is doing with this walking fieldtrip, he activates or develops prior knowledge of the lesson's concepts. This practice gives students an opportunity to organize information in their minds, as well as to add new information to existing schema. Choice B, creating a mood for the lesson, is a plausible choice, but not the best response according to principles of teaching and learning. Choices C and D are not "prior to instruction" options as the questions requires.

14. **D.** Mnemonics is an instructional strategy often used to help students remember challenging bits of information. Common examples of mnemonics include "*i* before *e* except after *c*" in spelling and "Every Good Boy Does Fine" (EGBDF) to help a student remember the notes on a treble clef in a music class.

15. **B.** The opportunities provided at Prout School show that this school sees itself as a resource to its school community. While the teachers may be a resource at this school (Choice D), this is not the best response because several of the activities listed could be facilitated by others who are not teachers.

16. **D.** In this situation, Miss Nelson sees herself as a resource to families as well as to her students, Choice D. While Miss Nelson most likely must use respectful communication with families (Choice C), this is not the best answer choice.

17. **C.** Once more and more children began to attend school, the one-room schoolhouse design no longer met the needs of the children and teachers. At first, most schools grouped children by age—ages 6–8 in one room and ages 9–14 in another. Once a child moved beyond the upper-level room, he or she either attended college or joined the workforce.

18. **A.** The National Education Association (NEA) was started in 1857 as the National Teachers Association. The NEA is currently the largest educational association in the world. The other plausible response, Choice C, The American Federation of Teachers, was formed in 1916 and has as its motto, "Democracy in Education and Education for Democracy."

Case III

19. **Suggested content:** Ms. Horm's kindergarteners may have found the film clip from *The Lion King* motivating for several reasons, primarily because it appealed to their learning styles or multiple intelligences. Children who are visual, tactile, or auditory learners would find the film clip appealing because of the wonderful use of color and music in the opening segment of the film, the feeling one gets from the stampede of animals, and the sounds of the animals and the incredible orchestra music that accompanies the film. Children's multiple intelligences may also be appealed to with this motivating opening. Students with musical intelligence would appreciate the orchestra. Students with visual/spatial intelligence would appreciate the art of the film. Students with naturalist intelligence would appreciate observing the nature in the African desert.

    Content categories: Students as Learners, Instruction and Assessment

20. **Suggested content:** Ms. Horm could read aloud a children's literature book that emphasized color words, such as *Planting a Rainbow* by Lois Elhert, and create a reader response activity to emphasize the use of colors and color words. In Ms. Horm's response activity, instead of plants, as found in the Elhert text, the children could plant their own rainbow of animals. The children could draw the animal, color it any way they would like, and then describe the animal, its color, and why they made it this color (as this relates to habitat and camouflage).

    Content category: Instruction and Assessment

21. **Suggested content:** Ms. Horm tried to have her students work cooperatively at the butcher block paper, but did not thoroughly plan for and teach her young students to work in this format. Since teaching cooperation is an important social skill that leads to academic success, Ms. Horm should continue to try this activity, but break it into smaller steps for her students. Instead of the whole class working on the paper at once, she could send five students at a time and teach the students to take an appropriate amount of space, what cooperation looks like and sounds like. She could ask students to model this for the rest of the class, and then, once each group of students gets their chance at the butcher block paper, the teacher could show evidence of success at cooperation. A win-win for all!

    Content categories: Students as Learners, Instruction and Assessment, Communication Techniques

Case IV

22. **Suggested content:** Jessica seems to know several sight words, the use of capitals to start a sentence, and periods to end a sentence. These are great accomplishments that can be built upon. In the spelling of Jessica's sight words, she knows several words with consonant/vowel/consonant pattern, such as mom and dad. Mrs. Kent and Mrs. Duffy could build on this knowledge by teaching Jessica to sort words by word families such as the –om family and the –ad family. Since Jessica seems to know where sentences begin and end, she may be ready to write questions and exclamatory sentences.

    Content categories: Students as Learners, Instruction and Assessment, Communication Techniques

23. **Suggested content:** Jessica seems to be having difficulty spelling words with long vowels, such as *made* (she had *mad*) and *pancakes* (she had *pancks*). Mrs. Kent and Mrs. Duffy could plan word building activities that help Jessica learn the rule of silent *e* when it comes at the end of a word. Teaching Jessica about word families, such as the –ake and –ade families will also help her to remember this rule. Labeling objects in the classroom or creating a word wall with these words will also help students like Jessica.

    Content categories: Students as Learners, Instruction and Assessment, Communication Techniques

24. **Suggested content:** Mrs. Kent and Mrs. Duffy could initiate a family message journal with Jessica's family and any other interested families. The first step would be to invite the families in to learn about the purpose of the journal and to understand that the initial goal is to write together, not correct spelling. By writing in the journal and experiencing the model of the parent and teacher, and with explicit spelling lessons by the teachers to correct any patterns of spelling error, Jessica's writing and spelling will improve. This journal could strengthen the home/school relationship and payoff for Jessica, too!

    Content categories: Teacher Professionalism, Communication Techniques

Discrete Multiple-Choice Questions

Answer Key, Test II, Questions 25–36			
Question	Answer	Content Category	Where to Get More Help
25.	A	Students as Learners	Chapter 7
26.	C	Students as Learners	Chapter 7
27.	A	Students as Learners	Chapter 7
28.	C	Students as Learners	Chapter 7
29.	A	Instruction and Assessment	Chapter 8
30.	A	Instruction and Assessment	Chapter 8
31.	D	Instruction and Assessment	Chapter 8
32.	A	Instruction and Assessment	Chapter 8
33.	B	Teacher Professionalism	Chapter 10
34.	D	Teacher Professionalism	Chapter 10
35.	B	Teacher Professionalism	Chapter 10
36.	A	Teacher Professionalism	Chapter 10

Explanations

25. A. Learning modalities, also known as learning styles, are important to consider when planning lessons. Students have strengths in at least one of the modalities—tactile (touching), kinesthetic (doing, movement), visual (seeing), and auditory (hearing).

26. C. Learning disabilities are determined by a multi-disciplinary team—a team of educators, administrators, specialists, and the child's parents—or by a physician. There are three main areas of learning disability: reading, writing, or mathematics. Some common characteristics of students with learning disabilities include, but are not limited to, the following: dislikes being touched, limited vocabulary, impulsivity, short attention span, poor coordination, and distractibility.

27. A. Erikson's eight stages of human development are based on a crisis or conflict that the person resolves during that period of their lives. Brandon is healthily mastering the Early Childhood conflict of Initiative vs. Guilt (Choice A), which can be seen in his ability to cooperate with peers, not being overly reliant on adults, and use of a healthy imagination in his play. Erikson's stages and conflicts are as follows:

Stage	Age range	Crisis or Conflict	Key event
Stage 1: Infancy	Ages 0–1	Trust vs. Mistrust	Feeding
Stage 2: Toddler	Ages 1–2	Autonomy vs. Doubt	Toilet training
Stage 3: Early Childhood	Ages 2–6	Initiative vs. Guilt	Independence
Stage 4: Elementary & Middle	Ages 6–12	Competence vs. Inferiority	School
Stage 5: Adolescence	Ages 12–18	Identity vs. Role Confusion	Sense of identity
Stage 6: Young Adulthood	Ages 19–40	Intimacy vs. Isolation	Intimate relationships
Stage 7: Middle Adulthood	Ages 40–65	Generativity vs. Stagnation	Support next generation
Stage 8: Late Adulthood	Age 65–death	Integrity vs. Despair	Reflection and acceptance

28. C. The question asks for the previous stage to the Early Childhood Stage (ages 2–6), which would be Choice C, The Toddler Stage. Erikson's theory suggests that Rose needs social experiences in this stage to help her become more confident, less guilty, and more independent before she can tackle the key conflict of the Early Childhood stage—Initiative vs. Guilt.

29. A. Mrs. Bergman is reinforcing and providing recognition to her students because she believes there is a relationship between a student's attitudes and beliefs and his or her achievement. Choice B—numbered heads together—is a cooperative learning structure in which students are assigned the same number to work together to become experts on a segment of content. Choice C—homework and practice—is an "essential nine" research-based instructional strategy, but it is not the best choice for this situation. Choice D is too narrow for the scenario presented. Mrs. Bergman is identifying strengths here, not weaknesses.

30. A. Mr. Christie's unit plans are best described as interdisciplinary because they involve reading, literature study, science goals, and health goals. You may have been tempted to choose thematic unit (Choice B), but a thematic unit has one overall theme, which this unit has within one component, but not across the entire unit of study. Choice C—literature unit—is tempting, but this is not the best way to describe Mr. Christie's unit plans. Choice D—inquiry-based—is similarly incorrect to Choice B. There may be an inquiry-based science component to Mr. Christie's unit plans, but this is not the case across the entire unit of study.

31. D. Project-based learning, like the unit Mr. Forte is teaching on patterns, involves in-depth investigation of a real-world, authentic topic or problem that is meaningful to students. The students work in small groups or pairs to solve a problem or to learn more about the topic. The teacher serves as facilitator and supports the students' projects and discoveries.

32. A. Anecdotal records are an authentic assessment used by teachers to record each student's progress and plan next best lessons for the student. Choice B—portfolio assessment—is too broad, but it is plausible in this teaching situation. Choices C and D are similar to other assessment practices, but they are not actually principles of assessment.

33. B. Latin Grammar Schools were established in 1635 to prepare boys for leadership positions in the church, state, and judiciary establishments. The practical purpose for these schools was to prepare the boys for the Harvard College entrance examinations. Choices A —Hornbook School—is a nonsense response based on the Hornbook used by children as a learning tool during this time period. Choice C—early elementary school—appears to be a logical response, but schools during this time period were not called elementary schools. Choice D—Common School—was a type of school initiated during the Common School period (1840–1880), not the Colonial period (1600–1776). The Common School had a very different philosophy of education than the Latin Grammar School described in the multiple-choice question.

34. D. The Superintendent of Schools was suggested by Horace Mann, an education reformer concerned with school policy and leadership. The terms *superintendent* and *principal* are derived from Industrial Revolution terminology similar to Superintendent of Railroads, Factory Superintendent, etc.

35. B. Teachers must understand the awesome responsibility placed upon them in the teaching profession. Professional associations and local school districts provide guidance on ethical standards for teachers. Choice B—code of ethics—is the credited response. Teachers are responsible for creating and sustaining a positive, challenging, and safe school environment.

36. A. A reflective practitioner possesses many reflective characteristics such as those presented in this multiple-choice question—collaboration, willingness to discuss experiences, and ability to critically analyze practice. Choice B—instructional practitioner—is a fictitious term. Choices C and D are plausible responses, but are not the best response—reflective practitioner.

PLT Grades K–6 Practice Tests

This chapter contains two full-length PLT Grades K–6 practice tests. These tests will provide you with an overall sense of the format of the actual test and help you determine content areas that you need to brush up on. You should practice your timing and pacing while working through these tests. Remember, you will have a total of 2 hours to complete the PLT test.

When you complete the practice test, score your answers and use the explanations to self-diagnose content areas to study in Part III of this guide. You also may want to complete the full-length practice tests located in Chapters 11, 13, and 14 to determine additional content areas to study. Even though these practice tests are written for other PLT test grade levels, the topics of the questions—Students as Learners, Instruction and Assessment, Communication Techniques, and Teacher Professionalism—remain the same.

-- CUT HERE --

(Remove these sheets and use them to mark your answers to the multiple-choice questions.)

ANSWER SHEET FOR TEST 1

7 Ⓐ Ⓑ Ⓒ Ⓓ		25 Ⓐ Ⓑ Ⓒ Ⓓ	
8 Ⓐ Ⓑ Ⓒ Ⓓ		26 Ⓐ Ⓑ Ⓒ Ⓓ	
9 Ⓐ Ⓑ Ⓒ Ⓓ		27 Ⓐ Ⓑ Ⓒ Ⓓ	
10 Ⓐ Ⓑ Ⓒ Ⓓ		28 Ⓐ Ⓑ Ⓒ Ⓓ	
11 Ⓐ Ⓑ Ⓒ Ⓓ		29 Ⓐ Ⓑ Ⓒ Ⓓ	
12 Ⓐ Ⓑ Ⓒ Ⓓ		30 Ⓐ Ⓑ Ⓒ Ⓓ	
13 Ⓐ Ⓑ Ⓒ Ⓓ		31 Ⓐ Ⓑ Ⓒ Ⓓ	
14 Ⓐ Ⓑ Ⓒ Ⓓ		32 Ⓐ Ⓑ Ⓒ Ⓓ	
15 Ⓐ Ⓑ Ⓒ Ⓓ		33 Ⓐ Ⓑ Ⓒ Ⓓ	
16 Ⓐ Ⓑ Ⓒ Ⓓ		34 Ⓐ Ⓑ Ⓒ Ⓓ	
17 Ⓐ Ⓑ Ⓒ Ⓓ		35 Ⓐ Ⓑ Ⓒ Ⓓ	
18 Ⓐ Ⓑ Ⓒ Ⓓ		36 Ⓐ Ⓑ Ⓒ Ⓓ	

ANSWER SHEET FOR TEST 2

7 Ⓐ Ⓑ Ⓒ Ⓓ		25 Ⓐ Ⓑ Ⓒ Ⓓ	
8 Ⓐ Ⓑ Ⓒ Ⓓ		26 Ⓐ Ⓑ Ⓒ Ⓓ	
9 Ⓐ Ⓑ Ⓒ Ⓓ		27 Ⓐ Ⓑ Ⓒ Ⓓ	
10 Ⓐ Ⓑ Ⓒ Ⓓ		28 Ⓐ Ⓑ Ⓒ Ⓓ	
11 Ⓐ Ⓑ Ⓒ Ⓓ		29 Ⓐ Ⓑ Ⓒ Ⓓ	
12 Ⓐ Ⓑ Ⓒ Ⓓ		30 Ⓐ Ⓑ Ⓒ Ⓓ	
13 Ⓐ Ⓑ Ⓒ Ⓓ		31 Ⓐ Ⓑ Ⓒ Ⓓ	
14 Ⓐ Ⓑ Ⓒ Ⓓ		32 Ⓐ Ⓑ Ⓒ Ⓓ	
15 Ⓐ Ⓑ Ⓒ Ⓓ		33 Ⓐ Ⓑ Ⓒ Ⓓ	
16 Ⓐ Ⓑ Ⓒ Ⓓ		34 Ⓐ Ⓑ Ⓒ Ⓓ	
17 Ⓐ Ⓑ Ⓒ Ⓓ		35 Ⓐ Ⓑ Ⓒ Ⓓ	
18 Ⓐ Ⓑ Ⓒ Ⓓ		36 Ⓐ Ⓑ Ⓒ Ⓓ	

Practice Test I

Case I

Directions: Questions 1–3 require you to write short answers, or "constructed responses." You are not expected to cite specific theories or texts in your answers; however, your knowledge of specific principles of learning and teaching will be evaluated. Be sure to answer all parts of the question. Write your answers in the space provided.

Scenario: Miss Chandler

Miss Chandler is a fifth-grade teacher who has just started teaching a unit on the Civil War with her students. Her principal, Mrs. Dougherty, has planned to observe Miss Chandler's teaching, one of the district's requirements on personnel review. Prior to the lesson observation, Miss Chandler and Mrs. Dougherty meet to discuss Miss Chandler's instructional objectives, her instructional methods, and her areas of focus for the observation. Document 1 is a copy of the lesson plan that Miss Chandler provides to Mrs. Dougherty, and Document 2 is a transcript of the pre-observation conversation.

Document 1: Civil War 1861–1862

Objectives

The student will discuss at least two of the social, political, and economic issues Americans faced during the start of the Civil War between 1861 and 1862.

The student will share personal connections and/or reactions about what they learned about the Civil War's social, political, and economic issues.

Resources

- Civil War photographs and timeline found at the following website: http://memory.loc.gov/ammem/cwphtml/cwphome.html
- Photographs of Civil War soldiers found at the following website: http://memory.loc.gov/learn/features/timeline/civilwar/soldiers/photos.html
- Computer with Internet connection and LCD monitor
- Map of the United States with the Mason-Dixon Line labeled

Motivation

Show photo of railroad wrecked when Confederate soldiers retreated. Discuss definition of political, social, and economic issues as they relate to the Civil War; then compare these issues to those of today.

Procedures

1. Preview
2. Warm-up
3. Motivation
4. Teach
5. Discuss/Assessment
6. Homework

GO ON TO THE NEXT PAGE

Warm-up

Show map of the United States and help students to identify the Union and Confederate states. Show the Mason-Dixon Line. Describe the name's origin—named for the astronomer Charles Mason and the surveyor Jeremiah Dixon, who were called in to settle a land dispute.

Preview

Teacher states, "In this lesson, we will discuss the start of the Civil War, which began in 1861. At the end of the lesson, you will be able to share your knowledge and opinions on two issues during this time. We'll look at real pictures from the war to help you understand and envision what the issues were like for U.S. citizens, just like you and me."

Teach

Using the photographs as a backdrop, the teacher shares content knowledge about the first two years of the Civil War and stops frequently to check for student understanding and to discuss the social, political, and/or economic impact of these events of the Civil War.

Timeline Highlights

1861:

- Inauguration of President Lincoln (political) who opposes slavery (social).
- The South secedes and forms its own government (political).
- Attack on Fort Sumter—start of Civil War (social, political, economic).
- Blockade of the South (economic).

1862:

- Lincoln authorizes a war order ignored by his general (political).
- Battle of the Monitor and the Merrimac: 13,000 casualties (social).
- Battle of Shiloh—74,000 died (social).
- Bloodiest day of the war at Antietam: Union 2,108 killed and 9,549 wounded; Confederates 2,700 killed and 9,029 wounded (social).
- Battle of Antietam convinced the British and French, who were considering siding with the Confederates, not to take action, paving the way for Lincoln's Preliminary Emancipation Proclamation, which would free all slaves in areas rebelling against the United States, effective January 1, 1863 (social, economic, and political).

Assessment

At the close of the discussion, the students will move into small groups to discuss at least two social, political, and economic issues of the Civil War. In addition, the students will brainstorm ways that these issues relate to their lives or personal experiences today. The teacher will monitor the groups for participation and accuracy. The teacher will grade the independent work and homework for content accuracy.

Independent Work

For homework, the students will write two paragraphs about the social, political, and economic issues discussed during the first two years of the Civil War. In addition, the students will write a third paragraph about how the issues of the Civil War connect to or impact their personal experiences or views.

Document 2

Mrs. Dougherty: I look forward to spending time in your fifth-grade classroom, Lacey. Thanks for your lesson plan. It is quite thorough, and I like your use of technology to support your teaching. Can you please tell me a bit more about your instructional objectives, the methods you plan to use, and what areas you'd like me to focus on.

Miss Chandler: Certainly, Lynn. I really am looking forward to your feedback on my teaching. I have such a great class, and I also really enjoy the topic—the Civil War. I really want my fifth-graders to be able to understand the concepts of social, political, and economic issues as they relate to the Civil War and to their lives. In addition, I want them to be active participants in their discussion of this topic. My methods include: 1. Using primary source photos to provide motivation and authentic context for the lesson; 2. discussion; and 3. writing to summarize two economic, social, and political issues of the war, as well as their personal connections.

Mrs. Dougherty: Sounds really interesting, Lacey. What parts of the lesson would you like me to focus on to help you reflect on your teaching?

Miss Chandler: Oh, right. Would you pay close attention to the children's discussion at the end of the lesson and then take a look at a few samples of their written homework. I am concerned about several students' ability to analyze and synthesize information into the three-paragraph format I've assigned. I've explicitly taught the children how to structure this type of writing assignment, and I've provided models in at least two previous assignments. We have a chart in the room with the format for the paragraph: a topic sentence, three main points or ideas, and a conclusion sentence. This is still difficult for many of my fifth-graders. Any advice on this would be helpful.

Mrs. Dougherty: OK, I'll see you tomorrow at 10 am. I'll plan to stay until the close of the lesson, and then look forward to reviewing the student writing samples with you.

Miss Chandler: Great. Thanks so much. See you in the morning.

1. Identify ONE strength of Miss Chandler's teacher professionalism and discuss why this is important based on the principles of teacher professionalism.

2. Suggest TWO additional resources Miss Chandler could use to teach her objectives and why these resources would be useful in the lesson.

3. Suggest ONE additional way Miss Chandler could strengthen her homework assignment and be sure to discuss the principles of learning or teaching that support the use of this suggestion.

GO ON TO THE NEXT PAGE

_____

_____

_____

_____

_____

_____

_____

_____

_____

_____

_____

_____

_____

_____

Case II

Directions: Questions 4–6 require you to write short answers, or "constructed responses." You are not expected to cite specific theories or texts in your answers; however, your knowledge of specific principles of learning and teaching will be evaluated. Be sure to answer all parts of the question. Write your answers in the space provided.

Scenario: Jack

Upon his entrance into the third grade, Jack's teacher, Miss Burke, noticed that Jack's academic and social development was advanced compared to his peers. Academically, Jack was reading at a sixth-grade level, writing well-developed essays with use of dialogue and complex sentences, computing complex math problems with ease, and sharing knowledge of science topics studied in the fifth grade or beyond. Socially, Jack had many friends, both boys and girls; he worked well in groups and participated in several activities outside of school such as Boy Scouts and city sports leagues. Jack's physical development was on grade level, although his athletic abilities were again advanced. He was the fastest runner in the third grade and showed exceptional talent on his baseball team, the Red Sox. Emotionally, Jack's development was on grade level. Jack's confidence, happiness, ability to cooperate, and sense of self and identity were all developing in a healthy way, as expected for a third-grade child.

Miss Burke noticed that Jack preferred to work alone during math, writing, and reading because his peers often slowed him down, and they also relied on his help as a peer tutor. Jack worked more collaboratively with peers during science, especially during hands-on science experiments.

4. Miss Burke would like to meet Jack's academic needs more effectively. Suggest ONE instructional method that will support this goal. Be sure to base your response on the principles of effective instruction and meeting students' learning needs.

5. Suggest ONE way that Miss Burke could involve a community member or Jack's parents in helping him socially and emotionally. Be sure to base your response in principles of teacher professionalism and meeting students' learning needs.

6. Suggest ONE way that Miss Burke can use questioning techniques to support Jack's deeper understanding in reading, writing, and mathematics. Be sure to base your response in principles of best instructional and communication practice.

GO ON TO THE NEXT PAGE

Discrete Multiple-Choice Questions

Directions: Questions 7–18 are not related to the previous cases. For each question, select the best answer and mark the corresponding letter space on your answer sheet.

7. Madison has been having difficulty at recess time on the playground. She used to like to talk with her friends and to play tag, but she has recently taken an interest in playing kickball with a new set of children. At first she just stood along the sidelines to watch the game, secretly hoping she would be invited to play. When this did not happen, Madison lodged a complaint with the teacher that one of the children playing kickball had intentionally thrown the ball at her. Erikson suggested that children in elementary and middle school (ages 6–12) work to resolve which of the following conflicts that Madison appears to be struggling with at this time?

    A. Identity vs. role confusion
    B. Pre-operational vs. operational thinking
    C. Generativity vs. stagnation
    D. Competence vs. inferiority

8. Steven enjoys talking with his sixth-grade friends as well as listening to popular music. He takes pride in his new sneakers—an expensive, popular brand—and his hooded sweatshirt from a skateboarding company. Which of the following needs would Maslow suggest Steven is striving to meet?

    A. Esteem needs
    B. Self-actualization needs
    C. Love and belongingness needs
    D. Physiological need

9. Which of the following theorists suggested that people possess multiple intelligences, such as intrapersonal, interpersonal, and musical intelligences?

    A. Gardner
    B. Howarth
    C. Epstein
    D. Binet

10. Sean is a kindergartener who enjoys working with clay, playing catch to learn letters, and making things. Which of the following modalities is Sean's preferred way to learn?

    A. Tactile
    B. Visual
    C. Musical
    D. Auditory

11. Mark is making patterns with counters shaped like teddy bears. His teacher asks him questions as he works, such as, "How many teddy bears are yellow?" and "What kind of pattern are you making?" Mark also notes that some teddy bears are not yellow. He tells his teacher that there are blue and green teddy bears, too. Which of the following instructional strategies is Mark's teacher using to help Mark better understand patterns?

    A. Summarizing
    B. Identifying similarities and differences
    C. Cause and effect
    D. Providing recognition and reinforcing effort

12. Nishita is a gifted second-grader who accurately and thoroughly completes her assignments 30 minutes earlier than her peers. Recently, Nishita appears to be bored with her schoolwork and is spending time visiting classmates while they are trying to complete their work. Nishita has also started to forget to hand in her classwork. Which of the following instructional strategies may be most helpful to Nishita?

    A.   Cooperative learning

    B.   Jigsaw

    C.   Chunking curriculum

    D.   Curriculum compacting

13. Mrs. Horton is teaching a reading lesson to her second-grade students. She has already discussed the story's beginning, middle, and end, and next she would like her students to be able to identify main characters, the setting, and the basic plot elements of the story. Which of the following graphic organizers would be most helpful in Mrs. Horton's lesson?

    A.   Sequence chart

    B.   Story map

    C.   Hierarchical array

    D.   Venn diagram

14. The primary purpose of using mnemonic devices, such as imagery and acronyms, is to help students

    A.   make a connection between the new information to be memorized.

    B.   build prior knowledge.

    C.   make notes in a way to be memorized.

    D.   build upon active thinking and new information.

15. Teachers must follow their school district's code of ethics, which guides professional responsibilities, EXCEPT under which of the following circumstances?

    A.   Collaborating with student's caregivers

    B.   Following U.S. laws

    C.   Providing information unrelated to employment

    D.   Committing to lifelong learning for all

16. Corporal punishment is not unconstitutional, but it may be _____ and only administered according to the laws of the state.

    A.   illegal

    B.   ineligible

    C.   punishment

    D.   punitive

17. Students have limited freedom of speech in schools. For example, student newspapers supported solely by the school may be edited by school personnel. School newspapers supported solely by student groups

    A.   may be edited by school personnel.

    B.   may be limited to distribution in school only.

    C.   may not be distributed to student groups at other schools.

    D.   may not be edited by school personnel.

GO ON TO THE NEXT PAGE

18. In 1957, a group of Black students asserted their right to attend the local high school. They were met with racial slurs, a mob mentality among some of the bystanders, and a cascade of rocks and bottles thrown at them. Federal soldiers had to escort the children through the doors of the school. The courageous students who advanced the Civil Rights movement became known as the

    A. Little Rock 9.
    B. Black Panthers.
    C. Memphis 5.
    D. Montgomery Bus Riders.

Case III

Directions: Questions 19–21 require you to write short answers, or "constructed responses." You are not expected to cite specific theories or texts in your answers; however, your knowledge of specific principles of learning and teaching will be evaluated. Be sure to answer all parts of the question. Write your answers in the space provided.

Scenario: Matt and Ryan

Matt and Ryan are twins attending first grade at Peaceful Elementary School. Matt and Ryan's parents have requested that the boys be placed in the same classroom, although usually the school prefers to place twins in separate classes. Although the boys are identical in appearance, they have very different learning styles and achievement.

Matt is a child who likes to move, to make things, and to play sports, especially basketball and bike riding. Matt has great interpersonal skills, many friends, and enjoys working in groups. He has difficulty sitting still, though, and often forgets to raise his hand or to take turns when he knows an answer. His teacher has noticed that Matt seems to forget to think before he speaks. Matt often forgets his school papers and his lunch money. He prefers to have clear routines at home and in the classroom and when these routines are broken he appears stressed, forgetful, and anxious. Academically, Matt is performing at grade level, but he does not seem to like to practice his reading. He also has a difficult time concentrating and sitting still when the teacher reads aloud to the class. Matt's mom tries to read aloud to him each night, but Matt often fidgets or tries to avoid reading together.

Ryan is a child who likes to work alone, to have quiet times, and to work on puzzles. He prefers working one-to-one and has one close friend besides his twin brother. Ryan is organized, meticulous, and well-prepared for his lessons each day. Sometimes Ryan is moody, sullen, and quiet for no apparent reason. At these times, Ryan does best when he is left alone to work and, after a short time, his mood improves and he is able to interact with the class appropriately. Academically, Ryan is an advanced reader, but he needs extra help with mathematics concepts such as numbers, counting, and patterns. He also has great difficulty with handwriting and is receiving support from the occupational therapist in this area.

19. Suggest ONE instructional method to best help Matt learn in the classroom at Peaceful Elementary. Be sure to base your response on the principles of student learning and instruction.

20. Suggest ONE instructional method to best help Ryan learn in the classroom at Peaceful Elementary. Be sure to base your response on the principles of student learning and instruction.

21. Identify ONE aspect of Matt's learning style and ONE aspect of Ryan's learning style that may need further assessment. How would you communicate your concerns to Matt and Ryan's parents? Be sure to base your response on principles of teacher professionalism and effective communication techniques.

_____

_____

_____

_____

_____

_____

_____

_____

_____

_____

_____

_____

_____

_____

_____

_____

_____

_____

Case IV

Directions: Questions 22–24 require you to write short answers, or "constructed responses." You are not expected to cite specific theories or texts in your answers; however, your knowledge of specific principles of learning and teaching will be evaluated. Be sure to answer all parts of the question. Write your answers in the space provided.

Scenario: Miss Arrighie

Miss Arrighie is a third-grade teacher in an urban elementary school that has been cited by the Board of Education as needing improvement. Document 1 shows the third-grade students' reading achievement scores for the last three school years.

GO ON TO THE NEXT PAGE

Document 1

Woonton School					
Grade 3	**School Year**	**Above Standard**	**Meets Standard**	**Nearly Achieved Standard**	**Below Standard**
Reading for High-Level Comprehension					
	2003–04	1%	10%	25%	64%
	2004–05	3%	10%	30%	57%
	2005–06	2%	7%	40%	51%
Reading for Basic Understanding					
	2003–04	25%	15%	41%	19%
	2004–05	36%	21%	42%	1%
	2005–06	38%	24%	38%	0%
Vocabulary					
	2003–04	5%	13%	33%	49%
	2004–05	6%	15%	37%	42%
	2005–06	2%	21%	29%	48%

Miss Arrighie has a diverse group of students. For example, 89% of her students receive free or reduced lunch; 76% of her students are Hispanic, 13% are Black, and 5% are Native American; 37% of her students receive special education services; and 61% of her students spoke another language before learning English (PLNE).

Miss Arrighie has been attending several professional development workshops and courses to better understand the diverse needs of her students and to learn strategies to improve her students' reading achievement, particularly in the areas of vocabulary and higher-level comprehension. She has tried reading in small groups, guided reading, and phonics programs, but she knows she needs to add more effective instructional methods to her teaching repertoire.

22. Suggest ONE strategy or method for improving her students' reading vocabulary. Be sure to base your response on the principles of learning and teaching.

23. Suggest ONE effective way that Miss Arrighie can connect home and school for her students. Be sure to base your response on effective communication techniques and teacher professionalism.

24. Discuss the pattern of student reading achievement in the area of "Reading for High Level Comprehension" for the past three years at Woonton School and suggest ONE strategy to improve high-level reading comprehension for Miss Arrighie's third graders. Be sure to base your response on the principles of assessment and instruction.

_____

_____

_____

_____

Discrete Multiple-Choice Questions

Directions: Questions 25–36 are not related to the previous cases. For each question, select the best answer and mark the corresponding letter space on your answer sheet.

25. Which of the following is a federal law prohibiting discrimination on the basis of a person's disability for all services, programs, and activities made available by state or local governments?

A. NCLB

B. Section 504

C. ADA

D. P.L. 94-142

26. Madison is a fourth-grader who enjoys school, especially when the teacher uses films, graphic organizers, or the computer projection machine during lessons. Which of the following learning modalities best describes Madison?

A. Auditory learner

B. Visual learner

C. Tactile learner

D. Kinesthetic learner

GO ON TO THE NEXT PAGE

Question 27 is based on the following passage.

Jamie is a sixth-grader who dislikes mathematics assigned to an honors-level mathematics class. She has set a goal to get a B in the class so that she can be placed in the honors-level track at the middle school. She completes course requirements that are graded, but she does not offer any additional effort if her grade is not at stake. Jamie rarely completes the extra credit opportunities and spends little time studying for tests and quizzes in this math class.

27. Based on the principles of teaching and learning, which of the following best describes Jamie's motivation in this class?

   A. Extrinsic
   B. Self-centered
   C. Intrinsic
   D. Achievement

28. Which of the following theorists suggests that females are socialized to highly value social relationships and to take responsibility for the well-being of others?

   A. Hoffman
   B. Gilligan
   C. Kohlberg
   D. Piaget

29. Mr. Ellson, a third-grade teacher, likes to have his students work in groups to complete projects together. He also tends to use the overhead projector to display examples of student work or specific examples of high quality projects. Which of the following theorist's work influences Mr. Ellson's practice?

   A. Erikson
   B. Dewey
   C. Bandura
   D. Maslow

30. Survey, Question, Read, Recite, and Review (SQ3R) is a method used most often in which of the following strategies?

   A. Phonemic awareness
   B. Cooperative learning
   C. Nonlinguistic representations
   D. Summarizing and note taking

31. Which of the following cooperative learning activities involves a "home team" of heterogeneously grouped students who then work in small groups to become experts on a portion of the content to be learned. After the students become "experts," they return to the home team to share important information.

   A. Think-Pair-Share
   B. STAD
   C. Numbered Heads Together
   D. Nonlinguistic representation

32. Mrs. Basel, a sixth-grade science teacher, assigns at least three lab experiments to her students each week. She highly values an inquiry-based approach to teaching science and believes that her students more deeply understand when she uses which of the following instructional approaches?

    A. Sequencing and repetition
    B. Generating and testing hypotheses
    C. Standardized-based instruction
    D. Differentiated instruction

33. Before a student can be suspended or expelled, he or she must be afforded a

    A. meeting with the teacher.
    B. trial.
    C. due process hearing.
    D. lawyer.

34. Jennifer Smith is a fifth-grade teacher who strives to meet the needs of all of her students, and she persists when faced with challenging teaching or learning circumstances. She possesses an awareness of her own culture and those of her students. Her principal describes Jennifer as a

    A. beginning teacher.
    B. master teacher.
    C. reflective practitioner.
    D. collaborative educator.

35. Which of the following reports, issued in the 1980s, suggested that current education majors and those in the teaching force were not all highly academically qualified to teach, especially in the content areas?

    A. A Nation at Risk
    B. No Child Left Behind
    C. Report of the National Reading Panel
    D. Elementary and Secondary Education Report

36. The Stanford Achievement Test and the Stanford-Binet intelligence tests were introduced by Lewis Terman, who used a scientific approach to determine and classify student ability. Terman's work is considered by many to have started the _____ in the United States.

    A. Scientific Period
    B. Intelligence Period
    C. Performance Movement
    D. Testing Movement

Answers and Explanations, Test I

Case I

1. **Suggested content:** Miss Chandler shows her teacher professionalism when she prepares thoroughly for her lesson observation and when she asks her principal for specific feedback on an aspect of her teaching. For example, Miss Chandler plans her Civil War lesson plan completely with objectives, motivating activities, teaching procedures, assessment plans, and instructional resources. Her resources, particularly the online primary documents such as the Civil War photographs, are authentic and intrinsically motivating to her students. Miss Chandler also shows her professionalism in this lesson when she asks her principal to focus on the students' homework assignment to improve her instruction. This is known as using formative assessment effectively.

   Content categories: Teacher Professionalism

2. **Suggested content:** Miss Chandler is teaching a lesson on the first two years of the Civil War. In addition to using a map and a website with Civil War photographs, she could use an up-to-date Social Studies textbook and a quality children's literature selection.

   A high-quality, up-to-date textbook written for fifth-graders would be an excellent additional resource in this lesson. For example, Miss Chandler could teach her students to read for information and to take notes on a timeline graphic organizer. The Social Studies textbook might include a timeline, additional photos and graphs, or tables sharing more information about the Civil War. In addition, a Social Studies textbook adopted for this grade level would generally offer reading materials at or close to the fifth-grade reading level.

   The second resource Miss Chandler could use to achieve her lesson objectives is a children's literature book. Patricia Polacco's *Pink and Say* would be a motivating and powerful way to open her lesson. This story, about two friends—one black, the other white—who serve on opposite sides of the Civil War, is a poignant and captivating one that fifth-graders would relate to and most likely be moved by. Miss Chandler's objective about "sharing personal connections and reactions" would definitely be supported by such a high-quality and appropriate children's literature selection.

   Content categories: Instruction and Assessment

3. **Suggested content:** Miss Chandler could strengthen her homework assignment—two paragraphs summarizing the social, political, and economic issues of the first two years of the Civil War—by providing more modeling and in-class guided practice for this assignment before she asks the students to complete this assignment alone at home. The content for this lesson is appropriately challenging for fifth-graders. Taking the information from the lesson and transferring this new knowledge into a written summary is complex for a fifth-grader and may require more scaffolding of support for students who have learning differences, English language learner development issues, and organizational issues. Miss Chandler could model how to approach the task explicitly using a whiteboard or a chart and give the students some time to start the assignment with peer support and her supervision. Once she is certain that all students fully understand how to approach the assignment, she could assign the summary for independent homework.

   Content categories: Students as Learners, Instruction and Assessment

Case II

4. **Suggested content:** Jack is an advanced third-grader in many areas and may benefit from an instructional method called curriculum compacting. When Miss Burke "compacts" the curriculum, she examines her instructional objectives and what a third-grader must do to demonstrate mastery or acceptable knowledge or skill in the area of study. Once Miss Burke determines what a student "needs to know," she then could develop a pre-test either in written or oral form to individually administer to Jack and other students who are also academically advanced in the area of study. Depending on how Jack performs on the pre-test, Miss Burke provides assignments specifically on what Jack needs to know and allows him to skip any unnecessary repetition, drill, or practice in areas that Jack has mastered. Curriculum compacting will allow Jack to feel more challenged in the classroom, offering him a confidence boost and recognition for his high-quality academic work.

   Content categories: Instruction and Assessment

5. **Suggested content:** Miss Burke could train a volunteer community member to become a mentor for Jack and other students especially interested in science. This might help Jack socially and emotionally in several ways. First, he could work with a smaller group of peers and receive more adult supervision, which would allow more opportunity for support if Jack needs it to get along with his peers. In addition, the mentor's science expertise could offer Jack the enrichment he may be looking for in the classroom. Lastly, Jack's confidence may be positively affected when the mentor makes a regular commitment to Jack and his science group, remembering important things Jack did and sharing in the joy of learning together.

   Content categories: Students as Learners, Teacher Professionalism

6. **Suggested content:** Miss Burke could use higher-level questioning from Bloom's taxonomy to challenge Jack in his thinking about reading, writing, or mathematics. For example, she could ask Jack an analysis-level question, such as "What are the features of the pattern you just created?" or "How do you know this answer?" Another type of high-level question she could ask is a synthesis question, such as "What can you infer here?" Or, put another way, "What is the hidden message here, Jack? What are the characters really saying even if they didn't use these specific words?" Making sure that Jack is being challenged is important, and probing for his understanding with these higher-level questions will help Jack to continue to grow as a thinker in the classroom.

   Content categories: Instruction and Assessment, Communication Techniques

Discrete Multiple-Choice Questions

Answer Key, Test I, Questions 7–18			
Question	*Answer*	*Content Category*	*Where to Get More Help*
7.	D	Students as Learners	Chapter 7
8.	C	Students as Learners	Chapter 7
9.	A	Students as Learners	Chapter 7
10.	A	Students as Learners	Chapter 7
11.	B	Instruction and Assessment	Chapter 8
12.	D	Instruction and Assessment	Chapter 8
13.	B	Instruction and Assessment	Chapter 8
14.	A	Instruction and Assessment	Chapter 8
15.	C	Teacher Professionalism	Chapter 10
16.	A	Teacher Professionalism	Chapter 10
17.	D	Teacher Professionalism	Chapter 10
18.	A	Teacher Professionalism	Chapter 10

Explanations

7. **D.** Madison appears to be struggling with her sense of competence versus her sense of inferiority, which Erikson suggests children in elementary and middle school (ages 6–12) work to resolve. In this stage, students strive to master sets of skills, which can lead either to a sense of competence or feelings of inferiority.

8. **C.** Maslow's levels or hierarchy of needs include the love and belongingness needs in which people need to belong to groups such as a church or social organization. Steven's interest in talking with friends, listening to popular music, and wearing clothing associated with sports teams all show Steven's attempts to fit into a particular peer group and to receive recognition or "love" from them.

9. **A.** Howard Gardner is the theorist who suggested multiple intelligences. There are eight multiple intelligences, according to Gardner's theory—linguistic, logical-mathematical, spatial, musical, bodily-kinesthetic, interpersonal, intrapersonal, and naturalist.

10. **A.** There are four learning modalities—auditory, visual, kinesthetic, and tactile. Sean appears to be a tactile learner—one who prefers to learn by touching or feeling something.

11. **B.** Mark is working on identifying similarities and differences in his work with patterns and teddy bear counters.

12. **D.** Of the choices offered, Nishita would benefit most from curriculum compacting, which is determining the key components of the curriculum that must be met and offering a compacted version of the work. Students like Nishita may become bored or even develop discipline problems when the work is too easy and not challenging. Curriculum chunking is not a correct method for Nishita, as this instructional technique requires the teacher to check in more frequently with students having difficulty with the content being studied. Jigsaw is a cooperative learning method that might be beneficial to Nishita, but it is not the best choice among the four. When a teacher "jigsaws" curriculum, he or she offers a portion of information to be learned by an individual student, who then reports the information learned to a small group. The group discusses and learns the material together to complete the jigsawed puzzle of information.

13. **B.** A story map is the best graphic organizer to present information such as characters, plot, and setting, which are also known as story elements or story grammar. Choice A, sequence chart, is best used to support instruction about the beginning, middle, and ending events in the story. Choice C, hierarchical array, shows the relationship between a concept/term and its related elements, which are presented below the concept or term. Choice D, Venn diagram, is best used to show the similarities and differences among elements in a story.

14. **A.** Mnemonics help students make a connection between the new information to be memorized. Encouraging students to connect prior knowledge to new information can help students retain this new information.

15. **C.** Teachers have the right to withhold information unrelated to employment, such as marital status, sexual preference, and number of children. Choices A, B, and D are common elements in a district's code of ethics for teachers.

16. **A.** Corporal punishment is not unconstitutional, but it may be illegal in the state in which you teach.

17. **D.** Student periodicals, such as newspapers, yearbooks, or magazines, may not be edited by school personnel if they are fully supported by student groups.

18. **A.** The Little Rock 9 was comprised of nine Black students from Little Rock, Texas, who nonviolently and bravely decided to challenge their right to attend the all-white Rock Central High in Little Rock, Texas.

Case III

19. **Suggested content:** Matt is a first-grade student who is active, athletic, and outgoing. His teacher could design instructional activities that appeal to his areas of strength—bodily-kinesthetic activities. For example, the teacher could teach letter formations by asking Matt to stand up and make the letters in the sky or use shaving cream to form the letters. For counting activities, the teacher could make a hop-scotch type game to jump certain numbers of spaces. It is important for the teacher to view Matt's learning styles and preferences as strengths, not deficits. While Matt may need special supports, and perhaps even special-education instruction in the future, the classroom teacher can set Matt up for success by teaching to his strengths, not highlighting his deficits.

    Content categories: Students as Learners, Instruction and Assessment

20. **Suggested content:** Ryan is a first-grade student who prefers to work alone in a quiet setting and use his mind to work on puzzles. His teacher could design instructional activities that support his strength—intrapersonal awareness. According to Gardner's theory of multiple intelligences, people like Ryan with intrapersonal intelligence know themselves well and are aware of their thoughts, feelings, and moods. Ryan would benefit from activities that

require him to use this knowledge—this strength—to interpret other people's feelings in a story or in a classroom situation. This will help Ryan's comprehension and social skills. His teacher could ask one other student to work on a puzzle with Ryan and, after a short time, ask them about what worked when creating the puzzle, how did they feel working together, etc. This will provide Ryan with the opportunity to practice his social skills in a one-to-one setting; it also will demonstrate his strength at thinking about his thoughts, feelings, and moods.

Content categories: Students as Learners, Instruction and Assessment

21. **Suggested content:** Matt and Ryan have several strengths that they bring to their first-grade classroom. In addition, they both show some patterns of behavior that may warrant observation and further assessment. Matt has considerable difficulty sitting still and showing impulse control when responding to the teacher's questions. These behaviors can be perfectly normal and healthy in a first-grader, but they could also signal differences in learning, such as a learning disability, attention deficit disorder, or a mood disorder. Ryan has an introverted personality in the classroom, which once again could be perfectly healthy and normal development for this first-grader. On the other hand, if the teacher notes a continued pattern of moodiness, a need to work alone, or a difficulty in group settings, she may want to seek the advice of her teacher support team. In both boys' cases, the teacher is responsible for reporting observations professionally to the school personnel who help teachers to problem solve and meet children's individual needs. The classroom teacher does not make a diagnosis of a learning disability or other learning differences a child may have.

Content categories: Teacher Professionalism, Communication Techniques

Case IV

22. **Suggested content:** Miss Arrighie has a diverse group of third-grade students, and she wants to improve her vocabulary instruction. One method to do this is to use graphic organizers such as a continuum. The continuum graphic organizer is a horizontal line with an arrow at either end. Near one end of the continuum, the teacher places a word, such as *sad,* and near the other end of the continuum the teacher places a word with the opposite meaning, such as *happy.* With the students' help, the teacher places other words that are synonymous with happy and sad, and they place the words along the continuum. Miss Arrighie can keep this graphic organizer posted and remind students to use exciting words instead of *happy* and *sad* in their written and spoken language.

Content categories: Students as Learners, Instruction and Assessment

23. **Suggested content:** Miss Arrighie teaches in an urban classroom in which 76% of her students are from an Hispanic ethnic group, 13% are Black, and 5% are Native American. Of these students, 61% of her students did not speak English as their first language in their home. Miss Arrighie can strengthen home and school connections by creating a one-page newsletter that is published in English, Spanish, and any other languages spoken in the children's homes. She can involve members of the parent community in helping with several aspects of publishing the newsletter—translating, deciding on the content, photocopying, and distributing. Miss Arrighie can show her respect for her students and their families by communicating respectfully and professionally with each of them on a regular basis.

Content categories: Teacher Professionalism, Communication Techniques

24. **Suggested content:** The pattern of "Reading for High-Level Comprehension" is improving in some areas and not improving in other areas. For example, in 2003–2004, 1% of the students were reading above the standard in this area and, during 2004–2005, 3% of the students were reading above the standard. In 2005–2006, this same area dropped to 2%. More dramatically, in 2003–2004, 64% of the students were not achieving the standard, but by 2005–2006 the percentage of students reading below the standard had reduced to 51%. While there has been some improvement at Woonton School, clearly more students need to meet or exceed the standard for reading for high-level comprehension. One method to use is to provide direct instruction on specific comprehension strategies, such as inferencing and summarizing. The teacher offers many specific lessons on these strategies with models and then lots of guided practice to scaffold support for students.

Content categories: Students as Learners, Instruction and Assessment

Discrete Multiple-Choice Questions

Question	Answer	Content Category	Where to Get More Help
		Answer Key, Test I, Questions 25–36	
25.	C	Students as Learners	Chapter 7
26.	B	Students as Learners	Chapter 7
27.	A	Students as Learners	Chapter 7
28.	B	Students as Learners	Chapter 7
29.	C	Instruction and Assessment	Chapter 8
30.	D	Instruction and Assessment	Chapter 8
31.	C	Instruction and Assessment	Chapter 8
32.	B	Instruction and Assessment	Chapter 8
33.	C	Teacher Professionalism	Chapter 10
34.	C	Teacher Professionalism	Chapter 10
35.	A	Teacher Professionalism	Chapter 10
36.	D	Teacher Professionalism	Chapter 10

Explanations

25. C. The Americans with Disabilities Act (ADA) is a federal law that prohibits discrimination on the basis of a person's disability for all services, programs, and activities provided by state and local governments. Choice A, NCLB, is No Child Left Behind Act of 2001, as reauthorization of the Elementary and Secondary Education Act (ESEA). Choice B, Section 504 of the Rehabilitation Act of 1973, is a civil rights law prohibiting discrimination against individuals with disabilities by federally assisted programs or activities. Choice D is Public Law 94-142, passed in 1975, now codified as IDEA (Individuals with Disabilities Education Act).

26. B. Madison's preferred learning modality is visual learning—learning by seeing. Visual learners are more successful when teachers use methods such as film, Power Point, overheads, notes on a chalkboard, or whiteboard.

27. A. Jamie appears to be motivated by extrinsic rewards for learning, not the intrinsic reward of learning for learning's sake.

28. B. Carol Gilligan's work questions the male-centered personality, psychology, and moral development theorists. She suggests three stages in the ethic of care—pre-conventional, in which the goal is individual survival; conventional, in which the goal is self-sacrifice to achieve goodness; and post-conventional, in which the goal is to uphold principles of nonviolence.

29. C. Bandura's social learning theory suggests that children learn by observing others. In the classroom, this may occur as modeling or learning vicariously through others' experiences.

30. D. Survey, Question, Read, Recite, and Review (SQ3R) is an instructional routine students can use to summarize and take notes effectively.

31. C. Numbered Heads Together is a cooperative learning strategy in which activities involve a "home team" of heterogeneously grouped students, who then work in small groups to become experts on a portion of the content to be learned. After the students become experts, they return to the home team to share important information.

32. B. Generating and testing hypotheses has become known as one of the 9 Essential Strategies. When using this strategy, students more deeply understand concepts being taught and must clearly explain their hypotheses and conclusions.

33. C. Students must be offered a hearing as part of due process established in the *Goss v. Lopez* case of 1971. Students facing suspension or expulsion must be afforded a hearing before their rights to an education are denied.

34. C. Reflective practitioners show persistence during challenging teaching situations, along with an understanding of their own and others' cultures. There are several other attributes of a reflective practitioner, such as a willingness to collaborate, good interpersonal skills, and an ability to critically analyze his or her own practice.

35. A. A Nation at Risk report was issued during the Reagan Administration and called for the creation of teaching, teacher education, and education standards.

36. D. The Testing Movement in U.S. education is thought to have begun with Terman's introduction of the Stanford-Binet intelligence test in 1916, along with other tests, such as the Stanford Achievement Test. Progressive educators of this time overwhelmingly supported such testing as a method of "scientifically" proving minorities and immigrants scored lower than whites on these tests.

Practice Test II

Case I

Directions: Questions 1–3 require you to write short answers, or "constructed responses." You are not expected to cite specific theories or texts in your answers; however, your knowledge of specific principles of learning and teaching will be evaluated. Be sure to answer all parts of the question. Write your answers in the space provided.

Scenario: Miss Egan

Miss Celia Egan is a fifth-grade teacher who has just introduced a science lesson on cloud formation to her students. The children are excited about the lesson because it involves hands-on learning and setting up an experiment to see how clouds actually form. In addition, Miss Egan has planned for a local television celebrity—Katie King, the weather person—to answer the students' questions about clouds and weather at the end of the unit. As part of her school system's evaluation process, Miss Egan will be observed by the Assistant Principal, Mrs. Kathy Egan (no relation!). Miss Egan has prepared her lesson plan (Document 1) and shared it with her Assistant Principal in preparation for the observation.

Document 1: Observing Cloud Formations

Objective

The students will summarize orally and in writing the key concept of the lesson—that clouds are formed when warm, humid air rises and cools, which causes water vapor in the air to condense.

Resources

- 4 clean mayonnaise-size jars
- 4 zip-seal plastic bags (sandwich size)
- Ice
- 4 liquid measuring cups
- Warm water
- 4 pieces of black construction paper
- Tape
- 4 flashlights
- Matches (for adult use only)
- 4 parent volunteers to support instruction and to light matches
- VCR/TV
- TV film clip of Katie King from a day that was cloudy
- Water cycle diagram
- Science journal and pencil

Procedures

1. Motivation—film clip & discussion
2. Warm-up
3. Preview
4. Teach
5. Experiment/discuss
6. Independent practice—write summary

Motivation

Show students the film clip of Katie King, the local TV weatherperson. Discuss the weather for that day (cloudy) and probe for background knowledge on how clouds are formed.

Warm-up

Observe types of cloud formations and discuss the prefixes and meanings of cloud types to help students understand cloud formations (e.g., *cirrus* means curly or fibrous; *cumulus* means lumpy or piled).

Preview

Show a water cycle diagram/poster depicting cloud formation, water vapor, condensation, and heat source (the sun).

Teach

1. Divide the class into four groups and ask parent volunteers to work with each of the groups. Demonstrate procedures for setting up the experiment.
2. Place black construction paper on the back of the mayo jar.
3. Place 1 cup of warm water in the jar.
4. Adult lights match, holds it at the mouth of the jar for a few moments, and then drops match in the water.
5. Quickly place a sandwich bag full of ice over the mouth of the jar.
6. Students observe cloud formation.
7. Students write down observations in science journals.

Assessment

The teacher informally checks the student science journals for participation and effort in the observation process. Next, the teacher formally assesses the homework summaries using the following criteria for an exemplary summary:

- Clear and concise summary of cloud formation process; no intrusive errors in mechanics or spelling.
- Paragraph format with main idea sentences, 3-5 detail sentences, and a closing sentence.
- Accurate science content that contains definitions for condensation, water vapor, and heat source.
- On time with neat handwritten or typewritten copy.

Independent Work

For homework, students will write a summary that shows their understanding of the cloud formation process.

After the lesson, Miss Egan was disappointed with many of her students' ability to stay focused during the experiment. Miss Egan felt that she had lost control of the classroom's management at several points in the lesson, including the showing of the film clip of Katie King and demonstrating the procedures of the experiment. Two groups had to repeat the experiment because they did not follow the sequence. In addition, one parent volunteer expressed frustration that two girls were continuously bickering over whose turn it was to manipulate the science materials. Mrs. Egan not only noted similar issues in her observation, but she also added that the students' independent work on writing summaries of their understanding of the content of the lesson were below school standards for mechanics and spelling, as well as for content knowledge.

1. Identify ONE strength of Miss Egan's lesson planning and base your response on the principles of learning and teaching addressed.

GO ON TO THE NEXT PAGE

2. Suggest TWO ways Miss Egan could improve her classroom management of this science lesson. Be certain to base your suggestions on the principles of instruction and assessment as well as best communication techniques in the classroom.

3. Suggest TWO ways Miss Egan can look to Mrs. Egan, her Assistant Principal, for professional development and guidance in her efforts to grow as a teacher. Be certain to base your answer on the principles of teacher professionalism.

_____

_____

_____

_____

_____

_____

_____

_____

_____

_____

_____

_____

_____

_____

_____

_____

_____

_____

_____

_____

_____

_____

_____

_____

_____

_____

Case II

Directions: Questions 4–6 require you to write short answers, or "constructed responses." You are not expected to cite specific theories or texts in your answers; however, your knowledge of specific principles of learning and teaching will be evaluated. Be sure to answer all parts of the question. Write your answers in the space provided.

Scenario: Jeffrey

Jeffrey is a third-grader who is struggling to learn in school. He is having great difficulty learning to read and is having social difficulty with many of his peers. Jeffrey is grossly overweight for a boy his age and height, and he often comes to school in the same ill-fitting and unclean outfits. His teacher, Mrs. Dion, has planned to observe Jeffrey at regular intervals and take notes about his contributions to class discussions so that she can share these observations at the next Teacher Support Team meeting. Document 1 contains Mrs. Dion's observations of Jeffrey over the period of a week in third grade.

Document 1

3/16/04, 9:15 am: At opening group meeting, Jeffrey sits off to the side of his peers, facing away from the group, and looking withdrawn and sad. When Clarissa asks Jeffrey if he wants to have a turn at changing the calendar, Jeffrey angrily answers no and tells Clarissa that she is bossy and nosy.

3/16/04, 12:10 pm: In the cafeteria, Jeffrey eats his lunch with one boy who is in first grade. The boys are neighbors and both of their families own farms. The boys talk about riding the tractor and helping out around the farm.

3/17/04, 1:00 pm: Jeffrey is looking at a magazine article about animals. He excitedly shows Johnny the picture of the goats and tells him that he has 15 goats at his house. Johnny tells Jeffrey that he is lying and the boys start to tussle over the magazine.

3/18/04, 10:35 am: During a cooperative group writing activity, Clarissa complains to the teacher that she does want to work with Jeffrey because he is mean and because he is not clean.

3/18/04, 11:15 am: Jeffrey asks the teacher for help reading the word pineapple. After the teacher helps him decode this word, Jeffrey asks, "What is a pineapple?"

Mrs. Dion brings her notes to the Teacher Support Team. Mrs. Dion has decided to place Jeffrey in a seat by himself and to create an individual reading group for Jeffrey because he is having so much difficulty reading and cooperating with his peers. The Teacher Support Team suggests that this may not be the most effective way to help Jeffrey make progress in the classroom.

4. Suggest ONE instructional method that might better help Jeffrey learn to read in his third-grade classroom. Be certain to base your response on the principles of instruction and assessment.

5. Suggest ONE resource that Mrs. Dion could use to help Jeffrey socially. Be sure to base your response on principles of communication techniques and teacher professionalism.

6. Identify ONE area of strength that Jeffrey brings to this classroom and suggest an instructional method to support his progress in third grade. Be sure to base your response on principles of student learning and instruction.

GO ON TO THE NEXT PAGE

_____
_____
_____
_____
_____
_____
_____
_____
_____
_____
_____
_____
_____
_____
_____

Discrete Multiple-Choice Questions

Directions: Questions 7–18 are not related to the previous cases. For each question, select the best answer and mark the corresponding letter space on your answer sheet.

7. Mrs. Manning has regular class meetings to discuss classroom rules, procedures, and policies. If students are having difficulty following a rule or if a policy seems too strict, the meeting is a place where the students and teacher can review concerns and come up with alternate solutions. Mrs. Manning's class meeting is grounded in

   A. Canter's assertive discipline theory.
   B. Kounin's with-it-ness theory.
   C. Glasser's choice theory.
   D. Jones' time on task theory.

8. Mrs. Benton likes to have a friendly relationship with her students and brings a *laissez-faire* approach to classroom management. For example, she prefers that the students take charge of the classroom procedures, and she allows them to go to the restroom, use the office phone, or visit the school nurse or another teacher's classroom whenever the students want to. Between teaching lessons, Mrs. Benton uses the Internet to order from catalogs and to check her email while the students work on seatwork. Based on this situation, which of the following is NOT a strength of Mrs. Benton's teacher professionalism?

   A. Understanding her role as a teacher
   B. Viewing diversity as positive and enriching
   C. Understanding her own culture
   D. Valuing the importance of empowering learners

Question 9 is based on the following passage.

Michelle enjoys school, especially this fourth-grade school year, because she is learning more about U.S. history, geometry, and earth science. She asks many questions of her teacher and often talks to her family about the things she has learned at school. Yesterday, Michelle brought a drawing of 3D objects to school that she had made at home.

9. Which of the following describes Michelle's motivation in fourth grade?

    A. Teacher-centered

    B. Parent-centered

    C. External

    D. Intrinsic

10. The primary purpose of a school-to-work program is

    A. to help students choose a college.

    B. to prepare students for future living.

    C. to prepare students for graduation.

    D. to help students engage in community service.

11. Mr. Murray has planned a health lesson in which his third-grade students must write a summary on a health-related article found in a magazine or on the Internet. He has planned for an assessment that looks at the overall quality of the students' work. This type of assessment plan is called

    A. norm-referenced scoring.

    B. achievement scoring.

    C. holistic scoring.

    D. objective scoring.

12. The sixth-grade teachers at North Central Elementary have their students switch classes in order to prepare them for the changing of classes and teachers next year at the middle school. For example, one sixth-grade teacher teaches science, another teaches language arts, another teaches social studies. The teachers have written a unit of study collaboratively in order to help students make connections between classes and content areas. This type of unit is known as

    A. interdisciplinary.

    B. content planning.

    C. thematic.

    D. standards-based.

13. Mrs. Eberly, a fifth-grade teacher, looks to which of the following professional associations for standards and best practice in mathematics instruction?

    A. National Accreditation of Mathematics Programs

    B. Addison and Wellesley

    C. National Association of Mathematics Instruction

    D. National Council of Teachers of Mathematics

GO ON TO THE NEXT PAGE

14. Miss Whitman likes to involve her students in the process of exploring the natural world in an effort to help students better understand science and the natural world. Recently, she had her students build a cardboard model house with four rooms and then wire the home with electricity to light it. Which of the following approaches is Miss Whitman using in her teaching of science?

   A. Inquiry model
   B. Hypothesis model
   C. Scientific process
   D. Standards-based approach

15. This professional association was formed in 1916. Its motto is "Democracy in Education and Education for Democracy." Which of the following associations is being described here?

   A. Democratic Teachers for American Education
   B. National Education Association
   C. Congress of Teachers and Industrial Organization
   D. American Federation of Teachers

16. Miss Southwick is a first-year teacher of fifth-grade who is planning a new unit for her social studies class. She is unsure of what her students must know and be able to do at this age level and in this content area. She has looked at the district curriculum guide, but it is outdated and not helpful. Which of the following will best aid Miss Southwick when planning this lesson?

   A. Teachers' union
   B. Teacher assistants
   C. Content standards
   D. School handbook

17. Which of the following laws advanced education as a social responsibility, not just a parental responsibility?

   A. Massachusetts Laws of Education 1642 and 1647
   B. No Child Left Behind and ESEA
   C. P.L. 94-142 and Section 504 of the Rehabilitation Act
   D. ADA and *Brown v. the Board of Education*

18. Which of the following school positions is rooted in Horace Mann's concept of a teacher leader and started in the secondary schools, years later spreading to the primary schools.

   A. Head teacher
   B. Superintendent
   C. Principal
   D. Teacher assistant

Case III

Directions: Questions 19–21 require you to write short answers, or "constructed responses." You are not expected to cite specific theories or texts in your answers; however, your knowledge of specific principles of learning and teaching will be evaluated. Be sure to answer all parts of the question. Write your answers in the space provided.

Scenario: Ms. Maher

Ms. Maher has involved her students in a community service project that involves cleaning up the river behind the school as well as checking the water quality of the river and reporting this data to the River Preservation Association. During the kickoff of the project, she invites parents and students to walk down to the river on a "walking fieldtrip."

The children observe the litter and debris polluting the river and react in disgust. The children also observe box turtles sunning themselves on a fallen log, fish near the surface of the water, and a mallard duck and their babies out for an afternoon swim.

When the class returns to school, she asks her students to work in small groups to discuss what they saw on the walking fieldtrip and brainstorm what they can do to make a difference to improve the life of the river right next to their school. The children unanimously agree that they would like to lead a community cleanup of the river project.

Over the next few days, besides planning for the community service River Cleanup Project that includes writing posters and letters to the editor of the local newspapers, Ms. Maher engages the children in a series of science lessons on the river's habitat and how to test for water quality.

The children begin to collect water samples weekly and then submit the data to an online website for the classroom as well as to the local River Preservation Association website. On the day of the river cleanup, over 100 community members don boots and gloves to assist the children in their efforts to clean the river. Ms. Maher congratulates the children for their successful community service project. She acknowledges their success in the classroom and in the community. The community members who helped with the cleanup all cheer the children's leadership and success as everyone takes a break for hot cider and cookies.

19. Identify ONE theory about student learning that guides Ms. Maher's instructional practice. Give a description of the theory and specific examples from Ms. Maher's practice.

20. Suggest TWO ways that Ms. Maher is motivating her students to learn socially, academically, and/or emotionally. Be sure to base your response on the principles of teaching and learning.

21. Suggest ONE extension activity that Ms. Maher could implement after the River Cleanup Project ends. Base your extension activity idea on your careful reading of the scenario and on the principles of instruction and assessment.

_____

_____

_____

_____

_____

_____

_____

_____

_____

_____

GO ON TO THE NEXT PAGE

_____

_____

_____

_____

_____

_____

Case IV

Directions: Questions 22–24 require you to write short answers, or "constructed responses." You are not expected to cite specific theories or texts in your answers; however, your knowledge of specific principles of learning and teaching will be evaluated. Be sure to answer all parts of the question. Write your answers in the space provided.

Scenario: Dwayne

Dwayne is a sixth-grader who is in Mr. Stafford's classroom. Dwayne appears to be underachieving, especially in the areas of reading and writing. He has great difficulty reading his social studies and science textbooks, and he rarely completes homework assignments involving reading. Dwayne enjoys mathematics, science, and social studies, especially when simulations, hands-on learning, or real-life scenarios are used in the lessons. He often earns A's and B's on the in-class assignments from science and math, but his overall grade is lower because of his inconsistent homework completion and difficulty reading independently.

Dwayne is an 11-year-old from a Native American and Black ethnic background who receives reduced lunch pricing at school. He has lived in this community his whole life with his mother and father. He has a large extended family that has also lived in the area for many years, and he enjoys much support from his family, especially his cousins who attend the same school. He has not been tested for special education and does not receive ESL services. Dwayne uses a local dialect of Black English Vernacular (BEV), which is noticeable in his classroom conversations and in his written work. Dwayne is athletic—he likes to play kickball, football, and soccer—and he appears confident and self-assured on the playground. He appears less confident in the classroom, often laying his head down on his desk or looking frustrated or overwhelmed by the task at hand.

22. Suggest ONE way to support Dwayne's social or emotional growth in the classroom. Be sure to base your response on the principles of student learning and teaching.

23. Suggest ONE way to involve Dwayne's family in his schoolwork. Be sure to base your response on principles of effective communication and teacher professionalism.

24. Suggest ONE reason why Dwayne might be having difficulty in the areas of reading and writing. Discuss the principles of student learning and instructional methods that may be involved in Dwayne's development as a learner.

_____

_____

_____

_____

_____

_____

_____

_____

_____

_____

_____

_____

_____

_____

_____

_____

_____

_____

_____

Discrete Multiple-Choice Questions

Directions: Questions 25–36 are not related to the previous cases. For each question, select the best answer and mark the corresponding letter space on your answer sheet.

25. Zachary is a third-grader who is working on a science experiment that involves balance and weights of objects. With his group at his side, Zachary places a lump of green clay on one pan of the balance and a lump of red clay on the other pan. His group notes that the lumps nearly balance the scale, and they decide that each lump of clay weighs almost the same amount. Then the teacher asks the group to flatten the green lump of clay and roll it into a "snake." She asks the children to predict which will weigh more now—the green or the red clay. Zachary is convinced that the red lump that has not been flattened and rolled will definitely weigh more. According to Piaget, which of the following stages best captures the level of Zachary's thinking?

  A. Deductive
  B. Pre-operational
  C. Concrete operational
  D. Sensorimotor

26. Lee is a third-grade student whose family has had a difficult time making ends meet. His dad works third shift as a security guard, and his mom has been laid off from her position at the local jewelry factory. Lee and his two sisters and two brothers try to help out around the house while also keeping up with their schoolwork. Lee's mom has shared her concern that they may not be able to pay the rent next month. Based on Maslow's hierarchy of needs, which of the following may need to be met to ensure Lee's sense of security in school and at home?

  A. Esteem needs
  B. Physiological needs
  C. Basic needs
  D. Belongingness needs

GO ON TO THE NEXT PAGE

Questions 27–28 are based on the following passage.

Dimitri is a third-grader in Mrs. Kendall's classroom; Holly is a third-grader in the same classroom. Dimitri is an outgoing, musically talented, and happy child. His favorite subjects are music and science. Holly is a quiet girl who likes to wear her long bangs over her eyes. She is insightful and sensitive, as noted during a lesson on butterflies and the life cycle. Holly worked hard to care for the butterflies and made careful observations of them in her science notebook. Holly's favorite subjects are science and art.

27. According to Gardner's theory of multiple intelligences, which of the following multiple intelligences might Dimitri possess?

   A. Interpersonal and musical intelligences
   B. Visual-spatial and linguistic intelligences
   C. Intrapersonal and musical intelligences
   D. Linguistic and logical-mathematical intelligences

28. According to Gardner's theory of multiple intelligences, which of the following multiple intelligences might Holly possess?

   A. Visual-spatial and logical-mathematical intelligences
   B. Intrapersonal and naturalist intelligences
   C. Interpersonal and naturalist intelligences
   D. Bodily-kinesthetic and linguistic intelligences

29. Mr. McGillivray is preparing for an evaluation by his principal. He wants to more carefully focus on his ability to carefully plan a lesson and then assess student progress. He should work on which of the following to improve his lesson implementation in these areas?

   A. Creating standards-based units and gathering resources
   B. Opening the lesson and modeling
   C. Setting objectives and providing feedback
   D. Correcting student papers and giving homework

30. Mr. Bell is teaching a lesson on writing a lab report. He has set clear goals and objectives for the lab report and is presenting the parts of the report in small, attainable increments to make certain his students meet success on this assignment. Which of the following instructional methods is Mr. Bell using?

   A. Cooperative learning
   B. Demonstration
   C. Sequencing
   D. Direct instruction

31. Mrs. Rainy is using the book *The Three Little Pigs* to teach her students about a story's beginning, middle, and end. She has read the story book aloud to the children and had them role play the key scenes in the story. Next, she would like to have her students write one sentence about the beginning, a second sentence about the middle, and a third sentence about the end of the story. What type of graphic organizer might help her achieve her objective?

   A. Venn
   B. Sequence
   C. Cause and effect
   D. Brainstorm

32. Joshua excitedly arrives home from school to tell his dad about the "trip" his fourth-grade class is taking across the United States. Joshua is working with three other classmates to plan their route and pack their belongings so that they're the first "car" in the class to make the coast-to-coast trip out West. Joshua's dad teasingly asks how much this fieldtrip will cost, and Joshua tells his dad that it's not a real trip the class is going on, that this is _____ in his Social Studies class.

    A. a simulation

    B. a lesson plan

    C. an experiment

    D. a standards-based objective

33. This group wrote a report calling for changes to liberalize the American high school. They called for eight years of elementary education and four years of secondary education. What is the name of this group?

    A. The National Reading Panel

    B. The National Coalition of Schools

    C. The NEA Committee of Ten

    D. The High School Reform Committee

34. Mr. Monroe is concerned about one of his second-grade students who is having difficulty in his classroom. His student, Charles, is frequently absent or tardy and, when he is present, he is often shy or withdrawn. Mr. Monroe has tried several ways to address his concerns for Charles and to help Charles to be successful in the second grade. He has called Charles' parents on several occasions; he has met with the Teacher Support Team about Charles; and he has tried to get to know Charles individually through small talk and focused attention on him. Which of the following characteristics of a reflective educator best describes Mr. Monroe?

    A. Reflective educators show persistence

    B. Reflective educators attend professional development

    C. Reflective educators have good interpersonal skills

    D. Reflective educators possess an awareness of culture

35. Miss Florence is a first-year principal at San Martin Elementary. She has learned that her state laws allow paddling of students with permission of the child's parents and with good reason. Paddling involves choosing an appropriate size paddle (smaller for younger children and larger for older students), requiring the child to lean over a desk, and striking the child on the backside three times with force. While she is uncomfortable with this type of discipline, she is required to paddle students if they repeatedly violate school rules. Paddling, in this scenario, is also known as

    A. assertive discipline.

    B. control theory.

    C. negative reinforcement.

    D. corporal punishment.

36. Mrs. Denham has been a classroom teacher for two years and is missing the learning-filled environment of her university classes. She would like to stay current on best instructional practices, current education research, and up-to-date children's book lists. Which of the following professional development resources is most likely to be helpful to Mrs. Denham?

    A. School library

    B. Professional workshops

    C. Her principal

    D. Workshop

Answers and Explanations, Test II

Case I

1. **Suggested content:** Miss Egan has planned a lesson plan on observing cloud formations. One strength of her lesson plan is her use of the inquiry-based science instructional method, including clear procedures for teaching with this method. For example, Miss Egan does not lecture on how the experiment will turn out and specifically how the clouds will form before the science hands-on experiment. She allows the students to make connections between prior knowledge of clouds and this new information. Her procedures for teaching this lesson are clearly stated, step-by-step.

   Content categories: Students as Learners, Instruction and Assessment

2. **Suggested content:** Miss Egan taught a lesson on cloud formations that was not implemented well, primarily because of classroom management issues. Two suggestions for Miss Egan are: 1. Preview Film Clip and 2. Prepare Volunteers. To more thoroughly prepare students for the purpose of viewing the film clip of Katie King, Miss Egan should clearly state the objectives of her lesson and review appropriate behaviors when viewing the film. She could create a simple graphic organizer for students to write on while they view the film or immediately after. This will hold each student individually accountable for the viewing, and it helps students know that watching the film is purposeful. If Miss Egan spent a bit more time preparing the classroom volunteers to demonstrate the procedures of the experiment and manage the materials of the experiment, the students may have more effectively taken turns and completed the experiment successfully. Although this may take a bit more planning time than conducting this experiment for the whole group with only the teacher demonstrating, it is worth the effort because of safety (matches were in use) and also because the students are more able to observe closely in small groups.

   Content categories: Instruction and Assessment, Communication Techniques

3. **Suggested content:** Miss Egan can seek the expertise, advice, and support of her Assistant Principal, Mrs. Egan, by asking her to suggest professional reading and professional development ideas about classroom management. Professional literature can offer ideas to Miss Egan on her own time and can provide a variety of models and theories to guide her to discover what is right for her and her class. Mrs. Egan may even have a few specific titles from her own professional library to loan to Miss Egan. Miss Egan can also ask her Assistant Principal to support her efforts to locate and attend professional development workshops on the topic of classroom management. Mrs. Egan may know of local, statewide, or national opportunities for professional development and can advocate for the release time—and also possibly for the funds—for Miss Egan to attend.

   Content categories: Teacher Professionalism

Case II

4. **Suggested content:** Jeffrey is a third-grader who is struggling academically and socially in his classroom. One instructional method that his teacher could try to help Jeffrey improve his reading is a word bank in order to improve Jeffrey's vocabulary and background knowledge. The word bank is made up of a file box and index cards. To start the word bank, the teacher can encourage Jeffrey to write words he knows or really likes, such as those having to do with farming, an area of strength for Jeffrey. On the front, Jeffrey writes the word correctly with the teacher's help. On the back, he can draw a picture or write a few words that define or describe the word (whichever he prefers). After Jeffrey has several words in his word bank, the teacher shows Jeffrey some games to play to practice reading or remembering the words, and then she asks Jeffrey to teach this game to his first-grade friend or a classmate (if Jeffrey is comfortable). Ideally, as the word bank grows, so does Jeffrey's vocabulary, reading ability, confidence, and perhaps even social skills!

   Content categories: Instruction and Assessment

5. **Suggested content:** Jeffrey is a struggling third-grader who is having social and academic difficulty. One way that Mrs. Dion could help Jeffrey strengthen his social skills is to implement a unit of study around the theme of conflict resolution. Mrs. Dion could get the help of the school social worker, special education teacher, or school psychologist to get ideas for this unit or to perhaps even assist in teaching it. (In this case, the adults are modeling good problem-solving and conflict resolution!) Mrs. Dion could use literature with themes of conflicts resolved in positive ways and non-examples of good conflict resolution. Along with this study of conflict resolution, Mrs. Dion could implement a time each day to actually work on conflict resolution skills in real-life school situations. In this way, Mrs. Dion is helping all students learn an important life skill and specifically she is providing Jeffrey with the tools he needs to be more successful in school.

Content categories: Teacher Professionalism, Communication Techniques

6. **Suggested content:** Jeffrey appears to work well with younger students, as noted in Mrs. Dion's observation of Jeffrey at lunch time. Mrs. Dion can capitalize on this strength in several ways, including: 1. helping Jeffrey to see this strength and 2. providing Jeffrey with buddy tutoring situations. Jeffrey may have low self-concept or sense of belonging in his classroom. Helping Jeffrey to see his strength may help him to feel more confident about his abilities to help others and to learn. Mrs. Dion could collaborate with a lower grade level teacher to offer Jeffrey time to tutor a child less able and younger than him. These tutoring sessions offer the opportunity to help Jeffrey gain a sense of belonging and competence at school; moreover, they provide him with a chance to practice reading and rereading materials to strengthen his own reading skills and strategies.

Content categories: Students as Learners, Instruction and Assessment, Communication Techniques

Discrete Multiple-Choice Questions

Answer Key, Test II, Questions 7–18			
Question	**Answer**	**Content Category**	**Where to Get More Help**
7.	C	Students as Learners	Chapter 7
8.	A	Students as Learners	Chapter 7
9.	D	Students as Learners	Chapter 7
10.	B	Students as Learners	Chapter 7
11.	C	Instruction and Assessment	Chapter 8
12.	A	Instruction and Assessment	Chapter 8
13.	D	Instruction and Assessment	Chapter 8
14.	A	Instruction and Assessment	Chapter 8
15.	D	Teacher Professionalism	Chapter 10
16.	C	Teacher Professionalism	Chapter 10
17.	A	Teacher Professionalism	Chapter 10
18.	C	Teacher Professionalism	Chapter 10

Explanations

7. **C.** Glasser's choice theory calls for regular class meetings to discuss classroom rules and procedures in a collaborative and problem-solving setting. In this context, students and teacher co-negotiate their learning environment, building ownership and responsibility for all in the learning community.

8. **A.** Mrs. Benton appears to be having difficulty enacting and understanding the importance of her role as a teacher. While a *laissez-faire* approach to the classroom can be effective for several teachers, Mrs. Benton's attempts to befriend her students, rather than teach them, shows her lack of professionalism and misguided priorities in the classroom.

9. **D.** Michelle's motivation is intrinsic—from within. She learns for the sake of learning and does not appear to need external rewards for learning.

10. **B.** The primary purpose of a school-to-work program is to help prepare students for future living.

11. **C.** Holistic scoring is a way to assess the overall quality of a student's work. The teacher does not evaluate each individual part; instead, he or she focuses on providing feedback about the whole piece of work.

12. **A.** A unit that incorporates content areas, such as science and language arts as described in this situation, is considered interdisciplinary. The goal of an interdisciplinary unit is to help students make connections between content areas and classes in hopes that the student will transfer learning beyond the classroom walls.

13. **D.** Mrs. Eberly will look to the National Council of Teachers of Mathematics for professional standards for teachers of mathematics.

14. **A.** Miss Whitman is using an inquiry model of instruction to help her students discover science concepts and how things work in science. In an inquiry model approach, the teacher provides hands-on experiences for the students to discover meaning. The teacher does not lecture or tell in this instructional model.

15. **D.** The American Federation of Teachers was formed in 1916 with the motto "Democracy in Education and Education for Democracy."

16. **C.** Content standards are more likely than the school handbook to guide Miss Southwick's instruction in this scenario. School handbooks usually contain school policies and sometimes brief outlines of what is taught at each grade level. Miss Southwick will get more reliable information about content she can teach from the content standards of her professional association.

17. **A.** The Massachusetts Laws of Education 1642 and 1647 established social responsibility to teach children to read and write.

18. **C.** Horace Mann established the role of the principal as a teacher leader and instructional leader.

Case III

19. **Suggested content:** Ms. Maher is using project-based learning to teach her students the value of devoting time to community service, working together to solve real problems, and, at the same time, learning more about science. John Dewey, known as the father of Progressive Education, believed that learning by experience was most important for people. Ms. Maher's river cleanup project, which started with a visit to the nearby river and an opportunity for the children to observe the problems and the beauty of the river, provided her students with the chance to determine a project that they felt was important and purposeful.

    Content categories: Students as Learners, Instruction and Assessment

20. **Suggested content:** Ms. Maher's community-based service project focusing on a local river cleanup proved to be very motivating for her students. Ways that this project is motivating to her students include: 1. the intrinsic motivation of learning science for real purposes and 2. the socially rewarding experience of working together and gaining recognition for an important job done well. The river project was intrinsically motivating, which means that the children were rewarded from within (not with stickers or tokens). The children learned the power of learning science to inform others, while also making a positive impact by cleaning up the river. The project also provided social recognition from their teacher and community members for their hard work. The children also felt the reward of working cooperatively for a good cause—the health of their river.

    Content categories: Teacher Professionalism, Communication Techniques

21. **Suggested content:** After such a successful lesson on river ecology, Ms. Maher could have her students complete an extension activity using more mathematical skills, such as representation of data. Her students could return to the website with their raw data and use computer software, or simply chart paper, to create a table of information about the river's water quality. Ms. Maher could teach her students how to calculate means, modes, and medians. In addition, she could have her students then compare their data to that of another river in the world for which they find data on the Internet. As a closing activity to this extension, Ms. Maher could invite a scientist to class to discuss how mathematics plays a key role in his or her work as a scientist.

    Content categories: Students as Learners, Instruction and Assessment

Case IV

22. **Suggested content:** Dwayne appears to be having the most difficulty with reading and writing in his sixth-grade classroom. One way to support Dwayne to experience more success in these areas is to "chunk" the curriculum materials for him. Curriculum chunking is a way to differentiate instruction for Dwayne that involves breaking down more complex assignments into smaller parts, and by providing immediate support and feedback on a section of work before Dwayne begins to struggle or fail with an assignment. This type of modification does not "water down" the curriculum or set a lower standard for Dwayne—he will still complete the assignments that his peers complete. This method provides the supports for Dwayne to succeed with challenging sixth-grade materials.

    Content categories: Students as Learners, Instruction and Assessment

23. **Suggested content:** Dwayne is a sixth-grader who is struggling with completing homework assignments, perhaps because the reading materials are difficult for Dwayne to read on his own. This child has the strength of having a large extended family and support system in town, so Mr. Stafford could help Dwayne find a "homework buddy" in an older cousin to provide a role model for him. In addition, Dwayne may need help with reading to learn, which may be something an older cousin or his parents can help him with. If Dwayne's reading needs are so great that he needs further support in this area, Mr. Stafford can work with the family to provide tutoring support or a referral for diagnostic testing with the school system's support.

    Content categories: Teacher Professionalism, Communication Techniques

24. **Suggested content:** Dwayne is a sixth-grader who is having difficulty with reading and writing. The demands of reading to learn in the sixth grade are great; if Dwayne did not have a strong foundation in these areas before this time, he may need further support to help him strengthen these areas. One reason why he may be experiencing difficulty could be based on cultural background. Dwayne may be having a challenging time writing in Standard, or "mainstream," English because of his rich background of language, which uses a Black Vernacular of English. Dwayne might be having difficulty "code-switching," or knowing when to use home language versus school language. Mr. Stafford can support Dwayne's progress in these areas by first understanding his own cultural background and language development, and by then seeking to respect and better understand Dwayne's linguistic pattern of language. Dwayne may need to have opportunities to write for a variety of purposes and to understand the strength of writing in both Standard English and Black Vernacular English. This recognition and appreciation of Dwayne's language may help him to take more risks with writing in the classroom.

    Content categories: Students as Learners, Instruction and Assessment

Discrete Multiple-Choice Questions

Answer Key, Test II, Questions 25–36			
Question	**Answer**	**Content Category**	**Where to Get More Help**
25.	C	Students as Learners	Chapter 7
26.	B	Students as Learners	Chapter 7
27.	A	Students as Learners	Chapter 7
28.	B	Students as Learners	Chapter 7

Question	Answer	Content Category	Where to Get More Help
29.	C	Instruction and Assessment	Chapter 8
30.	D	Instruction and Assessment	Chapter 8
31.	B	Instruction and Assessment	Chapter 8
32.	A	Instruction and Assessment	Chapter 8
33.	C	Teacher Professionalism	Chapter 10
34.	A	Teacher Professionalism	Chapter 10
35.	D	Teacher Professionalism	Chapter 10
36.	B	Teacher Professionalism	Chapter 10

Explanations

25. C. Zachary is showing his level of development at the concrete operational level when he does not recognize the conservation of weight principle. According to Piaget, concrete operational level thinkers have an ability to formulate and test hypotheses. In addition, concrete operational thinkers often try to confirm or disprove an hypotheses by changing two or more variables.

26. B. According to Maslow's hierarchy of needs, Lee's physiological needs must be met or he will have difficulty with higher level needs, such as love, sense of belonging, and esteem needs.

27. A. According to Gardner's theory of multiple intelligences, Dimitri shows strengths in the areas of musical and interpersonal intelligences.

28. B. According to Gardner's theory of multiple intelligences, Holly shows strengths in the areas of naturalist and intrapersonal intelligences.

29. C. Mr. McGillivray should focus on setting objectives and providing feedback to his students in his efforts to strengthen his lesson planning.

30. D. Mr. Bell is using direct instruction, which is an overarching method that involves carefully planned lessons presented in small, attainable increments with clearly defined goals and objectives.

31. B. Mrs. Rainy would use a sequence diagram to best teach her students how to note a story's beginning, middle, and end.

32. A. Joshua seems to really enjoy the simulation his teacher is using in social studies class. A simulation involves students actively experiencing real-life situations through scenarios and dramatization of events.

33. C. The NEA Committee of Ten created the report which resulted in the U.S. education school configuration of eight years of elementary education and four years of secondary education.

34. A. In this situation, Mr. Monroe shows his professionalism through his persistence in helping to find a way to assist his student.

35. D. Corporal punishment is that which involves striking a child. Corporal punishment is considered constitutional according to federal laws, but it may be considered illegal in schools according to state laws.

36. B. Mrs. Denham would most likely benefit from attending a professional development series of workshops to expose her to new ideas outside of her building and to new colleagues with whom she could build relationships.

PLT Grades 5–9 Practice Tests

In this chapter, you will find two full-length practice tests for the PLT Grades 5–9 designed to give you a sense of the test's format and scope. You may also want to practice your timing and pacing for the test by using these practice tests. Remember, you will have a total of 2 hours to complete the test.

After you finish each practice test, score your answers in the section that follows the test. Use the sample responses and explanations provided to figure out your strengths and weaknesses and assess which content areas you need to study in Part III of this book. You may also want to complete the full-length practice tests in Chapters 11, 12, and 14 to help you determine further content areas to study. Even though these additional practice tests are written for other grade levels, the topics of the questions—Students as Learners, Instruction and Assessment, Communication Techniques, and Teacher Professionalism—remain the same.

-------------------------------- CUT HERE --------------------------------

(Remove these sheets and use them to mark your answers to the multiple-choice questions.)

ANSWER SHEET FOR TEST 1

7 Ⓐ Ⓑ Ⓒ Ⓓ	25 Ⓐ Ⓑ Ⓒ Ⓓ
8 Ⓐ Ⓑ Ⓒ Ⓓ	26 Ⓐ Ⓑ Ⓒ Ⓓ
9 Ⓐ Ⓑ Ⓒ Ⓓ	27 Ⓐ Ⓑ Ⓒ Ⓓ
10 Ⓐ Ⓑ Ⓒ Ⓓ	28 Ⓐ Ⓑ Ⓒ Ⓓ
11 Ⓐ Ⓑ Ⓒ Ⓓ	29 Ⓐ Ⓑ Ⓒ Ⓓ
12 Ⓐ Ⓑ Ⓒ Ⓓ	30 Ⓐ Ⓑ Ⓒ Ⓓ
13 Ⓐ Ⓑ Ⓒ Ⓓ	31 Ⓐ Ⓑ Ⓒ Ⓓ
14 Ⓐ Ⓑ Ⓒ Ⓓ	32 Ⓐ Ⓑ Ⓒ Ⓓ
15 Ⓐ Ⓑ Ⓒ Ⓓ	33 Ⓐ Ⓑ Ⓒ Ⓓ
16 Ⓐ Ⓑ Ⓒ Ⓓ	34 Ⓐ Ⓑ Ⓒ Ⓓ
17 Ⓐ Ⓑ Ⓒ Ⓓ	35 Ⓐ Ⓑ Ⓒ Ⓓ
18 Ⓐ Ⓑ Ⓒ Ⓓ	36 Ⓐ Ⓑ Ⓒ Ⓓ

ANSWER SHEET TEST 2

7 Ⓐ Ⓑ Ⓒ Ⓓ	25 Ⓐ Ⓑ Ⓒ Ⓓ
8 Ⓐ Ⓑ Ⓒ Ⓓ	26 Ⓐ Ⓑ Ⓒ Ⓓ
9 Ⓐ Ⓑ Ⓒ Ⓓ	27 Ⓐ Ⓑ Ⓒ Ⓓ
10 Ⓐ Ⓑ Ⓒ Ⓓ	28 Ⓐ Ⓑ Ⓒ Ⓓ
11 Ⓐ Ⓑ Ⓒ Ⓓ	29 Ⓐ Ⓑ Ⓒ Ⓓ
12 Ⓐ Ⓑ Ⓒ Ⓓ	30 Ⓐ Ⓑ Ⓒ Ⓓ
13 Ⓐ Ⓑ Ⓒ Ⓓ	31 Ⓐ Ⓑ Ⓒ Ⓓ
14 Ⓐ Ⓑ Ⓒ Ⓓ	32 Ⓐ Ⓑ Ⓒ Ⓓ
15 Ⓐ Ⓑ Ⓒ Ⓓ	33 Ⓐ Ⓑ Ⓒ Ⓓ
16 Ⓐ Ⓑ Ⓒ Ⓓ	34 Ⓐ Ⓑ Ⓒ Ⓓ
17 Ⓐ Ⓑ Ⓒ Ⓓ	35 Ⓐ Ⓑ Ⓒ Ⓓ
18 Ⓐ Ⓑ Ⓒ Ⓓ	36 Ⓐ Ⓑ Ⓒ Ⓓ

Practice Test I

Case I

Directions: Questions 1–3 require you to write short answers, or "constructed responses." You are not expected to cite specific theories or texts in your answers; however, your knowledge of specific principles of learning and teaching will be evaluated. Be sure to answer all parts of the question. Write your answers in the space provided.

Scenario: Ms. Manning

Ms. Manning is an eighth-grade English teacher at Broad Leaf Middle School. Several of her students have documented IEPs for learning disabilities in the area of reading, and two of her students have been diagnosed with attention deficit hyperactivity disorder (ADHD). One of her students receives English as a second language services from the ESL teacher. Ten of her 25 students receive free or reduced lunch.

As required by her teacher contract, Ms. Manning must create a professional portfolio containing clear evidence that she is achieving her professional goals. Later this month, Ms. Manning will be evaluated by her principal.

Document 1

Professional Goals

- Create effective bridges between students' experiences and the eighth-grade curriculum goals.
- Improve classroom discussions to help students share their thinking at a variety of levels for a variety of purposes.
- Develop and utilize active partnerships with parents, colleagues, and school leaders.

Document 2

Unit Goals

- Students will analyze the qualities of a good friend.
- Students will read about a variety of friendships, from destructive to healthy, and make connections between literature and real-life experiences.
- Students will write a comparative essay about the similarities and differences between healthy and destructive friendships.

Document 3

Project Directions

A primary assignment in Ms. Manning's friendship unit involves students responding to two texts: *Give a Boy a Gun* by Todd Strasser and *Freak the Mighty* by Rodman Philbrick. The friends in *Give a Boy a Gun* have a destructive relationship that culminates in a school shooting and massacre. The friends in *Freak the Mighty* are an unlikely pair who share a mutually rewarding friendship, even though they are very different. After reading and discussing each of the texts from a variety of perspectives and levels, the students are given an assignment to reflect on the friendships in the literature and to write a series of five to seven interview questions to ask a peer and a family member about friendships—both destructive and healthy ones.

GO ON TO THE NEXT PAGE

Document 4

Project Assessment Rubric

Ms. Manning established the following guidelines for an exemplary comparative essay:

- Three to four in-text citations about *Freak the Mighty* and *Give a Boy a Gun* that use quotation marks and other punctuation properly and include a page number.
- Your interpretation of or personal connection to each in-text citation and an explanation of why you included these specific quotes.
- Five to seven interview questions that pursue deeper, higher-level understanding of destructive and healthy friendships.
- Conducted interviews with a family member and a peer (evidence of interview notes attached).
- Typewritten, double-spaced, two-paragraph comparative essay. The first paragraph describes the nature of healthy friendships with details/supports from the texts and interviews. The second paragraph describes the nature of destructive friendships with details/supports from the texts and interviews.

1. Identify ONE instructional method that Ms. Manning could use to help her students achieve the eighth-grade curriculum objectives. Be sure to base your response on principles of instruction and assessment.

2. Suggest TWO teaching methods that Ms. Manning could implement to stimulate discussion about friendships among her diverse learners. Be sure to base your response on principles of best communication techniques and instructional methods.

3. Suggest ONE additional criterion that Ms. Manning could include in her rubric. Be sure to cite principles of instruction and assessment that this additional criterion would offer.

_____

_____

_____

_____

_____

_____

Case II

Directions: Questions 4–6 require you to write short answers, or "constructed responses." You are not expected to cite specific theories or texts in your answers; however, your knowledge of specific principles of learning and teaching will be evaluated. Be sure to answer all parts of the question. Write your answers in the space provided.

Scenario: Miss Kelly

Miss Kelly knows that the upcoming school year will be fraught with challenges, so she has started planning her long-term and short-term goals for her sixth-grade students. Miss Kelly's neighborhood elementary school has been consolidated with another elementary school in the district because of declining school enrollments and school budgets. Miss Kelly is used to knowing many of her new students' parents and siblings, as she has been at the same neighborhood school for several years. This year, she will know only two of her 25 families. In addition, Miss Kelly's school district has adopted a new mathematics series that promotes the use of complex problem-solving, algebra, and higher-level thinking. Her new principal has decided to analyze data on student performance in mathematics this school year. Miss Kelly is a bit anxious about all these changes in the upcoming teaching year.

Miss Kelly plans to focus her efforts on helping her students meet or exceed standards in mathematics problem-solving. She has obtained and carefully read the teacher's manual for the new mathematics series and has attended two full days of professional development about implementing the new series.

Miss Kelly's long-term goals include the following:

- Students will meet or exceed sixth-grade mathematics standards in problem-solving.
- Each student will become a friend to a younger buddy to help build a sense of school community.

Miss Kelly's short-term goals include the following:

- Students will know how to locate important places and people in the school building.
- Students will meet with a buddy to establish relationships and to discuss mathematics problem-solving strategies.

4. Suggest ONE instructional method that will support one of Miss Kelly's long-term instructional goals. Be sure to cite principles of best practice in assessment and instruction.

5. Suggest ONE instructional method that will support one of Miss Kelly's short-term instructional goals. Be sure to cite principles of best practice in assessment and instruction.

6. Identify ONE way that Miss Kelly can approach the changes in her school district and teaching situation as a teaching professional. Be sure to base your response on principles of teacher professionalism and effective communication techniques.

GO ON TO THE NEXT PAGE

_____

_____

_____

_____

_____

_____

_____

_____

_____

_____

_____

_____

_____

_____

_____

_____

_____

_____

_____

_____

_____

Discrete Multiple-Choice Questions

Directions: Questions 7–18 are not related to the previous cases. For each question, select the best answer and mark the corresponding letter space on your answer sheet.

7. Celia and Alyssa are in the sixth grade at Wakeland Elementary School. Both girls take pride in looking their best at school and often seek the approval of their peers. Which of the following best describes the girls' stage of moral development according to Kohlberg?

   A. Over-conventional
   B. Pre-conventional
   C. Post-conventional
   D. Conventional

8. Mr. Conlin prefers instructional methods that enable his students to discover meaning. For example, in his recent lesson on measurement, he asked his students to plan and then enact their plan to draw three dinosaurs to scale on the school playground. He provided the materials and resources to help students learn more about the actual size of each dinosaur; otherwise, Mr. Conlin let his students discover their own solutions to the challenge of drawing such large animals. A guiding principle behind Mr. Conlin's practice is his educational philosophy about which of the following?

   A. Constructivism

   B. Behaviorism

   C. Nonviolence

   D. Self-actualization

Questions 9–10 are based on the following passage.

Phyllis is a third-grader who is making slower than average progress in her gross motor, fine motor, and language development. She has difficulty with handwriting, physical education activities, and speaking in class. Phyllis is receiving special services from the resource teacher, the speech and language teacher, and the occupational/physical therapist.

9. Phyllis' learning differences may be described as which of the following?

   A. Attention deficit disorder

   B. Autism

   C. Developmental delays

   D. Mental retardation

10. Which of the following federal laws protects Phyllis's rights and prohibits discrimination on the basis of her disability?

   A. Section 504 of the Rehabilitation Act

   B. Americans with Disabilities Act (ADA)

   C. P.L. 94-142

   D. IEP

11. Mrs. Whitman has planned a cooperative learning activity in which her students count off 1-2-3-4 to assign themselves to group 1, 2, 3, or 4. When all the children who counted off the number 1 get together, they read and discuss the first section of the social studies text chapter and answer the questions for section 1. When all the children who counted off the number 2 get together, they read and discuss the second section of the social studies text chapter and answer the questions for section 2. In a similar pattern, groups 3 and 4 read and complete questions for sections 3 and 4, respectively. After the groups complete their reading and questions, the children return to their regular seats, which are placed in groups of four, and share their "expertise" on the assignment. This cooperative learning structure is known as which of the following?

   A. Think-pair-share

   B. Student Teams Achievement Division

   C. Numbered Heads Together

   D. Advance organizers

12. Mrs. Brown strives to respond to the wide range of abilities of her second-grade learners by using methods such as tiered instruction and flexible grouping. Mrs. Brown is

   A. differentiating instruction.

   B. sequencing instruction.

   C. directing instruction.

   D. demonstrating instruction.

GO ON TO THE NEXT PAGE

13. Miss Wade is teaching vocabulary and shades of meaning. She uses the graphic organizer below to help her students learn a variety of ways to express feelings of happiness and anger. Which of the following types of graphic organizers best describes the "feelings visual" that Miss Wade is using?

furious	angry	frustrated	OK	content	happy	ecstatic

    A. Venn diagram
    B. Sequence chart
    C. Matrix
    D. Continuum

14. One approach to classroom management centers on effective lesson planning as the best way to manage classroom behavior. The teacher begins the lesson with an "anticipatory set" to help the students connect their background knowledge and experiences with the new information in the lesson. Next, the teacher models and provides guided practice for the new information to be learned. At the close of the lesson, the teacher provides opportunities for independent and extended practice. This approach is known as

    A. Hunter's Model.
    B. Canter's Model.
    C. Glasser's Model.
    D. Jones's Model.

15. In a report established by the Clinton administration and continued in the second Bush administration, officials established that all students will start school ready to learn; high school graduation rates will meet or exceed 90%; and teachers will have access to high-quality professional development. Which of the following reports is described?

    A. Goals 2000
    B. No Child Left Behind
    C. National Reading Panel Report
    D. A Nation at Risk Report

16. Teaching professionals who are working to build positive relationships with families ensure that they use which of the following?

    A. Empowerment of learners
    B. Advocacy for learners
    C. Respectful communication with caregivers
    D. Discrimination of students

17. Which of the following reports demonstrates the merits of a classical curriculum and was supported by those with a conservative view of education?

    A. No Child Left Behind
    B. Yale Report of 1828
    C. Morrill Report of 1862
    D. Goals 2000

18. The United States Supreme Court has ruled that the First Amendment of the U.S. Constitution requires public school officials to be neutral in their treatment of religion. In other words, schools can show neither favoritism nor hostility toward acts of religious expression, such as which of the following?

    A. Symbols
    B. Ministers
    C. Priests
    D. Prayer

Case III

Directions: Questions 19–21 require you to write short answers, or "constructed responses." You are not expected to cite specific theories or texts in your answers; however, your knowledge of specific principles of learning and teaching will be evaluated. Be sure to answer all parts of the question. Write your answers in the space provided.

Scenario: Mr. Dupré and Mr. Polhemus

Two middle-level social studies teachers at Lynnville School couldn't be further apart in their approaches, but both teachers are well respected for their eighth-grade students' success. Mr. Dupré involves students actively in learning content through history simulations, webquests, dramatic reenactments, and project-based learning. Mr. Dupré enjoys getting to know students as individuals through interactions with the students' families, by attending after school activities, and by leading the drama club. When his students have to prepare for tests, Mr. Dupré engages them in a *Jeopardy*-like game in which students work in teams to answer questions, from easy to most challenging, in a variety of categories. Mr. Polhemus uses lectures, worksheets, and textbook questions and answers to teach the same history content. Mr. Polhemus sees himself as an explainer of important historic events. He often uses an advance organizer to start a lesson and study guides to help students prepare for tests. The following documents show recent lesson plans on the Civil War written by each teacher.

Document 1: Mr. Dupré's Civil War Lesson Plan

Objective

The student will discuss the primary causes of the Civil War from a variety of perspectives.

Resources

- Costumes from Civil War era
- Music from the Civil War era
- Primary source documents
- Chart paper
- Markers

Motivation

Mr. Dupré opens the lesson dressed as President Abraham Lincoln and introduces his guests: Robert Barnwell Rhett of South Carolina (the principal dressed as this Southern political leader) and Henry Ward Brown of Connecticut (the physical education teacher dressed as this Northern abolitionist leader). The three adults lead a dramatic reenactment of a discussion on the causes of the Civil War.

Warm-up

Mr. Dupré thanks his guests to the students' applause and leads the students in creating a KWL chart (a chart to show what students Know, Want to know, and Learned) to elicit their prior knowledge of the Civil War and to help them set purposes for learning more about the Civil War's causes from multiple perspectives.

Preview

Mr. Dupré tells the students that they will learn about the causes of the Civil War and be able to discuss the causes from various perspectives, specifically from Abraham Lincoln's view and from the views of leaders from the North and the South.

GO ON TO THE NEXT PAGE

Teach

Mr. Dupré divides his class into three heterogeneous groups to read and discuss the primary documents found at their tables. One group studies Abraham Lincoln's view of the war's causes; one studies Northern leaders' views; and the third studies Southern leaders' views. The students use chart paper and markers to complete the following graphic organizer as a group:

Quote about cause of war	Who said it	What this means

Students discuss each quote, who said it, and what it means. Then, after giving the students time to write at least three ideas on the chart paper, Mr. Dupré has the groups change tables, read the information, and contribute additional ideas to the chart.

After the three groups have had the chance to contribute to all three charts, Mr. Dupré gathers the class as a whole group, and the class reviews the charts. Mr. Dupré closes the lesson by impersonating President Lincoln again. He summarizes what the students have learned so far and then assigns homework.

Assessment

Mr. Dupré observes the students' participation in the group discussion and evaluates students' individual contributions in the closing discussion. He also assesses the homework individually for content accuracy.

Independent work

The homework requires students to write three paragraphs summarizing the three different views on the causes of the Civil War as a review of the day's classwork.

Document 2: Mr. Polhemus's Civil War Lesson Plan

Objective

The student will discuss and write about the primary causes of the Civil War.

Resources

- Social studies textbook
- Online resources

Motivation

Mr. Polhemus provides an advance organizer with an outline of the textbook chapter on the causes of the Civil War.

Warm-up

Mr. Polhemus uses a computer projector to show the class a credible source website that discusses the causes of the Civil War. The students take turns reading the information from the website aloud and discuss important or difficult material as they go.

Preview

Mr. Polhemus tells the students that they will learn about the primary causes of the Civil War and will be able to discuss and write about those causes.

Teach

Mr. Polhemus asks his students to read the section of the social studies text chapter on the causes of the Civil War individually and use the advance organizer to guide their reading. After the students finish reading, Mr. Polhemus leads a lecture on the causes of the Civil War and asks questions of students to check for understanding. To close the lesson, Mr. Polhemus summarizes the primary causes of the Civil War and assigns homework.

Assessment

Mr. Polhemus observes student involvement in reading the online text as a group and reading the textbook individually. He informally assesses students' contributions to the discussion. He grades the homework individually for content accuracy.

Independent work

For homework, each student writes his or her answers to the four questions at the end of the chapter.

19. Identify ONE student learning style that may find success in Mr. Polhemus's classroom and ONE student learning style that may find success in Mr. Dupré's classroom. Be sure to base your response on principles of student learning and instruction.

20. Suggest TWO ways that Mr. Polhemus can learn more about Mr. Dupré's methods for teaching social studies and communicate with his colleague. Be sure to base your response on principles of teacher professionalism and communication techniques.

21. Suggest ONE way that Mr. Polhemus can modify his instruction to meet the needs of all learners. Suggest ONE way Mr. Dupré can modify his instruction to meet the needs of all learners. Be sure to base your response on principles of students as learners and instruction.

_____

_____

_____

_____

_____

_____

_____

_____

GO ON TO THE NEXT PAGE

_____

_____

_____

_____

_____

_____

_____

_____

_____

_____

Case IV

Directions: Questions 22–24 require you to write short answers, or "constructed responses." You are not expected to cite specific theories or texts in your answers; however, your knowledge of specific principles of learning and teaching will be evaluated. Be sure to answer all parts of the question. Write your answers in the space provided.

Scenario: Kelly

Kelly is a seventh-grader who is excelling in middle school. She has achieved high honors for three quarters and is involved in several school activities, including dance, volleyball, and student council. She is a member of the National Honor Society and the principal's student leader group. In English language arts classes, Kelly is reading books at least two years above her grade level, and she writes creatively and to inform with great success. She has served as the assistant editor of the school newspaper and hopes to be chosen for the yearbook committee. Kelly also performs well in science and social studies classes and in her unified arts courses, such as physical education, art, and music. She appears to enjoy recognition for her accomplishments, especially from her parents, peers, and teachers.

Kelly has to work hard for her A's in mathematics, which affects her confidence in this area. Sometimes she gets nervous before quizzes and tests. Kelly's teacher reports that Kelly has good mental math abilities but needs concrete objects, such as math manipulatives, to help her to solve complex math problems.

Kelly appears self-assured with her peers and often takes a leadership role. From time to time, she has minor conflicts with other peers who have strong leadership skills. Kelly tends to appreciate the kindness of her friends and often gives half her snack to friends or shares her latest music CDs. Her learning style is primarily visual, but she also shows strengths in the area of bodily-kinesthetic intelligence as noted in her exceptional dance ability.

22. Identify ONE strength of Kelly's and discuss this strength in terms of Kelly's development as an adolescent student.

23. Suggest ONE instructional method that would benefit Kelly based on the information provided in the case history. Be sure to base your answer on principles of student learning and instruction.

24. Suggest ONE way that Kelly's teacher can build a partnership with Kelly's family to support Kelly as a learner. Be sure to base your response on principles of student learning communication techniques and teacher professionalism.

_____

_____

_____

_____

_____

_____

_____

_____

_____

_____

_____

_____

_____

_____

_____

_____

_____

_____

_____

_____

_____

_____

_____

Discrete Multiple-Choice Questions

Directions: Questions 25–36 are not related to the previous cases. For each question, select the best answer and mark the corresponding letter space on your answer sheet.

_____

25. Effective classroom managers have a keen sense of awareness about all that is going on in the classroom simultaneously. Kounin calls this ability teacher

    A. perception.

    B. with-it-ness.

    C. professionalism.

    D. behavior modification.

GO ON TO THE NEXT PAGE

26. When a teacher plans a lesson, he or she should be aware of factors of the learning environment that he or she can control, such as _____, which may influence student achievement.

    A. school location
    B. classroom location
    C. seating arrangement
    D. class size

Questions 27–28 are based on the following passage.

Josiah is a seventh-grader who is having difficulty in school, primarily because of his limited vocabulary and poor reading habits. His social studies teacher, Mr. Enright, is concerned about Josiah's ability to pass the seventh grade and has asked for a meeting of the Teacher Support Team to discuss Josiah.

27. Mr. Enright's primary concern is most likely Josiah's

    A. health history.
    B. prior-year instruction.
    C. family background.
    D. readiness to learn.

28. Mr. Enright is concerned that Josiah may not have had the experiences, both learning and social, to have a vocabulary typically expected of a seventh-grader. Mr. Enright believes that if he helps Josiah develop his _____ for the social studies content, his vocabulary and understanding of the social studies content may improve.

    A. schema
    B. test-taking skills
    C. homework
    D. family

29. Mrs. Burt likes to use short speeches by famous people in history, as well as historical photographs from reputable websites. These materials are known as which of the following?

    A. Primary colors
    B. Primary media
    C. Primary websites
    D. Primary sources

30. In a unit of study on Black folktales, Mrs. Pates asks her class, "What are the features of American Black folktales?" On Bloom's taxonomy, this question is at which of the following levels?

    A. Literal level
    B. Analysis level
    C. Evaluation level
    D. Literature connection level

31. "The student will list and explain three causes of World War II" is known as which of the following in a lesson plan?

    A. Goal
    B. Behavioral objective
    C. Assessment
    D. Preview

32. Which of the following assessments measures a student's ability to develop or acquire skills and knowledge?

    A. Aptitude test
    B. Criterion-referenced test
    C. Standardized test
    D. Diagnostic test

33. Which of the following legal cases ruled that all students can be required to attend public *or* private schools?

    A. *Brown v. Board of Education*
    B. *Roe v. Wade*
    C. Oregon Case of 1925
    D. *Plessy v. Ferguson*

34. An attendance act passed in Massachusetts in 1852 was the first general law to control the conditions for children. It was the start of which of the following in the United States?

    A. National Education Association
    B. Compulsory education
    C. Separate but equal education
    D. Normal school education

35. Which of the following provided the foundation for vocational education in the United States and was seen as an enhancement to the traditional high school curriculum?

    A. Cardinal Principles of Secondary Education
    B. Progressive education movement
    C. No Child Left Behind
    D. Manual training movement

36. Which of the following dramatically changed U.S. education after October 4, 1957?

    A. Soviet launching of Sputnik
    B. U.S. launching of Apollo
    C. A Nation at Risk Report
    D. *Brown v. Board of Education* ruling

Answers and Explanations, Test I

Case I

1. **Suggested content:** Ms. Manning is teaching a unit on friendships using two books, *Freak the Mighty* and *Give a Boy a Gun*. One way that she could create an effective bridge between her students and the literature is to open the lesson by asking the students to visualize a good friend and then discuss that friend's character traits. After the students have a chance to widely respond, the teacher could write down a list of character traits of a friend. Finally, the teacher could give a brief overview of each book, highlighting the characters that have the same character traits of the students' friends or the ones who have traits opposite to their friends. This practice activates and builds upon students' schema of a friend and motivates students intrinsically to read and learn.

   Content categories: Instruction and Assessment

2. **Suggested content:** Ms. Manning is teaching two quality trade books to help her students more deeply comprehend text and better understand positive and destructive friendships. One way that she could have her students discuss the books' themes is to organize her class into literature circles. In this method, the teacher sets up groups of four to six students to discuss a literature selection. Each student has a role to play in the discussion (for example, leader, word finder, summarizer, illustrator, and so on), and each student is active in the discussion.

   A second discussion method that Ms. Manning could use is higher-level questioning techniques. For example, she could ask questions about the main themes in the book, ask the students to analyze the meaning of a portion of text, or ask them to draw conclusions about a character's motive. It is important for Ms. Manning to create a supportive environment for discussion and allow for alternative viewpoints.

   Content categories: Communication Techniques, Instruction and Assessment

3. **Suggested content:** Ms. Manning has created a rubric for her assignment to write interview questions, conduct an interview, and write a comparative essay. One criterion that Ms. Manning could add to her rubric is about the interview. She could be more specific about the types of questions the students must include, such as who, what, where, when, and why. In addition, she could be more specific about interview questions to help students more deeply examine healthy and destructive friendships. Ms. Manning could strengthen her rubrics by more closely aligning them to the project assignment. It is also important for Ms. Manning to ask students to self-assess their work using the project rubric.

   Content categories: Instruction and Assessment

Case II

4. **Suggested content:** Miss Kelly is experiencing a changing time in her school's and her students' history. As part of a long-term goal to adjust to a new school environment, Miss Kelly wants her students to learn to problem-solve and to befriend a younger buddy. One instructional method she could use to achieve these goals is to create a partnership with a classroom of younger students and teach them the reciprocal teaching procedure to learn problem-solving strategies. In reciprocal teaching, one student shares a problem and then asks questions about the problem-solving process. Then the students change roles and repeat this exercise.

   Content categories: Instruction and Assessment

5. **Suggested content:** One of Miss Kelly's short-term goals is that students will be able to locate important people and places in the school building. One way that she could help her students achieve this objective is to plan a series of guest speakers in the classroom and then mark that guest speaker's location in the school. After all the speakers' visits, the students could go on a scavenger hunt in small groups to follow the school map and locate these important people and places in the building. Miss Kelly could offer extrinsic rewards for students who complete the map successfully, use the best hallway behavior, or use the most respectful manners while visiting important people in the school.

   Content categories: Instruction and Assessment

6. **Suggested content:** Miss Kelly is facing a challenging, changing school year that she can embrace professionally. One way that she can get support is to turn to her professional association, such as the National Council of Teachers of Mathematics, to learn about problem-solving and mathematics. This association offers workshops, conferences, and professional journals to provide a variety of supports to flexibly meet her learning needs.

Content categories: Teacher Professionalism, Communication Techniques

Discrete Multiple-Choice Questions

Answer Key, Test I, Questions 7–18			
Question	**Answer**	**Content Category**	**Where to Get More Help**
7.	D	Students as Learners	Chapter 7
8.	A	Students as Learners	Chapter 7
9.	C	Students as Learners	Chapter 7
10.	B	Students as Learners	Chapter 7
11.	C	Instruction and Assessment	Chapter 8
12.	A	Instruction and Assessment	Chapter 8
13.	D	Instruction and Assessment	Chapter 8
14.	A	Instruction and Assessment	Chapter 8
15.	A	Teacher Professionalism	Chapter 10
16.	C	Teacher Professionalism	Chapter 10
17.	B	Teacher Professionalism	Chapter 10
18.	D	Teacher Professionalism	Chapter 10

Explanations

7. **D.** Celia and Alyssa are on the conventional level of moral development. According to Kohlberg, this level is characterized by seeking the approval of others or doing what will gain approval. This behavior is typical of middle school and high school students.

8. **A.** Mr. Conlin's practice is grounded in constructivism, a theory of learning that emphasizes a student's ability to solve real-life problems and make new meaning by reflecting on the learning experience.

9. **C.** Although some of her behaviors may be found in other answer choices, Phyllis's learning differences are appropriately called developmental delays in this situation.

10. **B.** The Americans with Disabilities Act prohibits discrimination against Phyllis based on her disabilities and protects her rights.

11. **C.** This cooperative activity is known as numbered heads together.

12. **A.** Tiered instruction is an instructional method to differentiate instruction in which the teacher plans tasks of varying complexity, but all with the same high standards and content expectations.

13. **D.** The diagram that Miss Wade uses is a continuum, which helps reveal the subtle shades of meaning of vocabulary words.

14. **A.** Hunter's Model is an approach to classroom management that centers on the teacher's planning for good lessons, not managing an individual child's behavior. Hunter's Model lessons include an anticipatory set, modeling, guided practice, independent practice, and extended practice.

15. A. The Goals 2000 Report calls for all students to start school ready to learn, for high school graduation rates to meet or exceed 90%, and for all teachers to have access to high-quality professional development. (There are additional recommendations in this report that are not mentioned in the question.)

16. C. Teaching professionals are expected to use respectful communication with children's caregivers.

17. B. The Yale Report of 1828 praises the merits of a classical curriculum.

18. D. According to the U.S. Supreme Court, schools must remain neutral on issues involving school prayer as religious expression. The school can neither promote school prayer nor punish it.

Case III

19. Suggested content: Mr. Dupré and Mr. Polhemus successfully teach social studies with very different instructional approaches. Students with a kinesthetic learning style may find more success in Mr. Dupré's approach. For example, his use of drama and movement will appeal to a student who learns by doing. Students with a visual learning style may find more success in Mr. Polhemus's approach. For example, his use of graphic organizers and computer projection equipment will appeal to students who learn by seeing information.

Content categories: Students as Learners, Instruction and Assessment

20. Suggested content: Mr. Polhemus can learn more about his colleague's practice in two ways. First, he can initiate an offer to observe and support each other's teaching. The two teachers could work together to learn about one another's strengths. Second, Mr. Polhemus could attend professional workshops to learn more ways to teach students with a kinesthetic learning style. Learning new techniques will help Mr. Polhemus differentiate instruction and vary his instructional routines to better meet the needs of all his students.

Content categories: Teacher Professionalism, Communication Techniques

21. Suggested content: Both Mr. Polhemus and Mr. Dupré could vary their instruction to meet the needs of all their students. Mr. Polhemus tends to use direct instruction and appeal to visual learners. One modification that he could make to his lesson is to add dramatization to the closing of his lesson. Near the end of the lesson, Mr. Polhemus summarizes the content for his students. Instead, he could have his students summarize the content by acting out key parts of the lesson. Mr. Dupré tends to add movement and drama to his lessons. One modification that he could make is to add more visual information, such as photos from the Civil War era. It is important for both teachers to add methods to their teaching repertoires in order to meet all students' needs.

Content categories: Students as Learners, Instruction and Assessment

Case IV

22. Suggested content: Kelly is a seventh-grader who is experiencing much success in middle school, especially with her academics. According to Piaget, Kelly has most likely developed to the level of formal operational thinking. For example, Kelly is reading above the seventh-grade level and is writing to inform others. Gardner might suggest that Kelly's strength in visual intelligence is helping her to excel in her academics. Lastly, Kelly appears to be attaining all of the age-level verbal and linguistic characteristics of a child her age. She is reading and writing well, and she demonstrates strength in her interpersonal communication.

Content categories: Students as Learners

23. Suggested content: Kelly would benefit from an instructional method that highlights one of her strengths—dance. One method that would most likely support Kelly's strength is incorporating nonlinguistic representations. Nonlinguistic representations have been found to stimulate and increase brain activity. Kelly's teacher can use nonlinguistic representations in a lesson by using words and symbols to show their relationships. Kelly's teacher can also teach words by using physical models and physical movement to represent the new information. This type of active involvement in the lesson is likely to engage and motivate Kelly.

Content categories: Instruction and Assessment

24. Suggested content: One way that Kelly's teacher can build a partnership with her family is to share Kelly's strengths with her family at a parent-teacher conference. As noted in the case history, Kelly is a strong student academically. Her teacher could share evidence of Kelly's work and let Kelly's parents know how this work exceeds standards for students in the seventh grade at this school. During the conference, the parents could have an opportunity to ask questions and get ideas about how they could support or enrich Kelly's academics at home. Once the parents and teacher build a trusting relationship with two-way communication, they may even be able to collaboratively work together to address Kelly's occasional difficulty working with peers who have strong leadership skills.

Content categories: Teacher Professionalism, Communication Techniques

Discrete Multiple-Choice Questions

Answer Key, Test I, Questions 25–36			
Question	**Answer**	**Content Category**	**Where to Get More Help**
25.	B	Students as Learners	Chapter 7
26.	C	Students as Learners	Chapter 7
27.	D	Students as Learners	Chapter 7
28.	A	Students as Learners	Chapter 7
29.	D	Instruction and Assessment	Chapter 8
30.	B	Instruction and Assessment	Chapter 8
31.	B	Instruction and Assessment	Chapter 8
32.	A	Instruction and Assessment	Chapter 8
33.	C	Teacher Professionalism	Chapter 10
34.	B	Teacher Professionalism	Chapter 10
35.	D	Teacher Professionalism	Chapter 10
36.	A	Teacher Professionalism	Chapter 10

Explanations

25. B. Kounin calls a teacher's ability to be aware of all that is going on in a classroom simultaneously as "with-it-ness." (Some folks think that teachers are born with eyes in the back of their heads, too!)

26. C. A teacher should plan for the classroom environmental factors that he or she can control, such as seating arrangement. For lessons involving the use of the chalkboard, all students must have a clear visual path to the chalkboard. For lessons involving conversation, student must face one another and sit in close enough proximity to be able to converse.

27. D. Based on the passage, Josiah is showing a lack of readiness to learn the content of seventh grade. Mr. Enright is most likely concerned about this and is seeking ideas to help Josiah from his Teacher Support Team.

28. A. Mr. Enright is going to try to develop Josiah's background knowledge or schema for the seventh-grade social studies content to help Josiah learn and remember the content.

29. D. Mrs. Burt is using primary sources to enrich her lessons.

30. B. According to Bloom's taxonomy, Mrs. Pate's question is at the analysis level, a higher-level question.

31. B. A behavioral objective focuses on observable student behaviors and is measurable.

32. A. An aptitude test measures a student's ability to develop or acquire skills and knowledge.

33. C. The Oregon Case of 1925, which is also known as *Pierce v. Society of Sisters,* established that the state of Oregon could not require all students to attend public school, as this violates a child's 14th Amendment rights of personal liberty. This case established that all students can be required to attend public or private schools, but not one or the other.

34. B. Compulsory education was started in the U.S. after a ruling in 1852 in Massachusetts that was the first general law to attempt to control the conditions for children.

35. D. The manual training movement provided the foundation of vocational education in U.S. schools today.

36. A. On October 4, 1957, the Soviet Union successfully launched Sputnik, which catapulted the United States into a "space race" to prove that the U.S. was more powerful than any other nation. This event also launched a major reform of mathematics and science education in the United States.

Practice Test II

Case I

Directions: Questions 1–3 require you to write short answers, or "constructed responses." You are not expected to cite specific theories or texts in your answers; however, your knowledge of specific principles of learning and teaching will be evaluated. Be sure to answer all parts of the question. Write your answers in the space provided.

Scenario: Tom

Tom is an 11-year-old sixth-grade student who loves nature, likes classifying and organizing things, and enjoys attention from his peers. His teacher, Mrs. Thompson, uses a science-based, interdisciplinary approach to instruction but has found that Tom is having difficulty completing his "science log" each day. Mrs. Thompson immerses her students in the lives of many living things by placing a variety of animal tanks around the perimeter of the classroom. She allows the students to move the animals to their desks for close-up views. She has a variety of information sources about animals in the classroom, including reference books, children's science magazines, online encyclopedias, and Internet access. Mrs. Thompson asks her mentor to observe Tom so that she can offer teaching suggestions to help Tom complete his written work.

Observation: Mrs. Thompson's Class, May 22

Pre-observation notes: Mrs. Thompson states, "The purpose of the 'science log' is to make daily observations of a living creature in our classroom, to document the use of classroom and library resources when new information is gathered, and to learn to express content knowledge clearly, in complete sentences, and thoroughly." She continues, "Tom has not completed his science log for several days now. When Tom remembers to turn in his log, or when he has not misplaced it, his entries often have a drawing of the living creature and a few words, not a few complete sentences. Clearly, the criterion on thorough work is not being met. I believe that Tom is capable of higher-level work than this." Mrs. Thompson then asks her mentor to observe his work and make some suggestions so that she can better help Tom achieve sixth-grade standards.

Mentor classroom observation focused on Tom

Mrs. Thompson begins the whole-group lesson by asking students to share what they wrote in their science logs yesterday. Tom does not offer to speak. Instead, he whispers to a friend nearby and then looks at the tanks of living creatures near him.

Next, the teacher makes a KWL chart on the chalkboard and asks students to share what they want to know about the living creature they are observing. The teacher writes these facts under the K, or Know, column. Tom excitedly contributes that he knows that a hermit crab can move from one shell to another and that he has seen hermit crabs at the beach. After several students share, Mrs. Thompson instructs the students to turn to the next clean page of their logs and write a sentence about what they would like to know. Tom appears to think during this time and then begins to draw a picture of a hermit crab. After a short time, Mrs. Thompson asks three students to share what they want to know, and then she writes these sentences in the W, or Want to know, column. Tom does not offer to share his sentence, as he does not have a sentence written, only a drawing. He shows his drawing to a girl nearby, and she praises his artistic ability.

Next, Mrs. Thompson instructs her students to break into small groups and use the classroom and library resources to answer their questions about the living creatures they are studying.

Mrs. Thompson moves to her desk to correct spelling papers while the students complete their science log entries. Tom completes his drawing of the hermit crab with careful attention to detail and then writes a brief sentence about a hermit crab with many misspellings and limited content. He does not seek out any of the classroom resources to learn more about his living creature. Once he has finished (or thinks he has finished) his work, he talks with a boy near him about the hermit crab and asks the friend if he knows what a hermit crab eats.

GO ON TO THE NEXT PAGE

Mrs. Thompson closes the lesson with time to discuss what the students have learned about their living creatures. Once again, Tom is silent and appears to be uncomfortable with the written work in his science log. When Mrs. Thompson calls on Tom to share, he appears nervous and says that he does not want to. Mrs. Thompson reminds the students to turn in their science logs on their way out of class. Tom puts his log in his backpack and hurries to catch up to a friend in the lunch line.

Post-observation notes

Mrs. Thompson shares that she believes Tom is a bright boy who loves science. She expresses her concerns that Tom does not complete his science log as instructed; instead, he draws, talks, and writes at a much lower level than his peers. Mrs. Thompson also mentions that Tom's talking to friends during class may be one reason he does not complete his work. Her mentor suggests, "Perhaps Tom is completing the assignment to the best of his ability at this time. Let's talk about strategies to help Tom be more successful when writing in his science log."

1. Suppose Mrs. Thompson and her mentor discussed alternative ways to monitor and teach during the science log writing time.

   - Identify TWO alternative ways to teach *during* the lesson so that Tom might be more successful in completing his science log.
   - Explain how each way to develop the lesson that you have identified could benefit Tom's learning needs. Base your response on principles of student learning and instruction.

2. Next, Mrs. Thompson and her mentor discuss ways to support Tom before the science log observation and writing time.

   - Identify TWO specific ways to actively engage Tom in the lesson so that he might be more successful.
   - Explain how each way that you have identified could benefit Tom's learning needs, basing your response on principles of student learning and assessment.

3. Finally, Mrs. Thompson and her mentor discuss ways to assess Tom's work and provide helpful feedback to Tom and his family about his progress.

   - Identify TWO criteria for scoring the science log in this sixth-grade classroom and ONE way to share this information with the student or his parents.
   - Explain how the assessment ideas that you have suggested will make the science log more successful for Tom.

_____

_____

_____

_____

_____

_____

_____

_____

_____

Case II

Directions: Questions 4–6 require you to write short answers, or "constructed responses." You are not expected to cite specific theories or texts in your answers; however, your knowledge of specific principles of learning and teaching will be evaluated. Be sure to answer all parts of the question. Write your answers in the space provided.

Scenario: Terrance

The Teacher Support Team (TST) is designed to support teachers' attempts to resolve instructional problems for their students with academic, emotional, social, or behavioral issues. The team is comprised of the school principal, the team guidance counselor, a reading specialist, a special education teacher, a school psychologist, a classroom teacher, and the teacher who refers a student. Caregivers, a school social worker, and the school nurse are invited to attend when appropriate. The TST's goal is to offer instructional strategies to classroom teachers in an effort to provide education services in a student's least restrictive environment. For students who are not making adequate yearly progress, the TST may recommend further testing by specialists.

Mrs. Peacock is an experienced seventh-grade teacher who has requested a meeting of the TST to discuss a student named Terrance. The TST reviewed the background information prepared by Mrs. Peacock on Terrance, a 13-year-old seventh-grader in her classroom. Terrance lives with his mother, his father, and his two older sisters. His primary language is English, and he appears to be in good physical health based on records from the nurse's office. Terrance did not attend preschool; he stayed home with his mother while his two older sisters attended school. He attended the public school district's half-day kindergarten, where he had limited success learning the alphabet, had difficulty with concepts about print, and experienced difficulty exhibiting appropriate social and emotional behaviors when he faced academic or social challenges in the classroom. In first grade, Terrance lagged behind his peers in reading and writing development. He had limited success, especially in the areas of reading and writing, in grades 2–6, and retention was considered several times, but he was never held back. Now in seventh grade, Terrance loves when his teacher reads aloud, but he rarely reads independently. He avoids reading and never agrees to read aloud when the class is taking turns doing so. His writing is poor—equivalent to that of a second-grader.

At the TST meeting, Mrs. Peacock described the problems Terrance is experiencing in seventh grade. He is becoming a classroom bully, and he has frequent outbursts when asked to complete his reading or writing work. In addition, Mrs. Peacock has noticed that Terrance has difficulty hearing rhythm, rhyme, and syllables in poetry and during language arts exercises. Mrs. Peacock added that she has met with Terrance's parents, who share her concerns about Terrance's lack of reading progress and his increasing outbursts during homework time at home. Terrance's parents mentioned that they recently purchased a workbook-based home-study program on writing to help their child and would appreciate any support or ideas that Mrs. Peacock can give them.

GO ON TO THE NEXT PAGE

Mrs. Peacock has tried the following strategies to support Terrance's reading and writing development:

- Moved his seat to the front of the classroom, near the teacher
- Set him up with a partner who is a strong reader

After meeting with the TST team and Terrance's parents, Mrs. Peacock would like suggestions for new strategies to try in the classroom, and she would like the support of her colleagues' expertise. She has requested that a reading specialist or special educator conduct an in-depth evaluation of Terrance's strengths and weaknesses.

4. Identify ONE strategy that Mrs. Peacock hasn't tried to support Terrance's diverse learning needs. Be sure to base your response on principles of learning and teaching.

5. Suggest ONE reason why Terrance may benefit from an evaluation for reading intervention or special education. Be sure to base your rationale on principles of student learning.

6. Suggest ONE way, not already offered in the scenario, that Terrance's parents can support his literacy development at home. Be sure to base your response on principles of teacher professionalism and communication techniques.

Discrete Multiple-Choice Questions

Directions: Questions 7–18 are not related to the previous cases. For each question, select the best answer and mark the corresponding letter space on your answer sheet.

7. Jessica tends to make decisions based on what actions will please others, especially her teachers and her peers. She places a lot of emphasis on maintaining relationships with others and listens carefully to others' views when making decisions. According to Kohlberg's theory, which of the following best describes Jessica's level of moral development?

    A. Post-conventional
    B. Pre-conventional
    C. Anti-conventional
    D. Conventional

8. Maddie works in the resource classroom for her writing and mathematics instruction as stated in her IEP. Maddie's resource teacher often helps Maddie see the real-life purpose behind the writing or math lesson and helps her see when and where she can use this lesson again in another learning situation. Her classroom teacher and her resource teacher communicate about Maddie's progress and frequently share materials and lesson plans to help Maddie do which of the following?

    A. Master skills
    B. Exit from special education
    C. Transfer learning
    D. Satisfy state and federal requirements

Questions 9-10 are based on the following passage.

Carrie is a seventh-grader with delayed speech who dislikes being touched and has difficulty following simple directions. She also has a limited vocabulary and is quite distractible.

9. Which of the following special education labels most closely matches Carrie's learning and developmental behaviors?

    A. Learning disabled
    B. Functionally mentally retarded
    C. Autistic
    D. Gifted

10. Carrie is eligible to receive instruction in her _____ as mandated by federal special education laws.

    A. neighborhood school
    B. private school
    C. self-contained classroom
    D. least restrictive environment

11. Which of the following measures of central tendency is defined as the midpoint of a set of numbers, such as scores from a classroom?

    A. Mode
    B. Median
    C. Mean
    D. Average

GO ON TO THE NEXT PAGE

12. Which of the following is most likely to be read by a teacher but not corrected for spelling, grammar, or mechanics?

    A. Free-response journal

    B. Science lab report

    C. Reader response entry

    D. Summative essay

13. Mrs. McGuire reads aloud to her students every day after lunch. She chooses a book that is beyond the instructional reading level for the majority of her students, with rich vocabulary and many personal connections for her students. Which group formation would most likely be most effective for reading aloud to her class?

    A. Jigsaw

    B. Flexible group

    C. Whole group

    D. Cooperative group

14. Mrs. Faella has asked Paul and Denise to read together. She has instructed Paul to read the first passage and for Paul to ask Denise questions. When they are done discussing the first passage, Denise then reads aloud and asks Paul questions about the text. Which of the following best describes this instructional routine?

    A. Fluency reading

    B. Echo reading

    C. Scaffolded teaching

    D. Reciprocal teaching

15. Mrs. Josephson enjoys learning from the diverse experiences of her students, and her peers see her as a highly professional and reflective teacher. Which of the following views is most likely held by Mrs. Josephson, who is seen as a reflective professional?

    A. Diversity is a challenge that she can overcome.

    B. Diversity is a positive, enriching aspect of teaching.

    C. Diversity is a necessary evil in teaching.

    D. Diversity is a problem in American schools today.

16. Which of the following landmark cases found that "separate educational facilities are inherently unequal"?

    A. *Brown v. Board of Education*

    B. Oregon School Case of 1925

    C. Land Ordinance of 1785

    D. P.L. 94-142

17. A founding father of America advanced formal education by establishing a plan for an English-language grammar school. This school would teach not only Latin but also English. Which of the following founding fathers created this plan for schools (which never was fully enacted in his lifetime)?

    A. Thomas Jefferson

    B. George Washington

    C. Benjamin Franklin

    D. John Hancock

18. Which of the following colleges was established in 1636 to ensure that the leaders of the church, state, and judicial systems were well prepared and learned?

    A. Harvard College
    B. Colgate College
    C. Simmons College
    D. Providence College

Case III

Directions: Questions 19–21 require you to write short answers, or "constructed responses." You are not expected to cite specific theories or texts in your answers; however, your knowledge of specific principles of learning and teaching will be evaluated. Be sure to answer all parts of the question. Write your answers in the space provided.

Scenario: Michael

Michael is an eighth-grade student in Mr. King's health class. Michael shows great interest in the course content, actively participates in class, and responds well to Mr. King's enthusiastic and positive teaching style. Michael does very well with an assignment that Mr. King designed for a test grade and then repeats once a month throughout the marking period. Below is a brief synopsis of the assignment:

> Use the Internet or a magazine to find an article related to health and fitness. Write a summary of the article that includes at least three main health-related points of the article and then make one connection between the article and your knowledge/experiences. Be sure to include the proper citation of your article and its source.

Mr. King introduced the assignment by providing a model and then offering direct instruction on how to write the summary. He also gave examples of personal connections between the article and his knowledge and experiences and showed the students how to add this information to the end of the summary. Mr. King modeled his writing process by thinking aloud and actually demonstrating his writing using the overhead projector. Mr. King's eighth-grade English-teaching colleague teamed with Mr. King and planned to carefully teach how to cite Internet sources and periodicals. The two devised a guide sheet, which they provided to students and turned into a poster for both of their classrooms.

Michael earned a B on his first health summary because he misunderstood or did not carefully read some of the directions. In addition, the assignment was one day late. Michael got discouraged that he forgot his homework on his desk, which is a problem he often has with schoolwork. Mr. King has noticed that Michael's health binder is usually disorganized, and Michael frequently forgets to bring a pencil to class. Mr. King reviewed the second health summary assignment individually with Michael and checked with Michael to be sure he had an appropriate article a week before it was due. He also had his whole class work in pairs to discuss real-life connections to the topics of their articles during class a few days before the next summaries were due. On the second assignment, Michael earned an A. He continued to earn A's on his summary assignments, with the exception of one, which was late. Michael became an active class contributor and appeared confident in his abilities to find health-related information on the Internet and in magazines, as well as in his ability to write a summary.

19. Identify TWO strengths of Mr. King's health assignment and explain how each strength demonstrates aspects of effective planning. Be sure to base your response on principles of planning instruction.

20. Suggest TWO ways that Mr. King could communicate to Michael to encourage him to achieve academic excellence. Be sure to include communication techniques based on teacher professionalism.

21. Identify TWO ways to make accommodations for a student with Michael's learning style. Be sure to base your response on principles of teaching students with diverse needs.

GO ON TO THE NEXT PAGE

_____
_____
_____
_____
_____
_____
_____
_____
_____
_____
_____
_____
_____
_____
_____
_____
_____
_____
_____
_____

Case IV

Directions: Questions 22–24 require you to write short answers, or "constructed responses." You are not expected to cite specific theories or texts in your answers; however, your knowledge of specific principles of learning and teaching will be evaluated. Be sure to answer all parts of the question. Write your answers in the space provided.

Scenario: Mr. Poulin

Mr. Poulin is a ninth-grade teacher of algebra. His class is comprised of average-achieving students, although, as one might imagine, his students still have a wide range of knowledge, skills, and dispositions in mathematics. Several of his students have been identified as having diverse learning needs; they include students with attention deficit hyperactivity disorder (ADHD), bilingual language learners, and students with learning disabilities.

For a lesson on operations and numbers, Mr. Poulin has the following objective:

- The student will use the order of operations to accurately evaluate an expression and to complete a word problem.

At the opening of the lesson, Mr. Poulin reads aloud the following situation:

Jason, Josh, Mary, and Elizabeth are playing in a local golf tournament. For the first two days, Jason's scores were 2 under par, or under zero. Josh also had scores under par. Mary's scores were lower than Jason's scores, and Elizabeth's scores were zero (par) or greater.

Mr. Poulin asks his students how they might begin to solve this problem. After probing for student background knowledge and strategies, he states: "In order to solve this real-life problem, we're going to need to understand the order of operations." He lectures for five minutes and writes notes on the chalkboard. He summarizes the steps:

1. Evaluate all powers.
2. Do multiplications and/or divisions from left to right.
3. Do all additions and/or subtractions from left to right.

Next, Mr. Poulin assigns the students to work individually to draw a graph showing all the possible scores for Josh and to compare all the golfers' scores.

At the close of the lesson, Mr. Poulin assigns page 36, odd numbers only, in the mathematics textbook. He assesses students' participation in the lesson discussion and then plans to grade homework individually, making corrections as needed.

22. Identify ONE strength of Mr. Poulin's algebra lesson. Explain how he demonstrates an aspect of effective planning. Be sure to base your response on principles of planning instruction.

23. Suggest ONE way that Mr. Poulin could make additional accommodations for the diverse learners in his algebra class. Be sure to base your response on principles of teaching diverse learners.

24. Suggest ONE additional way that Mr. Poulin can assess students' understanding of the lesson. Be sure to base your response on principles of assessment.

_____

_____

_____

_____

_____

_____

_____

_____

_____

GO ON TO THE NEXT PAGE

_____
_____
_____
_____
_____
_____
_____
_____
_____

Discrete Multiple-Choice Questions

Directions: Questions 25–36 are not related to the previous cases. For each question, select the best answer and mark the corresponding letter space on your answer sheet.

25. Which of the following theorists' work focuses on children learning by observing others?

   A. Kohlberg
   B. Bandura
   C. Maslow
   D. Jones

26. Which of the following theorists suggested that children learn through two complementary processes called assimilation and accommodation?

   A. Small
   B. Piaget
   C. Glasser
   D. Freud

Questions 27–28 are based on the following passage.

Maria is an eighth-grader who is learning about the Harlem Renaissance in her English class. Her teacher has set up opportunities for the students to read and learn more about this period in small groups by using quality websites. Maria shares her enthusiasm when she finds an excellent source of information on the Internet and explains to her teacher, "As I think back about my reading, I realize it was like I was there in Harlem! I could hear Nora Zeale Hurston and Langston Hughes reading their recent works. In my mind, I was thinking that this was the birth of the Jazz Age and the Beat Poets. What a great website, and what a great time in history!"

27. Which of the following describes Maria's thinking about her own reading of this website?

   A. Reciprocal
   B. Rote
   C. Metacognitive
   D. Literal

28. Maria's teacher most likely set up the students in peer groups to research the Harlem Renaissance for which of the following reasons based on principles of learning and teaching?

    A. To be sure that each student had a chance on the computer

    B. To help each student complete a worksheet on the assignment

    C. To minimize classroom disruption

    D. To help each student find his or her zone of proximal development

29. Which of the following study strategies involves surveying text, questioning, and then reading, reciting, and reviewing the text to better comprehend it?

    A. 4 MAT

    B. SQ3R

    C. Summarizing and note-taking

    D. Cooperative learning

30. Bobby is having difficulty completing his homework and practice activities in mathematics. He makes several errors in his work and has worked more slowly than his peers. Which of the following instructional modifications might help Bobby complete his math work with more success?

    A. Curriculum compacting

    B. Tiered instruction

    C. Curriculum chunking

    D. Jigsaw

31. Mr. Matthews likes to immerse his students in the social studies content that he teaches. During a recent unit on Westward Expansion, the students took a covered wagon ride, and then they read and reenacted a story from this period and charted their course across the country. Which of the following methods is Mr. Matthews employing?

    A. Simulation

    B. Whole language

    C. Project-based learning

    D. Demonstration

32. At the end of the school year, Mrs. Lahiri provided which of the following evaluations to her supervisor to demonstrate her progress toward her professional goals?

    A. Summative evaluation

    B. Formative evaluation

    C. Diagnostic evaluation

    D. Remedial evaluation

33. Mrs. Basel modifies her teaching practice to meet the unique needs of several of her seventh-grade students. For example, she incorporates a basketball-like game into studying for a unit test in science. In addition, Mrs. Basel attends meetings about those of her students who are struggling academically, socially, or emotionally. Which of the following best describes Mrs. Basel's reason for her teaching practice?

    A. She desires to receive good evaluations.

    B. She likes to play games.

    C. She advocates for all students.

    D. She wants more free time to plan.

GO ON TO THE NEXT PAGE

34. If a teacher could reasonably have foreseen a negative teaching situation, or if a teacher acted differently than a reasonable teacher placed in a similar situation would have, then which of the following is true for this teacher?

    A. The teacher can freely associate with whomever he or she chooses.

    B. The teacher can be recommended for tenure.

    C. The teacher cannot be fired.

    D. The teacher can be sued and found liable for negligence.

35. The National Council of Teachers of English, the International Reading Association, and the National Science Teachers Association are all

    A. seminars.

    B. journals.

    C. conferences.

    D. professional associations.

36. Which of the following federal laws prohibits discrimination on the basis of a person's disability for all services, programs, and activities provided or made available by state or local governments?

    A. Americans with Disabilities Act

    B. P.L. 94-142

    C. Individualized Education Plan Act

    D. No Child Left Behind

Answers and Explanations, Test II

Case I

1. **Suggested content:** Mrs. Thompson is a sixth-grade teacher who is having a difficult time meeting the needs of her student, Tom. Two ways that she could improve her instruction during the science log lesson are to take an active role in the monitoring of students and to ask probing questions to guide students to look more deeply at the information about their living creatures. When Mrs. Thompson actively monitors the class, she can help improve Tom's and other students' time on task. This also demonstrates her with-it-ness—her ability to monitor all students at the same time. When Mrs. Thompson asks probing questions—such as "How do you know?" or "What makes you think so?"—she is helping her students think more deeply. Tom may need more guidance in learning with the resources in the classroom or rehearsing what he has read before he can write it down in his science log.

   Content categories: Students as Learners, Instruction and Assessment

2. **Suggested content:** Mrs. Thompson can actively engage Tom in the lesson by setting him up with a partner and providing a volunteer tutor for him. Tom likes to talk about what he is learning, and allowing him to work with a partner will provide an opportunity for him to do so. Tom may also need more help with directions and redirections, so the partner can help here as well. Tom also appears to be writing at a lower level than his peers. Establishing a time for Tom to work with a volunteer on his writing may provide the necessary supports for Tom to complete his science log.

   Content categories: Students as Learners, Instruction and Assessment

3. **Suggested content:** The goal of the science log is to record observations clearly and thoroughly. One criterion Mrs. Thompson could include in a rubric is about *thorough* writing in the science log. Mrs. Thompson could explain that a thorough entry has a heading, an illustration, three to five sentences with information about the living creature, and the source of the information. Setting clear criteria helps students know explicitly how they will be assessed and how they can improve their work.

   Content categories: Students as Learners, Instruction and Assessment

Case II

4. **Suggested content:** Terrance is a seventh-grade student reading and writing far below grade-level. One strategy that Mrs. Peacock could try is to reinforce and provide recognition. When using this method, the teacher shares stories of people who did not give up and who ultimately succeeded. She is also personalizing recognition by letting Terrance know when he is making progress in his reading and writing. Lastly, she should provide adequate support to Terrance when he is struggling to make progress in his reading or writing. This method utilizes a key aspect of Vygotsky's theory of the zone of proximal development. In this theory, a student needs to be offered support from a teacher or a more capable peer to learn the "just right" next lesson he or she needs to learn, even if this lesson is far below grade-level.

   Content categories: Students as Learners, Instruction and Assessment

5. **Suggested content:** Terrance is a seventh-grader reading and writing at an elementary-school level. He would benefit greatly from a reading or special education evaluation in the following ways: 1. diagnostic information, 2. background information, and 3. suggested interventions. An evaluation could provide diagnostic information, which is an assessment of Terrance's areas of strength and weakness. In addition, an evaluation could provide background information about Terrance's family, his development, and his literacy background. For example, Terrance may have a medical condition or a family history that is contributing to his literacy difficulties. Lastly, an evaluation could offer Mrs. Peacock information on intervention programs to help Terrance close his literacy achievement gap.

   Content categories: Students as Learners, Teacher Professionalism

6. **Suggested content:** Mrs. Peacock can develop a partnership with Terrance's parents to support them in their efforts to help their child to read and write on grade level. Together they can collaborate on ways to give Terrance opportunities to be successful in reading and writing for authentic purposes. For example, Terrance could start a scrapbook of school and family events that requires him to organize events and label them. Another activity that would benefit Terrance is to listen to rap music or other music with clear rhythm and rhyme. His parents could then write out the rap or song lyric and ask Terrance to re-read it and discuss the lyrics.

Content categories: Teacher Professionalism, Communication Techniques

Discrete Multiple-Choice Questions

Answer Key, Test II, Questions 7–18			
Question	*Answer*	*Content Category*	*Where to Get More Help*
7.	D	Students as Learners	Chapter 7
8.	C	Students as Learners	Chapter 7
9.	A	Students as Learners	Chapter 7
10.	D	Students as Learners	Chapter 7
11.	B	Instruction and Assessment	Chapter 8
12.	A	Instruction and Assessment	Chapter 8
13.	C	Instruction and Assessment	Chapter 8
14.	D	Instruction and Assessment	Chapter 8
15.	B	Teacher Professionalism	Chapter 10
16.	A	Teacher Professionalism	Chapter 10
17.	C	Teacher Professionalism	Chapter 10
18.	A	Teacher Professionalism	Chapter 10

Explanations

7. **D.** Jessica is operating at the conventional level according to Kohlberg's theory of moral development.

8. **C.** Maddie's teachers are striving to help Maddie transfer learning from one classroom to another and beyond the classroom walls.

9. **A.** Carrie's behaviors are indications of a student who may have learning disabilities. It is important for a teacher to note such observations and report them to a teacher support team or another specialist in the school, but not to "label" the student as learning disabled. Teachers teach and report observations; diagnosticians and other specialists establish diagnoses.

10. **D.** Federal law mandates that children are to be educated in their "least restrictive environment."

11. **B.** The midpoint in a set of numbers is known as the median.

12. **A.** A free-response journal is intended to be used for rough drafts and short bits of writing that are not corrected for grammar, mechanics, or conventions. All other choices in this question may or may not be graded for grammar, mechanics, or conventions depending on a teacher's or a school's preference.

13. **C.** Reading aloud in this scenario is most effective when done as a whole group. This setup helps build community, offers a common text to discuss, and settles students for an afternoon of schoolwork.

14. **D.** Mrs. Faella is using an instructional strategy known as reciprocal teaching in which one student (or adult) reads aloud a portion of text and asks questions of another, and then the roles reverse.

15. **B.** To be considered a teacher with professionalism, Mrs. Josephson must see and believe that diversity is a positive, enriching aspect of teaching.

16. **A.** The *Brown v. Board of Education* case established that the long-held contention that separate but equal schools is inherently unequal. This case was a pivotal one in U.S. education history and advanced the integration and rights of all children in public schools.

17. **C.** Benjamin Franklin had the foresight to create a plan for schools that teach English-language grammar, not only Latin, as was the standard in schools of his time. Franklin's plan for an English-language grammar school was never fully accepted or enacted during his lifetime, but the idea certainly influenced schools of today.

18. **A.** Harvard College was established in 1636 to ensure that the leaders of the church, state, and judicial systems were learned and well prepared for their vocations.

Case III

19. **Suggested content:** Mr. King's health lesson demonstrates two strengths: 1. real-life purpose and 2. integration of content areas. First, this health assignment has a real-life purpose—to help students read to learn more about personal health and fitness. In addition, the Internet provides students with an opportunity to practice using a current technology to help them to read and learn more. Second, Mr. King's assignment helps students see the connection between health class and English class. Collaboration with the English teacher models the importance of working together, and it shows the students that school subjects are connected, not discrete, classes.

    Content categories: Instruction and Assessment

20. **Suggested content:** Mr. King could communicate with Michael to encourage him to achieve academically in two ways: 1. help Michael to set goals and 2. probe for student understanding. First, Michael could benefit from setting goals with the help of his teacher. Goal-setting may help Michael to muster the intrinsic motivation when learning gets difficult. Second, Mr. King could probe for Michael's understanding to ensure that Michael clearly understands the directions of a task. Each of these communication methods focuses on Michael's individual needs and offers Michael the chance to be successful in school.

    Content categories: Teacher Professionalism, Communication Techniques

21. **Suggested content:** Two accommodations that could help Michael include 1. differentiated instruction and 2. testing accommodations. Mr. King could differentiate his lessons to meet Michael's learning style, one that considers his attention difficulty. An example of differentiating instruction for Michael could be providing step-by-step directions for his health assignments, including the organization of his binder for this course. Michael could also benefit from testing accommodations, such as increased time for taking exams and more frequent breaks. Michael appears to have attention difficulties, and these accommodations may help Michael experience success in the classroom and beyond.

    Content categories: Students as Learners, Instruction and Assessment

Case IV

22. **Suggested content:** One strength of Mr. Poulin's lesson is that it aims to teach mathematics in the context of a real-life situation. Mr. Poulin asks his students questions about the situation and seeks to help his students solve the problem through discussion and collaborative problem-solving. He shares the steps for problem-solving and sets clear purposes for his lesson. Mr. Poulin's choice to provide purposeful and authentic tasks in mathematics class offers a chance for his students to be intrinsically motivated and to see the connections between mathematics and real-life situations.

    Content categories: Students as Learners, Instruction and Assessment

23. **Suggested content:** One additional way that Mr. Poulin could accommodate the diverse needs of his algebra students is to assign his students to work with partners of small groups instead of requiring them to work individually to solve the problem. Mr. Poulin could assign his students to work in cooperative learning groups so that they work collaboratively to solve the assigned problem. Slavin and Kagan have both found that student achievement is improved when students work cooperatively.

    Content categories: Students as Learners, Instruction and Assessment

24. **Suggested content:** Mr. Poulin could assess his students' learning by creating a rubric for scoring their assignment on graphing. The rubric might include the assignment criteria, as well as a scoring guide to determine an exemplary, acceptable, and unacceptable graph. It is important that Mr. Poulin share the graph assignment criteria and rubric with the students prior to the completion of the assignment so that students can self-assess their academic progress on the assignment.

    Content categories: Instruction and Assessment

Discrete Multiple-Choice Questions

Answer Key, Test II, Questions 25–36			
Question	*Answer*	*Content Category*	*Where to Get More Help*
25.	B	Students as Learners	Chapter 7
26.	B	Students as Learners	Chapter 7
27.	C	Students as Learners	Chapter 7
28.	D	Students as Learners	Chapter 7
29.	B	Instruction and Assessment	Chapter 8
30.	C	Instruction and Assessment	Chapter 8
31.	A	Instruction and Assessment	Chapter 8
32.	A	Instruction and Assessment	Chapter 8
33.	C	Teacher Professionalism	Chapter 10
34.	D	Teacher Professionalism	Chapter 10
35.	D	Teacher Professionalism	Chapter 10
36.	A	Teacher Professionalism	Chapter 10

Explanations

25. **B.** Bandura's work focuses on children's ability to learn by observing others.

26. **B.** Piaget suggested that children learn through two complementary processes called assimilation and accommodation.

27. **C.** Maria is showing her teacher that she is a metacognitive reader when she describes her awareness of her own reading process. Metacognition is the ability to think about one's own thinking.

28. **D.** Maria's teacher was optimizing Vygotsky's theory of a zone of proximal development, in which a more able peer (or teacher) helps a student learn something too challenging to learn alone. This practice embraces a social-constructivist view of teaching.

29. **B.** SQ3R is a study strategy that helps students take notes on and learn new information.

30. C. Bobby would benefit from curriculum chunking. His teacher can offer smaller, more manageable amounts of homework practice for Bobby. This way, the teacher can offer more frequent check-ins and support as needed. When Bobby demonstrates that he can handle more information with success, the teacher can offer more work.

31. A. Mr. Matthews is using simulation to teach his students during this social studies unit.

32. A. Mrs. Lahiri provided a summative evaluation, or an evaluation that reviews progress to date. A summative evaluation occurs at the end of a period and may not necessarily be used to inform practice or instruction.

33. C. Mrs. Basel is demonstrating her professional desire to meet the needs of all her students and advocate for all her students as learners.

34. D. In this case, the teacher could be sued and found liable for negligence.

35. D. Professional associations offer leadership and guidance to a group of professionals. Every content area taught in public schools has a professional association to guide it. Find out about your area's professional association as soon as you finish studying for this test!

36. A. The Americans with Disabilities Act, also known as Title II, prohibits discrimination on the basis of a person's disability for all services, programs, and activities provided or made available by state or local governments.

PLT Grades 7–12 Practice Tests

In this chapter, you will find two full-length practice tests for the PLT Grades 7–12 designed to give you a sense of the test's format and scope. You may also want to practice your timing and pacing for the test by using these practice tests. Remember, you will have a total of 2 hours to complete the test.

After you finish each practice test, score your answers in the section that follows the test. Use the sample responses and explanations provided to figure out your strengths and weaknesses and assess which content areas you need to study in Part III of this book. You may also want to complete the full-length practice tests in Chapters 11, 12, and 13 to help you determine further content areas to study. Even though these additional practice tests are written for other grade levels, the topics of the questions—Students as Learners, Instruction and Assessment, Communication Techniques, and Teacher Professionalism—remain the same.

-------------------------------- **CUT HERE** --------------------------------

(Remove these sheets and use them to mark your answers to the multiple-choice questions.)

ANSWER SHEET FOR TEST 1

7 Ⓐ Ⓑ Ⓒ Ⓓ	25 Ⓐ Ⓑ Ⓒ Ⓓ
8 Ⓐ Ⓑ Ⓒ Ⓓ	26 Ⓐ Ⓑ Ⓒ Ⓓ
9 Ⓐ Ⓑ Ⓒ Ⓓ	27 Ⓐ Ⓑ Ⓒ Ⓓ
10 Ⓐ Ⓑ Ⓒ Ⓓ	28 Ⓐ Ⓑ Ⓒ Ⓓ
11 Ⓐ Ⓑ Ⓒ Ⓓ	29 Ⓐ Ⓑ Ⓒ Ⓓ
12 Ⓐ Ⓑ Ⓒ Ⓓ	30 Ⓐ Ⓑ Ⓒ Ⓓ
13 Ⓐ Ⓑ Ⓒ Ⓓ	31 Ⓐ Ⓑ Ⓒ Ⓓ
14 Ⓐ Ⓑ Ⓒ Ⓓ	32 Ⓐ Ⓑ Ⓒ Ⓓ
15 Ⓐ Ⓑ Ⓒ Ⓓ	33 Ⓐ Ⓑ Ⓒ Ⓓ
16 Ⓐ Ⓑ Ⓒ Ⓓ	34 Ⓐ Ⓑ Ⓒ Ⓓ
17 Ⓐ Ⓑ Ⓒ Ⓓ	35 Ⓐ Ⓑ Ⓒ Ⓓ
18 Ⓐ Ⓑ Ⓒ Ⓓ	36 Ⓐ Ⓑ Ⓒ Ⓓ

ANSWER SHEET FOR TEST 2

7 Ⓐ Ⓑ Ⓒ Ⓓ	25 Ⓐ Ⓑ Ⓒ Ⓓ
8 Ⓐ Ⓑ Ⓒ Ⓓ	26 Ⓐ Ⓑ Ⓒ Ⓓ
9 Ⓐ Ⓑ Ⓒ Ⓓ	27 Ⓐ Ⓑ Ⓒ Ⓓ
10 Ⓐ Ⓑ Ⓒ Ⓓ	28 Ⓐ Ⓑ Ⓒ Ⓓ
11 Ⓐ Ⓑ Ⓒ Ⓓ	29 Ⓐ Ⓑ Ⓒ Ⓓ
12 Ⓐ Ⓑ Ⓒ Ⓓ	30 Ⓐ Ⓑ Ⓒ Ⓓ
13 Ⓐ Ⓑ Ⓒ Ⓓ	31 Ⓐ Ⓑ Ⓒ Ⓓ
14 Ⓐ Ⓑ Ⓒ Ⓓ	32 Ⓐ Ⓑ Ⓒ Ⓓ
15 Ⓐ Ⓑ Ⓒ Ⓓ	33 Ⓐ Ⓑ Ⓒ Ⓓ
16 Ⓐ Ⓑ Ⓒ Ⓓ	34 Ⓐ Ⓑ Ⓒ Ⓓ
17 Ⓐ Ⓑ Ⓒ Ⓓ	35 Ⓐ Ⓑ Ⓒ Ⓓ
18 Ⓐ Ⓑ Ⓒ Ⓓ	36 Ⓐ Ⓑ Ⓒ Ⓓ

Practice Test I

Case I

Directions: Questions 1–3 require you to write short answers, or "constructed responses." You are not expected to cite specific theories or texts in your answers; however, your knowledge of specific principles of learning and teaching will be evaluated. Be sure to answer all parts of the question. Write your answers in the space provided.

Scenario: Miss Matthews

Miss Matthews is an eighth-grade teacher at Curtis Junior High School. She has planned a lesson on problem-solving for her principal to observe as part of the district's teacher-evaluation procedure. Document 1 shows the plans that Miss Matthews submitted to the principal prior to the lesson.

Document 1

Lesson plan

Problem of the Day

Objective

The student will solve a two-step mathematics problem by using the guess-and-check strategy.

Resources

- "Problem of the Day" slips of paper
- Calculators

Motivation

Miss Matthews will read the problem of the day aloud and ask students to visualize this situation in their minds.

Procedures

Warm-up

Students will play a game of guess-and-check using mental math and then calculators. Miss Matthews will display math problems on the overhead projector. The students will discuss their strategies for solving problems.

Preview

Miss Matthews will tell the students that they will use the problem-solving strategy of guess-and-check to solve a problem.

Teach

1. A student distributes the problem of the day.
2. The students glue the problem into their math notebooks.
3. Miss Matthews asks a volunteer to read the problem aloud to the class.
4. She asks students to brainstorm ways to approach the problem.
5. The students solve the problem independently in their math notebooks.

GO ON TO THE NEXT PAGE

Assessment

Miss Matthews asks students to peer-review problems for accuracy and use of the guess-and-check strategy.

- The student earns a 3 if she solved the problem accurately and used guess-and-check.
- The student earns a 2 if she solved the problem accurately but did not use guess-and-check, or did not solve the problem accurately but did use guess-and-check.
- The student earns a 1 if she attempted to solve the problem but did not solve it accurately and did not use guess-and-check.
- The student earns a 0 if she did not turn in the work or turned in incomplete work.

Independent work

The homework assignment is a similar problem requiring the use of guess-and-check.

Evaluation

When the principal came to visit Miss Matthews's math class, she saw evidence of excellent planning but poor class-room management. Miss Matthews clearly knew her content, set clear expectations, and designed a good, standards-based math problem for students to solve. The problem was implementation. When Miss Matthews asked a student to pass out the problems at the beginning of the lesson, the student acted silly and pretended to be a "Problem of the Day Fairy" as she passed out the papers. Several students enjoyed the performance, and the class became noisy with laughter. Miss Matthews nervously laughed with the students and thanked the girl for handing out the papers with such drama and flair. Next, when the students were supposed to be brainstorming ways to solve the problem, several students were talking in the back of the class. Two students asked to go to their lockers for their forgotten math notebooks, and Miss Matthews allowed them to do so. When Miss Matthews collected the students' in-class responses, she noted a wide range of scores, from 3s to 0s. Several students who were present did not even hand in their classwork.

1. Identify ONE classroom-management strategy for Miss Matthews to implement in her math classroom. Be sure to base your response on principles of teaching and communication techniques.

2. Suggest TWO ways that Miss Matthews can involve her students more appropriately and actively in the lesson. Be sure to base your answer on principles of student learning and instruction.

3. Suggest ONE way that Miss Matthews's principal can support Miss Matthews's professional development. Be sure to base your response on principles of teacher professionalism or communication techniques.

_____

_____

_____

_____

_____

_____

_____

_____

_____

_____

_____

Case II

Directions: Questions 4–6 require you to write short answers, or "constructed responses." You are not expected to cite specific theories or texts in your answers; however, your knowledge of specific principles of learning and teaching will be evaluated. Be sure to answer all parts of the question. Write your answers in the space provided.

Scenario: Colin

Colin is a kind, athletic tenth-grader who loves music, spending time with friends, talking online, and Spanish class. A tutor helps him get average grades in science and mathematics. His tutor has noticed that Colin has organizational problems and needs a lot of help breaking down information when studying for tests. The tutor reports the following areas of strength and weakness for Colin:

Strengths:

- Visual learner
- Excellent memory
- Aptitude with languages

Weaknesses:

- Study habits
- Attention span
- Concentration when reading

Recently, Colin has started to skip classes and go to a local breakfast spot with friends. He seems to be prioritizing his social life above his academic life, and he is having a difficult time finding a balance between the two. His mother, a single parent, tries to help with Colin's schoolwork, but she works many hours at the local bank, so Colin is often responsible for completing his homework on his own.

GO ON TO THE NEXT PAGE

Colin's guidance counselor, Mr. Sweeney, asked to speak to Colin about his goals and progress in tenth grade. Colin stated that everything was fine, but Mr. Sweeney was not convinced and decided to set up a meeting with Colin's mother and teachers.

4. Suggest ONE way that Colin's teachers or guidance counselor can collaborate with others to provide supports for him. Be sure to base your response on principles of communication and teacher professionalism.

5. Identify ONE area of learning difference that could explain Colin's learning behavior at school and with his tutor. Suggest TWO teaching methods to support his learning needs. Be sure to base your response on principles of student learning and instruction.

6. Suggest ONE study strategy (or comprehension strategy) that Colin could learn to help him with his science reading homework and note-taking. Be sure to base your response on principles of instruction.

_____

_____

_____

_____

_____

_____

_____

_____

_____

_____

_____

_____

_____

_____

_____

_____

_____

_____

_____

Discrete Multiple-Choice Questions

Directions: Questions 7–18 are not related to the previous cases. For each question, select the best answer and mark the corresponding letter space on your answer sheet.

7. Mr. Craig is a first-year teacher of tenth-grade social studies. He feels successful in his knowledge of content, his ability to plan lessons, and his interactions with colleagues. He has reflected on his instruction and realizes that his students frequently talk off-task, especially during independent seat work. Which of the following suggestions would be most helpful to Mr. Craig in this situation?

    A. Call the students' parents, speak with the principal, and offer after-school help
    B. Offer after-school help, give students detention, and speak individually with students
    C. Create incentive systems, speak with the principal, and use more wait time
    D. Give the teacher "look," create incentive systems, and provide individual help

8. According to Erikson's theory of human development, adolescents ages 12–18 work to resolve which of the following conflicts?

    A. Peers versus parents
    B. Identity versus role confusion
    C. Social versus academic
    D. Guilt versus isolation

9. Mr. Sanderson believes that students need clear guidelines and expectations for homework. He does not allow any late homework, although he allows students to show him their homework the next day for no credit. For students who complete homework on time, he gives full credit. In addition, students who complete homework receive one extra-credit point for every five homework assignments completed. Which of the following principles of learning and teaching guides Mr. Sanderson's practice?

    A. Intrinsic motivation
    B. Operant conditioning
    C. Rewards
    D. Structure

10. Mrs. Gagliardi and her 11th-grade English students enjoy their discussions of the King Arthur legend. Mrs. Gagliardi prefers to help her students come to their own interpretations and meaning of the text through open-ended questions and through exposing her students to a variety of viewpoints on the legend's meaning. Mrs. Gagliardi is using which of the following theories to guide her educational practice?

    A. Constructivism
    B. Behaviorism
    C. Authoritarianism
    D. Moral development

GO ON TO THE NEXT PAGE

Questions 11–12 are based on the following scenario.

Ms. Salvatore is a special education resource teacher who provides services identified with IEPs in Mrs. Keen's heterogeneously grouped seventh-grade English classroom. Mrs. Keen has just completed a lesson on *The Outsiders* and has asked her students to complete a character-analysis activity in small groups. Ms. Salvatore helps any student who needs the support but pays particular attention to the students identified as having special needs. One student, Jeffrey, appears to be having difficulty getting along with the students in his group and quickly becomes angry. Jeffrey has been diagnosed with an emotional problem and has a behavior intervention plan to support him.

11. Ms. Salvatore and Mrs. Keen's work together is known as

   A. an individualized program.
   B. a resource room.
   C. an inclusion program.
   D. a self-contained room.

12. Students with identified emotional problems usually benefit from which of the following supports?

   A. Self-contained classrooms and strict rules
   B. A supportive environment and unlimited choices
   C. A strict environment and no-tolerance policies
   D. Structured choices and a positive environment

13. If a teacher wants to ask higher-level questions, which of the following types of questions from Bloom's taxonomy would she use?

   A. Comprehension and discussion
   B. Analysis and synthesis
   C. Knowledge and literal
   D. Open-ended and reflective

14. Which of the following types of tests are written for a variety of subjects and levels designed to measure a student's knowledge of or proficiency in an area that was learned or taught?

   A. Achievement tests
   B. Aptitude tests
   C. Criterion-referenced tests
   D. Essay tests

15. Mrs. Audette is a tenth-grade social studies teacher at Central High School. Recently, she has been experiencing personal problems related to the break-up of her marriage. The police have visited her home on several occasions, and charges of domestic assault have been filed by both Mrs. Audette and her estranged spouse. She has neither shared her personal problems at work nor missed any days of school. Which of the following teachers' rights pertain to Mrs. Audette's circumstances?

   A. She can be fired because of the charges.
   B. She can be suspended during a civil or criminal trial.
   C. She cannot be fired because she did not commit domestic assault.
   D. She cannot be fired unless her behavior interferes with her teaching effectiveness.

16. In 1918, secondary education was reorganized to include the following: health education, basic skills, good relationships, vocations, civic education, worthy use of leisure time, and ethical behavior. Which of the following is the name for this reorganization?

   A. American Federation of Teachers
   B. Manual Training Movement
   C. Testing Movement of Secondary Education
   D. Cardinal Principles of Secondary Education

17. Which of the following public laws mandates the regulation and formulation of Individualized Education Plans for students with identified learning differences?

   A. ADA
   B. NCLB
   C. P.L. 94-142
   D. Section 504 of the Rehabilitation Act

18. The Progressive Period of U.S. education is marked by an influence of which of the following revolutions?

   A. Industrial Revolution
   B. American Revolution
   C. Spanish Revolution
   D. New England Revolution

Case III

Directions: Questions 19–21 require you to write short answers, or "constructed responses." You are not expected to cite specific theories or texts in your answers; however, your knowledge of specific principles of learning and teaching will be evaluated. Be sure to answer all parts of the question. Write your answers in the space provided.

Scenario: Mrs. Horton

Mrs. Horton is thrilled to have the opportunity to teach in the town in which she was educated more than 20 years ago. A few of her former teachers at Lincoln Middle School are still teaching; the building looks the same; and the principal is the same; but the school's student body has changed over the years—racially, ethnically, linguistically, and economically. Half the student body is Hispanic; 13% is Caucasian; 31% is African American; 5% is Asian; and 1% is Native American. Fifteen percent of the student body receives English language learner or bilingual education services. The students in Mrs. Horton's seventh-grade class speak more than ten different languages besides English. Sixteen percent of the student body receives special education services, and 46% of the student body receives free or reduced lunch.

Mrs. Horton has set three professional goals for the school year:

- To create a positive, respectful learning environment in which all her students can achieve high standards
- To get to know each student and his or her family
- To actively engage students in meaningful learning experiences

Her first unit is called "That Was Then, This Is Now." The students will read S. E. Hinton's novel *That Was Then, This Is Now* in her reading/language arts class. The following activity demonstrates how Mrs. Horton has chosen to kick off the unit and begin to achieve her professional goals.

That Was Then, This Is Now

Mrs. Horton shares her own seventh-grade class picture from when she attended Lincoln School two decades ago. She tells a bit about her favorites—friends, subjects, activities, and teachers. She also explains a bit about the make-up of her

GO ON TO THE NEXT PAGE

nuclear family and some of their traditions. As she shares this information, she allows students to ask questions and adds the information to a large chart paper in order to provide a model for her students. Next, she asks her students to think back to their lives one decade ago, to when they were around three years old. She smiles and adds that they weren't born two decades ago! She asks the students to write down information about friends, activities, teachers (if they attended preschool), or caregivers who taught them something, who they lived with, and what some of their traditions were. For homework, she asks the students to speak with adults at home and review any baby books or photo albums to add to their visual. She also asks each student to bring a photo or drawing from this period. The students share their work the next day, and Mrs. Horton posts their photos next to each student's first-day-of-school photograph that she took.

19. Suggest ONE way that Mrs. Horton can achieve her first goal—to create a positive, respectful learning environment in which all students can achieve high standards. Be sure to base your response on principles of learning and teaching.

20. Suggest ONE way that Mrs. Horton can achieve her second goal—to get to know each student and his or her family. Be sure to base your response on principles of learning and teaching.

21. Suggest ONE way that Mrs. Horton can achieve her third goal—to actively engage students in meaningful learning experiences. Be sure to base your response on principles of learning and teaching.

Case IV

Directions: Questions 22–24 require you to write short answers, or "constructed responses." You are not expected to cite specific theories or texts in your answers; however, your knowledge of specific principles of learning and teaching will be evaluated. Be sure to answer all parts of the question. Write your answers in the space provided.

Scenario: Luke

Luke, a junior at West High School, is very bright and artistic. Recently, he has become turned off to school, much to the surprise of his parents and teachers. In the past, Luke has been on the honor roll every quarter, has been active in the school's art exhibitions, and even won an art award from the local press for a photograph that he entered into its contest.

Luke recently shared with his guidance counselor that high school is a chore. His academic performance has declined rapidly this year, and he is at risk of having to repeat several courses. Luke has changed his style of dress, his hairstyle, and the music he listens to, apparently to fit in with a new social group—considered the "bad" group of kids in town. This group skateboards on private property and hangs out on the streets downtown. Several of the students in this group have caught the attention of law enforcement officials for underage drinking and disorderly conduct.

Luke's guidance counselor calls a meeting with Luke's parents and teachers to share information and create a plan to support Luke. Luke's parents report that Luke has not been himself lately and that they have had to get after him to attend to his studies. His teachers also report a change in Luke's demeanor in class. At the start of the year, he seemed to be enjoying school and had several friends from the "art circle" of kids. In the past quarter, Luke has failed to turn in 50% of his homework and has become withdrawn and disengaged.

22. Identify ONE of Luke's behaviors that offers insight into his problems. Discuss at least TWO student learning issues that could be affecting Luke in school.

23. Suggest ONE support that Luke's counselor and parents could put into place to help Luke through this difficult time in school. Be sure to base your response on principles of communication and teacher professionalism.

24. Suggest ONE modification or support that Luke's teachers could implement in the classroom to help Luke through this difficult time. Be sure to base your response on principles of instruction and assessment.

GO ON TO THE NEXT PAGE

_____

_____

_____

_____

_____

_____

_____

_____

_____

_____

_____

Discrete Multiple-Choice Questions

Directions: Questions 25–36 are not related to the previous cases. For each question, select the best answer and mark the corresponding letter space on your answer sheet.

---

25. Pedro is a student who is new to the United States and just recently began to speak English. Spanish is his native language. Which of the following behaviors does a student often engage in when thought and language first come together?

   A. Babbling

   B. Self-talk

   C. Simultaneous play

   D. Zone of proximal development

26. Which of the following is the process through which social activities evolve into mental activities?

   A. Inner speech

   B. Internalization

   C. Tertiary activities

   D. Assimilation

27. Josh's family situation—living with a single mom who is dependent on alcohol and drugs—makes it difficult for him to be successful in school. Josh is the provider for this family at the young age of 13, and he is the authoritative voice for his younger siblings. Josh helps his siblings complete homework; he fixes dinner; he organizes all the school papers and even signs permission slips. Josh has a difficult time in school when he is treated "like a baby" and is told what to do by teachers and other authority figures. Which of the following best describes Josh's difficulty in school?

   A. Josh may have learning disabilities.

   B. Josh has a behavior problem.

   C. Josh is from a minority ethnic group.

   D. Josh has a cultural mismatch between home and school.

28. Mrs. Xavier plans her lessons so that her students work heterogeneously on similar assignments, but with varying levels of support. For example, she tiers the instruction of a summary writing assignment to provide more support and direction for the students who are still struggling with this type of writing, and she offers more creativity and freedom for the same assignment to the students who have mastered this style of writing. Which of the following best describes Mrs. Xavier's instructional practice?

   A. Grade-equivalent instruction
   B. Sequential instruction
   C. Differentiated instruction
   D. Scope and sequence instruction

29. Which of the following is an important comprehension strategy that involves teaching students to use a double-entry notebook or SQ3R to comprehend written materials that can be incorporated into lessons in the early grades through adulthood?

   A. Reinforcing and providing recognition
   B. Identifying similarities and differences
   C. Summarizing and note-taking
   D. Nonlinguistic representations

30. Which of the following strategies helps students tap into their natural curiosity to understand concepts more deeply?

   A. Generating and testing hypotheses
   B. Anchored instruction
   C. Tiered instruction
   D. Compacted instruction

31. 1. Anticipatory set, 2. Modeling, 3. Guided practice, and 4. _____. Which of the following comes next in Hunter's model of lesson planning?

   A. Motivation
   B. Independent practice
   C. Assessment
   D. Preview

32. Which of the following guides a teacher's instruction to ensure that he or she is following district requirements as well as not repeating content from a previous grade level?

   A. Unit plans
   B. Lesson plans
   C. Book lists
   D. Curriculum frameworks

33. Which of the following people is considered a founding father of the Progressive Period (1880–1920) of American education?

   A. Gardner
   B. Piaget
   C. Dewey
   D. Mann

GO ON TO THE NEXT PAGE

34. Which of the following reports provided evidence that education in the United States, particularly in secondary schools, was falling behind that in other countries?

    A. No Child Left Behind

    B. A Nation at Risk

    C. First Year Studies

    D. ESEA

35. Which of the following reports was written during the Clinton administration and included such issues as schools being drug free and schools promoting partnerships to increase parental involvement?

    A. Goals 2000

    B. National Reading Panel Report

    C. NEA Committee of Ten Report

    D. Title I Report

36. Mr. and Mrs. Smith attended a recent parent/teacher conference with Mrs. Rodrigues, their child's sixth-grade teacher. The Smiths are frustrated that their daughter is still not reading at grade level and blame the schools, teachers, and administration for her lack of success in this area. Mrs. Rodrigues used which of the following to show her professionalism and willingness to listen to the Smiths' concerns?

    A. Open communication

    B. Closed communication

    C. Multicultural communication

    D. Respectful communication

Answers and Explanations, Test I

Case I

1. **Suggested content:** Miss Matthews is a math teacher who is teaching a problem-solving lesson to her eighth-grade students. One classroom management strategy that Miss Matthews can implement is Canter and Canter's assertive discipline approach. With this approach, the teacher sets clear expectations for student behavior and follows through consistently and fairly with consequences. This approach is based on the tenet that students have a choice to follow the rules or face the natural consequences. One common sequence of consequences involves marking checks on the chalkboard or whiteboard:

   - 1 check = warning
   - 2 checks = detention
   - 3 checks = call home and detention
   - 4 checks = meeting with the principal, detention, and possible suspension

   Content categories: Instruction and Assessment, Teacher Professionalism

2. **Suggested content:** Miss Matthews can involve her students actively and appropriately in the lesson in two ways:

   - Allow the students to model the problem-solving by using the overhead projector during the warm-up section of the lesson
   - Pair up the students to solve the problem in step five of the teach portion of her lesson plan

   When Miss Matthews's students demonstrate their problem-solving abilities to open the lesson, the tone of the lesson—this is a serious class where we work hard to learn—is set, providing a strong context for the lesson to come. Allowing the students to work in pairs for the independent practice portion of the lesson supports students' social needs to talk and work together. It also offers students who may still be learning the problem-solving strategy an appropriate scaffold of instruction and offers students who are strong in this concept or skill the opportunity to strengthen their understanding by teaching.

   Content categories: Students as Learners, Instruction and Assessment

3. **Suggested content:** Miss Matthews appears to have a strong understanding of her content. She may benefit from more professional development in the area of classroom management. Her principal can support Miss Matthews by approving her request for attendance at a professional development workshop or to visit the classroom of another teacher who has more experience and proven effectiveness in classroom management. After Miss Matthews returns from her professional development, the principal could be supportive by asking Miss Matthews what approaches she learned and how she plans to implement them. After Miss Matthews has had some time to implement and gain confidence in the new approach, the principal could observe to offer encouragement for Miss Matthews's professional growth.

   Content categories: Communication Techniques, Teacher Professionalism

Case II

4. **Suggested content:** Colin is a tenth-grader who is losing focus on the purpose of his studies. He is having a hard time finding a balance between his academic and social priorities. Colin's guidance counselor, teachers, and mother could work together to provide more structure and support for Colin. One way to do so is to require Colin to use an assignment planner and write down each of his tests, quizzes, and homework assignments. After Colin writes down an assignment, he is responsible for asking the teacher to review his planner and sign it. When Colin goes home to do his homework independently, he has a clear idea of what his assignments are. When his mother gets home, she can look at the planner, review Colin's completed homework, and then sign the planner. This home/school/student communication system provides supports for Colin without shifting the responsibility of the work from Colin.

   Content categories: Teacher Professionalism, Communication Techniques

5. **Suggested content:** Colin's tutor has noticed his strengths as well as his weaknesses. His tutor reports that Colin has poor study habits, a short attention span, and poor concentration when reading. Colin's behavior could indicate attention deficit disorder or several other learning differences. Based on these observations (not a diagnosis for attention deficit disorder since teachers report learning observations and behaviors to change instruction and are not qualified to diagnose a student with a disorder or learning disability), the teacher could try two instructional strategies to help Colin with his academics. The first is to use graphic organizers to help Colin organize and synthesize information visually. Colin is a visual learner, so graphic organizers may be very helpful for him when studying for tests or trying to learn lots of information. The second strategy is to break down the assignments into two or three smaller parts—known as curriculum chunking—to provide more support, positive reinforcement, and instruction for Colin if needed.

Content categories: Students as Learners, Instruction and Assessment

6. **Suggested content:** Colin has been having difficulty studying for tests, especially in the area of science. One instructional strategy that the teacher could try is to explicitly teach Colin to summarize and take notes. Many students find the SQ3R method for note-taking very beneficial. This method involves the following five steps:

1. SURVEY—Colin previews the science reading by looking at the headings, illustrations, and other text features.
2. QUESTION—Colin writes or thinks of questions that he generated during the survey step.
3. READ—Colin reads the science textbook section, focusing primarily on reading to find the answers to his questions.
4. RECITE—Colin answers each question in his mind and then writes the answers in his notebook.
5. REVIEW—After Colin has repeated this sequence all the way through the assigned reading, he immediately reviews his notebook to improve his recall and comprehension of the information learned in the lesson.

Content categories: Students as Learners, Instruction and Assessment

Discrete Multiple-Choice Questions

Answer Key, Test I, Questions 7–18			
Question	*Answer*	*Content Category*	*Where to Get More Help*
7.	D	Students as Learners	Chapter 7
8.	B	Students as Learners	Chapter 7
9.	B	Students as Learners	Chapter 7
10.	A	Students as Learners	Chapter 7
11.	C	Instruction and Assessment	Chapter 8
12.	D	Instruction and Assessment	Chapter 8
13.	B	Instruction and Assessment	Chapter 8
14.	A	Instruction and Assessment	Chapter 8
15.	D	Teacher Professionalism	Chapter 10
16.	D	Teacher Professionalism	Chapter 10
17.	C	Teacher Professionalism	Chapter 10
18.	A	Teacher Professionalism	Chapter 10

Explanations

7. D. Mr. Craig can attempt to handle this discipline problem within the classroom first; therefore, choice D is the credited response. The teacher can first try to give a "look," or a stern glance; create incentive systems; and provide additional help.

8. B. According to Erikson's stages of human development, adolescents ages 12–18 work to resolve the conflict of identity versus role confusion. Adolescents consider the roles they play in the adult world and initially experience a sense of role confusion. Eventually, most adolescents achieve a sense of identity—better understanding of who they are and how they can contribute to the adult world.

9. B. Mr. Sanderson's practice is guided by an understanding of Skinner's theory of operant conditioning. Operant conditioning is a form of learning in which a learning response increases in frequency when followed by reinforcement.

10. A. Constructivism is theoretical perspective on learning that suggests learners create or construct knowledge from their experiences.

11. C. An inclusion program for special education students typically provides supports for students in as many general education classes as possible, such as this scenario with Ms. Salvatore and Mrs. Keen's class. Usually, the special education teacher works in the general education teacher's classroom to provide supports to students with IEPs and to offer expertise and assistance within the classroom.

12. D. Students with emotional and/or behavioral problems usually respond well to structured choices and a positive, supportive classroom environment. The teacher must strive to maintain a balanced perspective about the student and focus on the student's efforts at self-control and self-discipline. Answer choices A, B, and C all suggest a level of control and rigidity, which often results in an escalation of the student's emotional or behavioral issues rather than the more desirable de-escalation of behavior problems in the classroom.

13. B. Higher-level questions in Bloom's taxonomy include analysis and synthesis questions.

14. A. Achievement tests are written for a variety of subjects and levels and are designed to measure student knowledge or proficiency in the areas that were learned.

15. D. Mrs. Audette cannot be fired unless her behavior interferes with her teaching effectiveness. This is one of several rights that teachers have.

16. D. The Cardinal Principles of Secondary Education reorganized secondary schools to include health education, basic skills, good relationships, vocations, civic education, worthy use of leisure time, and ethics.

17. C. P.L. 94-142 mandates the regulation and formulation of Individualized Education Plans (IEPs) for students with identified learning differences.

18. A. The Progressive Period in U.S. education was influenced by the Industrial Revolution.

Case III

19. Suggested content: Mrs. Horton is returning to her former junior high school after being away from the community for many years. She has an instructional goal to create a positive, respectful learning environment in her classroom. One way that she can do so is to share her hopes and dreams for her year at the school. Then she can ask her students to think about their own hopes and dreams for seventh grade, quick- or free-write about these ideas, and then share their thoughts with a peer nearby. Once all the students have at least one hope or dream to share, each one can make a poster with his or her name in large print, his or her hope or dream in large print, and a collage of magazine cutouts, photos, or drawings that help others visualize what that hope or dream is about. Mrs. Horton can hang these posters around the room throughout the year and make a point to refer respectfully and positively to the class's hopes and dreams.

Content categories: Students as Learners, Instruction and Assessment

20. **Suggested content:** Mrs. Horton's second goal is to get to know each family from her classroom. One way that she could do so is to have her students interview each family member about "That Was Then, This Is Now." In class, Mrs. Horton can teach her students to write five good interview questions with the goal of getting to know something about that person's past and something about the person today. Each student will go home, conduct the interview, and then present it to the class in one of a variety of formats—a paper, a PowerPoint, a website, or a video.

    Content categories: Teacher Professionalism, Communication Techniques

21. **Suggested content:** Mrs. Horton's third goal is to involve her students actively in the learning process. One way that she can do so is to design a unit using a project-based learning approach. In this unit, the students will work on an in-depth investigation of a real-life, relevant, and meaningful topic. She can plan a variety of hands-on, visual, and auditory experiences to engage the students actively in problem-solving and inquiring. The students can be allowed to work in pairs or small groups to maximize active involvement.

    Content categories: Students as Learners, Instruction and Assessment

Case IV

22. **Suggested content:** Luke is a bright and artistic student who is beginning to disengage in school during his junior year of high school. One behavior of Luke's that is of particular interest is his change in social groups. Luke has recently changed his style of dress, his hairstyle, and his musical interests. One reason for this change could be that Luke is struggling to resolve the conflict of identity versus role confusion. According to Erikson, adolescents typically work to resolve this conflict between the ages of 12 and 18. A second reason for this change could be related to Luke's risk-taking and perhaps even experimentation with illegal substances, such as drugs or alcohol. In his effort to fit in, or for another reason that may be unclear to all involved, Luke may be trying drugs or alcohol, which is affecting his behavior and performance in school.

    Content categories: Students as Learners

23. **Suggested content:** Luke would benefit if his guidance counselor and parents formed a partnership to help Luke recognize his new pattern of behavior and understand the choices he is making. Open communication among Luke, school personnel, and Luke's parents will show Luke that he is important to many people, all of whom believe that he can achieve great things. The school personnel and parents can "double-team" Luke with the same message—that this effort and his achievement are connected and that his hard work in school will pay off. His counselor and parents may also want to communicate openly about the peers Luke is spending time with; Luke's family may need to address this at home based on their expectations and values.

    Content categories: Teacher Professionalism, Communication Techniques

24. **Suggested content:** Luke is at a crossroads near the end of his high school career. His teachers can have a tremendously positive impact on his decision to stay in school and his return to achieving the honor roll. One modification or support that Luke's teachers could implement is an advisory period for Luke (and perhaps the whole 11th grade, with administrative support). An advisory is a place for students to get to know one or two adults in school better, and vice versa. Advisories can be implemented in a variety of ways, such as just talking, reading a book together and discussing, playing board games, or taking a walk through the school's athletic fields. Adolescents need adult role models whom they can trust in school. Offering Luke a consistent way to get this time and attention from an adult in the course of a busy academic day is important for a student on the verge of a crisis, as Luke appears to be.

    Content categories: Students as Learners, Instruction and Assessment

Discrete Multiple-Choice Questions

Answer Key, Test I, Questions 25–36			
Question	*Answer*	*Content Category*	*Where to Get More Help*
25.	B	Students as Learners	Chapter 7
26.	B	Students as Learners	Chapter 7
27.	D	Students as Learners	Chapter 7
28.	C	Students as Learners	Chapter 7
29.	C	Instruction and Assessment	Chapter 8
30.	A	Instruction and Assessment	Chapter 8
31.	B	Instruction and Assessment	Chapter 8
32.	D	Instruction and Assessment	Chapter 8
33.	C	Teacher Professionalism	Chapter 10
34.	B	Teacher Professionalism	Chapter 10
35.	A	Teacher Professionalism	Chapter 10
36.	D	Teacher Professionalism	Chapter 10

Explanations

25. B. Self-talk is a behavior that students often engage in when thought and language first come together. Secondary teachers may see this behavior in students who are learning a language for the first time, such as English language learners.

26. B. Internalization is the process through which social activities evolve into mental activities.

27. D. Josh may be experiencing a cultural mismatch between home and school. At home, he is playing the role of an adult, being the caregiver for his mother and siblings. At school, he is required to switch to a more age-appropriate role, but one that is not a part of Josh's cultural experiences.

28. C. Mrs. Xavier differentiates her lesson instruction to meet the needs of individual students while maintaining high expectations for all students.

29. C. Summarizing and note-taking are essential instructional strategies that teach students to better comprehend materials.

30. A. Generating-and-testing-hypotheses strategies help students tap into their natural curiosity, study real-life problems, and understand concepts more deeply.

31. B. Hunter's model is a classroom management strategy that focuses on planning instruction. The next step in lesson planning, according to Hunter's model, is independent practice.

32. D. Curriculum frameworks help guide a teacher's instruction to help him or her follow the district requirements.

33. C. Dewey is considered the father of Progressive Education.

34. B. A Nation at Risk report, published in the 1980s, suggested that U.S. schools were falling behind those in other countries.

35. A. Written during the Clinton administration, Goals 2000 was a report on U.S. education that included recommendations for improving schools.

36. D. Mrs. Rodrigues is using respectful communication with Mr. and Mrs. Smith. Respectful communication is a key behavior of teaching professionals.

Practice Test II

Case I

Directions: Questions 1–3 require you to write short answers, or "constructed responses." You are not expected to cite specific theories or texts in your answers; however, your knowledge of specific principles of learning and teaching will be evaluated. Be sure to answer all parts of the question. Write your answers in the space provided.

Scenario: Mr. Robinson

Mr. Robinson is a high school English teacher who primarily teaches 12th grade. He strives to share his love of literature, especially theater, with his students. Each year, he takes his AP English class to the city's repertory theater to experience the art and joy of live theater. This year, the repertory theater is producing *Suddenly Last Summer* by Tennessee Williams. Mr. Robinson's students are primarily from a middle-class background, although some receive free lunch and a few live in multimillion-dollar homes. The majority of his students plan to attend college, although a few will remain in town to run family businesses.

Mr. Robinson plans to have his students study Williams's play, which is about a young, affluent man who mysteriously and tragically dies. The only witness to this horrific death is his cousin, who is committed to a mental institution soon after the event. The young man's mother is incensed by the "rumors" her niece is spreading about her beloved only son's death and calls in a doctor who specializes in lobotomies to assess the girl's mental state and see if she is a candidate for this last-resort treatment. This dark play explores themes of rich versus poor and good versus evil, as well as issues of race, class, and sexual preference.

Mr. Robinson knows that he wants his students to experience this play but is not certain how to approach his introductory lesson for the play.

1. Suggest ONE way that Mr. Robinson could introduce the lesson and play. Be sure to base your response on principles of instruction and student learning.

2. Suggest ONE objective that Mr. Robinson could have for teaching this play and viewing the play at the theater. Be sure to base your response on principles of instruction and student learning.

3. This play contains disturbing scenes about murder, race, and sexual preference. Suggest ONE way that Mr. Robinson could communicate with parents and administrators about this lesson. Be sure to base your response on principles of professional communication and teacher professionalism.

_____

_____

_____

_____

_____

_____

_____

_____

_____

_____

_____

Case II

Directions: Questions 4–6 require you to write short answers, or "constructed responses." You are not expected to cite specific theories or texts in your answers; however, your knowledge of specific principles of learning and teaching will be evaluated. Be sure to answer all parts of the question. Write your answers in the space provided.

Scenario: Miss Coates

Miss Coates is a first-year English teacher at Madison High School. Approximately 227 of the school's 500 students are ESL. Three languages besides English are primarily spoken by students: Spanish, Mandarin Chinese, and Vietnamese. Miss Coates teaches five English classes a day—one class of honors American literature, two classes of college-preparatory American literature, and one class of English/drama.

In her English/drama class, she has 25 students, ten of whom speak English as a second language. The ESL teacher, Mr. Sawyer, and Miss Coates have planned to team-teach during the next unit in an effort to integrate English language learning lessons into the context of the English classroom content. The teachers have chosen the next play to read and produce. They have decided to have the students read the play in cooperative groups in an effort to support the students who need it and offer leadership opportunities to the students who are excelling in English class.

The students read the play in small groups and then plan to act out the scene they were assigned. The teachers have created the following criteria for the cooperative group reading and the acting out of the scene (Document 1).

Document 1

Criteria for group work:

- Focus on the task
- Interact positively
- Work together cooperatively
- Read the play for meaning

GO ON TO THE NEXT PAGE

Criteria for acting:

- Focus on the task
- Interact positively
- Work together cooperatively
- Perform the play for meaning

4. Identify TWO key features of cooperative learning groups. What makes this type of grouping practice successful for ALL students? Be sure to base your response on principles of student learning and instruction.

5. Suggest ONE way that Miss Coates and Mr. Sawyer can strengthen the criteria for the reading or acting of the scene. Base your response on principles of instruction and assessment, as well as communication techniques.

6. Suggest ONE accommodation that the teachers can offer to support the students who speak English as a second language. Be sure to base your response on principles of student learning and instruction.

_____

_____

_____

_____

_____

_____

_____

_____

_____

_____

_____

_____

_____

_____

_____

_____

_____

_____

_____

_____

_____

_____

Discrete Multiple-Choice Questions

Directions: Questions 7–18 are not related to the previous cases. For each question, select the best answer and mark the corresponding letter space on your answer sheet.

7. Maria is participating in a classroom taught entirely in English even though she has just moved to the United States from Central America. Her lessons are offered in simplified English so that she can learn both English and the academic content. Which of the following best describes the type of instruction Maria is receiving?

   A. Primary language not English instruction
   B. Ebonics
   C. English as a second language instruction
   D. English immersion instruction

8. Stewart and Sarah are visual and auditory learners who also show multiple intelligences in the verbal-linguistic and musical areas. Which of the following instructional resources would most likely meet Stewart and Sarah's learning styles?

   A. Multimedia/technology
   B. Books
   C. Whiteboard and markers
   D. Art supplies

9. Which of the following theories espouses offering adequate support or scaffolding to enable students to perform challenging tasks with success?

   A. Behaviorist theory
   B. Social learning theory
   C. Motivation theory
   D. Classical theory

10. Boys usually enter adolescence at age _____; girls usually enter adolescence at age _____.

   A. Boys 10; Girls 12
   B. Boys 12; Girls 10
   C. Boys 15; Girls 13
   D. Boys 14; Girls 12

11. Which of the following types of assessment helps inform a teacher's day-to-day instruction with students?

   A. Summative assessment
   B. Norm-referenced assessment
   C. Formative assessment
   D. Achievement assessment

12. Which of the following types of assessment helps inform curriculum and school progress toward goals?

   A. Summative assessment
   B. Formative assessment
   C. Diagnostic assessment
   D. Behavior assessment

GO ON TO THE NEXT PAGE

13. Which of the following is typically an effective behavior reinforcer for students in grades 6–8?

    A. Colorful stickers for a job well done

    B. Short periods of free time with peers

    C. Classroom duties, such as leader or office helper

    D. Position in class lineup

14. Which of the following is usually an effective instructional modification for students with learning disabilities?

    A. Setting strict routines and rules

    B. Setting up homogeneous groups

    C. Setting clear but flexible limits

    D. Setting conflict resolution guidelines for the class

15. Which of the following is the federal document that establishes the responsibility for public education?

    A. *Brown v. Board of Education*

    B. *Plessy v. Ferguson*

    C. First Amendment

    D. U.S. Constitution

16. Which of the following states that it is legal for an employer to hire from underrepresented groups, but that an employer cannot dismiss a person from an underrepresented group by using this guideline?

    A. Civil rights

    B. Discrimination on the basis of race

    C. Discrimination on the basis of age

    D. Reverse discrimination

17. Which of the following entities is legally responsible for education in the United States?

    A. Federal government

    B. States

    C. School district

    D. U.S. Constitution

18. Teachers and students have legal rights. The U.S. courts have placed limits on a teacher's ability to disrupt the curriculum or the functioning of a school. Which of the following best describes teachers' and students' rights in this situation?

    A. Freedom of speech

    B. Freedom of religion

    C. Freedom to bear arms

    D. Freedom of the press

Case III

Directions: Questions 19–21 require you to write short answers, or "constructed responses." You are not expected to cite specific theories or texts in your answers; however, your knowledge of specific principles of learning and teaching will be evaluated. Be sure to answer all parts of the question. Write your answers in the space provided.

Scenario: Ashley

Ashley is a seventh-grade girl who has strengths in art (especially drawing), social studies, reading, and computer science. She has the physical challenge of hearing loss. Ashley's teachers have been instructed to use a multifaceted instructional approach that always includes information presented visually for Ashley. In addition, several of Ashley's teachers and friends have learned sign language, and Ashley is very capable of communicating through signing. She is able to read lips well also. She struggles with mathematics concepts and relies on manipulatives and mnemonic devices to help her remember basic facts and learn concepts. Ashley has age-appropriate social and emotional development. She has many friends and is invited to socialize with her peers after school and on weekends. She takes pride in her appearance and strives to wear the "in" styles to gain her peers' approval.

Ashley's social studies teacher, Miss Hopkins, is teaching a unit on the U.S. Constitution. She explains that the Constitution spells out the rules for our government, such as how we make laws and how long the president may stay in office. Miss Hopkins has a goal to teach higher-level thinking during this unit and has collaborated with her colleagues in math, science, and English to work on similar questioning techniques with the students. They plan to teach the students higher-level questions from Bloom's taxonomy, such as analysis, synthesis, and evaluation.

19. Identify ONE instructional modification that Miss Hopkins may want to employ to best meet Ashley's high-level abilities in social studies and reading as well as to provide appropriate instruction in regard to her physical challenge.

20. Suggest TWO instructional methods that Miss Hopkins could use to teach high-level thinking in this unit on the Constitution. Be sure to base your response on principles of instruction and assessment.

21. Identify ONE social development behavior of Ashley's and what level she appears to be at developmentally. Suggest ONE way that you could use this social development behavior to support Ashley's instruction. Be sure to base your response on principles of student learning and instruction and assessment.

GO ON TO THE NEXT PAGE

_____

_____

_____

_____

_____

_____

_____

_____

Case IV

Directions: Questions 22–24 require you to write short answers, or "constructed responses." You are not expected to cite specific theories or texts in your answers; however, your knowledge of specific principles of learning and teaching will be evaluated. Be sure to answer all parts of the question. Write your answers in the space provided.

Scenario: Mrs. Young

Mrs. Young is a tenth-grade social studies teacher who is teaching a lesson on current events. She has asked her class of 25 students to read the newspaper in print or online each day and to bring in a copy of an article of interest once a week. The students are to read the article and then write a summary of the article that includes the following information:

- Topic
- Main idea sentence
- Three to five interesting and important facts from the article
- Two ways that this article's content connects to your life or the life of someone you know well
- Bibliographic citation in MLA format

The paper must be typed, and the student must bring a copy of the article. Mrs. Young's class is a college-preparatory section of sophomores comprised of students from rich and diverse cultural backgrounds. She and her students have great discussions and learn a lot from one another. The classroom rules about discussion and listening to varying viewpoints are well established, and Mrs. Young's students behave well, treat one another with respect, and have come to look forward to their turn to discuss the article they chose to read and review.

22. Suggest ONE reason for Mrs. Young's success in this lesson. Be sure to base your response on principles of communication skills and teacher professionalism.

23. Suggest ONE instructional method that Mrs. Young could use to teach students to better comprehend and summarize their news articles. Be sure to base your response on principles of instruction and assessment.

24. Identify ONE aspect of adolescent cognitive development that is an important learning factor for Mrs. Young to consider when planning her lessons. How can she adapt instruction to meet her adolescents' developmental needs? Be sure to base your response on principles of student learning.

Discrete Multiple-Choice Questions

Directions: Questions 25–36 are not related to the previous cases. For each question, select the best answer and mark the corresponding letter space on your answer sheet.

25. According to Kohlberg, what moral behavior do adolescents usually exhibit in the conventional stage?

A. Antisocial behaviors
B. Deep levels of reflection
C. Attempts to gain approval from peers
D. Conformity to rules

GO ON TO THE NEXT PAGE

26. According to Piaget, what cognitive development behaviors do adolescents exhibit in the formal operational stage?

   A. Inability to separate and control variables
   B. Ability to demonstrate and develop concepts without concrete materials or images
   C. Inability to test multiple hypotheses
   D. Ability to depend on concrete reality to develop concepts

27. Ricky is a ninth-grade student who shows many at-risk behaviors for dropping out of high school. Even though Ricky has a history of academic failure, which of the following must the teacher do in Ricky's situation?

   A. Send Ricky to the school guidance counselor
   B. Submit a referral for counseling for Ricky
   C. Assign extra homework to help Ricky catch up
   D. Communicate high expectations for Ricky's success

28. Mrs. Martinez strives to understand her own culture and the culture of her students in her effort to meet all of her students' educational needs. Which of the following levels of culture will Mrs. Martinez better understand if she learns about the social roles in her students' home lives, their home languages, their nonverbal communication behaviors, and their family structures?

   A. Behavioral level
   B. Emotional level
   C. Cultural norms
   D. Concrete level

29. Which of the following correlates most highly with scores from norm-referenced assessments?

   A. At-risk behaviors
   B. Learning disability
   C. Academic achievement
   D. Socioeconomic status

30. When a teacher is working with a small group of students, which of the following classroom environment factors should the teacher consider most?

   A. Ability to hear the whole class
   B. Ability to see the small group
   C. Ability to see the whole class
   D. Ability to use the chalkboard

31. Which of the following is a formative assessment?

   A. Pre-test
   B. Hearing screening
   C. SAT I
   D. California Achievement Test

32. Ms. Weeks is an 11th-grade social studies teacher who recently learned that she is pregnant. Which of the following is her right as a teacher?

   A. She has the right to choose her substitute teacher.
   B. She must take maternity leave for six weeks.
   C. She must return to work immediately after the child's birth.
   D. She has the option to take maternity leave.

33. Brian is a freshman with Down's syndrome at Central High School. Brian receives his English, mathematics, and science instruction in a self-contained special education room. He attends regular education classes with his grade-level peers for all other subjects, including physical education and lunch. Which of the following describes the instructional setting to Brian's educational programming?

    A. Self-contained classroom

    B. Least restrictive environment

    C. Private school setting

    D. School-to-work program

34. A student with documented learning disabilities who has been found eligible for special education service must have an

    A. individual education process.

    B. independent education evaluation.

    C. individualized education plan.

    D. independent education program.

35. One of the predominant leaders during the Early National Period of U.S. education was

    A. Ulysses S. Grant.

    B. Benjamin Franklin.

    C. John Dewey.

    D. Horace Mann.

36. During the late 1800s, the laws of Massachusetts required that students attend school to control the conditions for children. By 1918, all U.S. states had regulations about students' school attendance. Which of the following is the term for required attendance in public schools?

    A. Mandatory requirements

    B. Truancy education

    C. Tardy education

    D. Compulsory education

Answers and Explanations, Test II

Case I

1. **Suggested content:** Mr. Robinson is a 12th-grade teacher who enjoys taking his literature students to the local repertory theater each season. Mr. Robinson could introduce their reading of the play *Suddenly Last Summer* by inviting one or two of the actors to his class for a sneak preview of a key dramatic scene. Mr. Robinson could set a brief context for the actors' preview with a brief biography of Tennessee Williams and his purpose for having the actors in class today. After the brief scene was performed, the students could have an opportunity to ask the actors questions. Mr. Robinson and the actors would be mindful not to give away too much of the storyline and to leave the students wondering what this play is all about. This is an excellent way to connect the play to the upcoming theater experience and would intrinsically motivate the students to read the play.

   Content categories: Students as Learners, Instruction and Assessment

2. **Suggested content:** One instructional objective that Mr. Robinson could plan for this lesson is:

   The students will read, view, and discuss Tennessee Williams's play *Suddenly Last Summer* and be able to interpret and analyze at least one theme of the play. Based on the scenario, the content of this play will require maturity and high-level discussion, which is appropriate for high school seniors. In addition, attending a live performance of the play offers another avenue for students to make sense of the play and provides a motivating experience for the students to continue to attend live theater beyond high school.

   Content categories: Teacher Professionalism, Communication Techniques

3. **Suggested content:** *Suddenly Last Summer* contains themes that some parents, students, and community members may be disturbed by, such as sexual orientation, violent murder (not shown on the stage, but described), and racial equity issues. A teacher has the right to select a text that he or she deems high quality that has not been formally excluded or "banned" from the curriculum by formal vote of the school committee. It would be professional for Mr. Robinson to keep his students' parents updated on the curriculum and other events related to English class; it would be very wise for Mr. Robinson to send parents information about this play before the unit of study begins. He can let parents know about the upcoming field trip, invite parents to join the field trip (if this is an option), and invite family members to read the play themselves and discuss it at home. This demonstrates respect for the families and shows that Mr. Robinson values each family's individual culture, values, and child-rearing beliefs. If a parent objects to his or her child reading the play, he or she can meet with Mr. Robinson to discuss alternatives for the student during the two weeks the class studies this play.

   Content categories: Students as Learners, Instruction and Assessment

Case II

4. **Suggested content:** Miss Coates is a first-year teacher using cooperative learning in her high school English/drama class. One key feature of cooperative learning is the positive interdependence fostered during the activity. Positive interdependence means that the students must rely on each other to complete the work in order to be successful. A second key feature of cooperative learning is the individual accountability that the teacher ensures in the activity. Students working in a cooperative group must be individually accountable to complete certain aspects of the project and share with both the group *and* the teacher. These two features make cooperative learning a method that helps students achieve and learn together.

   Content categories: Students as Learners, Instruction and Assessment

5. **Suggested content:** Miss Coates and Mr. Sawyer have created criteria for group work and for acting out the scene. One way that they could improve the criteria is to be more specific about what each criterion means. For example, "interact positively" could have a series of cartoon pictures or quotes that demonstrate what positive interaction looks and sounds like. Another way that they could make the criteria more specific is to have the students role-play or dramatize what each criterion means. This mixture of metacognition and dramatization will help ensure that all students understand the task before they begin it.

   Content categories: Instruction and Assessment, Communication Techniques

6. **Suggested content:** Miss Coates and Mr. Sawyer teach several students who do not speak English as their first language. One accommodation that they could make is to pre-teach major concepts, themes, and vocabulary prior to reading the play. It is important to have a visual of this content, so the teachers could create a *CliffsNotes*-style guide to the play and share it with students.

Content categories: Students as Learners, Instruction and Assessment

Discrete Multiple-Choice Questions

Answer Key, Test II, Questions 7–18			
Question	*Answer*	*Content Category*	*Where to Get More Help*
7.	D	Students as Learners	Chapter 7
8.	A	Students as Learners	Chapter 7
9.	B	Students as Learners	Chapter 7
10.	B	Students as Learners	Chapter 7
11.	C	Instruction and Assessment	Chapter 8
12.	A	Instruction and Assessment	Chapter 8
13.	B	Instruction and Assessment	Chapter 8
14.	C	Instruction and Assessment	Chapter 8
15.	D	Teacher Professionalism	Chapter 10
16.	D	Teacher Professionalism	Chapter 10
17.	B	Teacher Professionalism	Chapter 10
18.	A	Teacher Professionalism	Chapter 10

Explanations

7. **D.** English immersion instruction consists of classroom discourse conducted in English only, even if students speak other languages. The teacher offers simplified English so that Maria can learn both English and academic content.

8. **A.** Auditory learners benefit from the use of such instructional resources as multimedia and technology.

9. **B.** Social learning theory focuses on the concept that people learn from observing others.

10. **B.** Boys usually enter adolescence at age 12, and girls usually enter adolescence at age 10.

11. **C.** Formative assessment is used before or during instruction to inform instructional planning and enhance student achievement.

12. **A.** Summative assessment is used after instruction or teaching to evaluate a student's or teacher's achievement.

13. **B.** Students in grades 6–8 generally respond well to the reward of short periods of free time with peers.

14. **C.** Students with learning disabilities generally respond well to teachers setting clear but flexible limits.

15. **D.** The U.S. Constitution establishes the responsibility of public education.

16. **D.** Equal-opportunity policies state that it is legal to hire underrepresented groups, but that an employer cannot dismiss a person from an underrepresented group based on reverse discrimination policy.

17. **B.** The U.S. Constitution establishes that the legal responsibility for education in the United States falls on each of the states.

18. **A.** Teachers and students have the right to freedom of speech according to the U.S. Constitution.

Case III

19. **Suggested content:** Ashley is a tenth-grader in Miss Hopkins's class. She has several academic and social strengths. She also has the physical challenge of being hearing impaired. One instructional modification that Miss Hopkins could make to her social studies lesson is to face Ashley at all times when she is speaking to the whole class or to Ashley individually. Ashley can read lips as well as sign, so it is important to offer as many opportunities as possible for her to learn content. It would also be wise to seat Ashley close to wherever Miss Hopkins generally addresses the class as a group.

    Content categories: Students as Learners, Instruction and Assessment

20. **Suggested content:** Miss Hopkins is teaching a social studies unit on the history of the U.S. Constitution. She would like her students to demonstrate high-level thinking. She would like her students to use Bloom's taxonomy as a guide to help them ask questions that require them to analyze, synthesize, and evaluate when responding. One method that she could use in this lesson is the Socratic seminar. The students and teacher discuss the content as partners as they explore and evaluate the concepts and ideas behind the U.S. Constitution. Students and teachers strive to ask thoughtful, open-ended questions that will encourage others to analyze, synthesize, and evaluate the ideas being considered. A second method to promote higher-level thinking is to teach students to generate questions and test hypotheses. In this approach, the teacher taps into students' natural curiosity to help them more deeply understand the concepts being taught.

    Content categories: Communication Techniques, Instruction and Assessment

21. **Suggested content:** Ashley's social development appears to be that of a typical seventh-grade adolescent. Her behavior to dress "in style" to gain status and recognition from her peers is the main reason for the previous conclusion. According to Erikson, Ashley's desire to gain attention from her peers is a typical conflict that a student works to resolve in the "identity versus role confusion" stage. Ashley's behavior is also indicative of a child at Kohlberg's conventional stage of moral development. In this stage, a person wrestles with being a "good girl" by pleasing others—parents, teachers, and peers. Ashley's social development is typical for her age; her strong friendships and social life attest to this as well.

    Content categories: Students as Learners, Instruction and Assessment

Case IV

22. **Suggested content:** Mrs. Young is a tenth-grade social studies teacher who is teaching a lesson on current events. One key reason for her success in this lesson is her careful attention to the classroom environment, particularly as it relates to respecting diversity. Mrs. Young has set up a learning environment that is safe and comfortable for discussion. She appears to be influenced by Glasser's choice theory as her primary philosophy when organizing classroom discipline. This approach is centered on student choice and creating a culture of respect in the classroom.

    Content categories: Teacher Professionalism, Communication Techniques

23. **Suggested content:** Mrs. Young would like her students to comprehend and summarize current news articles that the students are truly interested in. One method that she could use to support this goal is summarizing and note-taking. In this instructional approach, the teacher teaches the students to take notes by using a method such as SQ3R, which stands for Survey-Question-Read-Recite-Review. The students survey the text to get a general sense of the headings, topics, and pictures and then formulate questions that they generate prior to reading. Next, the students read and then recite the answers to their questions. Finally, the students write down their responses to the questions and review them. This is an excellent strategy to teach students prior to completing the article assignment.

    Content categories: Instruction and Assessment

24. Suggested content: Mrs. Young should consider her students' cognitive development level as she plans for discussions in her classroom. According to Piaget's theory of the stages of cognitive development, most of her tenth-grade students will have achieved the formal operational level of thinking. Students who are thinking at this level are able to reason in hypothetical situations and to use abstract thought in discussions.

Content categories: Students as Learners

Discrete Multiple-Choice Questions

Answer Key, Test II, Questions 25–36			
Question	*Answer*	*Content Category*	*Where to Get More Help*
25.	C	Students as Learners	Chapter 7
26.	B	Students as Learners	Chapter 7
27.	D	Students as Learners	Chapter 7
28.	A	Students as Learners	Chapter 7
29.	D	Instruction and Assessment	Chapter 8
30.	C	Instruction and Assessment	Chapter 8
31.	A	Instruction and Assessment	Chapter 8
32.	D	Instruction and Assessment	Chapter 8
33.	B	Teacher Professionalism	Chapter 10
34.	C	Teacher Professionalism	Chapter 10
35.	B	Teacher Professionalism	Chapter 10
36.	D	Teacher Professionalism	Chapter 10

Explanations

25. C. According to Kohlberg's stages of moral development, adolescents usually attempt to gain the approval of peers during the conventional stage.

26. B. Piaget suggests that in the formal operational stage, adolescents show the ability to demonstrate and develop concepts without the use of concrete materials or images.

27. D. Teachers must communicate high expectations for Ricky's success in an effort to teach all children and do so professionally.

28. A. According to Hidalgo's theory on the three levels of culture, the behavioral level of culture is comprised of people's social roles, home languages, nonverbal communication behaviors, and family structures.

29. D. Norm-referenced assessment scores correlate most highly with socioeconomic status.

30. C. In an effort to manage the entire classroom environment and ensure the safety of students, the teacher should have the ability to monitor the whole class when working with a small group.

31. A. A pre-test is a type of formative assessment. A pre-test helps the teacher determine students' prior knowledge and plan instruction accordingly.

32. D. A teacher who is pregnant has the right to take a maternity leave that is not counted as sick time.

33. B. Brian is receiving instruction in his least restrictive environment. Brian needs a higher level of support in mathematics and science; therefore, he attends a self-contained classroom for these lessons. He does not need as much support in other subjects, so he attends these classes with his grade-level peers.

34. C. As legally guided in P.L. 94-142, students with documented learning disabilities who have been found eligible for special education must have an individualized education plan (IEP).

35. B. Benjamin Franklin was a predominant leader, as well as a leader in education, during the Early National Period of U.S. education.

36. D. Compulsory education began in the late 1800s in an effort to require students to attend school in order to control the conditions of children.

PART V

CLOSING THOUGHTS

Final Tips and a Study Planning Guide

The purpose of this final chapter is to offer you a few final test preparation tips and resources to help you achieve a passing score on the PLT.

Final Tips

Registration

If your state has more than one Praxis II test required for certification, consider taking only one test per test day. Several states now require a Praxis II Special Subjects Content test in addition to the PLT. Taking the 2-hour PLT is a fast-paced, intense, and exhausting experience. You may want to exercise your option of spreading out your testing time to improve your performance.

Plan ahead. Presently, Praxis II is only available in paper-and-pencil format, which requires registration a minimum of one month prior to the testing date. Check the ETS website (http://www.ets.org) for test dates in your area.

Registration is less expensive and more easily completed online.

Some colleges or universities will waive the fee for the PLT. Talk to a financial aid officer.

Bring proof of your registration, even if it's a printout of your online registration confirmation.

If you're eligible for testing accommodations, complete the required documentation prior to registering for the test and mail it to ETS early!

Studying

Don't wait until the last minute.

Self-assess your strengths and weaknesses as a test-taker and student from the past. Also, use this guide to help you determine the content you still need to know. If you're not a great multiple-choice person, study more of those items. If you're struggling with reading comprehension, writing, or knowing the fundamentals of education psychology, then study and practice more of the case studies and constructed responses.

Remember, all of the practice tests in this book can help you prepare for the content and format of the PLT.

Make a study plan and stick to it. The tables below provide suggested study plans for those with a longer timeline and those with a shorter timeline.

Test Day

Be sure to get a good night's sleep the night before your test.

Eat a healthy, adequate breakfast.

Remember your two forms of identification, pencils/pens, and proof of registration.

Arrive at least 15 minutes early.

Pass the PLT!

Study Planning Guide

If You Have a Longer Timeline	
When	*What You Need to Do*
3 months (or more) before the PLT	Register for the test. Complete paperwork for accommodations, if applicable. Complete paperwork or speak with your financial aid officer about the possibility of a fee waiver, if applicable. Read the Introduction and Part I of *CliffsTestPrep Praxis II: Principles of Learning and Teaching*. Dust off your education psychology textbook or borrow one from your library. More recent copies even have references to the Praxis II PLT test! Use your favorite Internet Browser (e.g. Google, Yahoo!) to search for websites using keywords such as "Praxis II" and "principles of learning and teaching." Look for sites that contain PowerPoint presentations or the names of colleges or universities. Many of these sites are created by professors and offer a wealth of information to shore up your weaknesses and help you prepare for the content of the test. Bookmark these websites for future use.
2 months (or more) before the PLT	Make sure you've already registered for your test. Also, be sure to set aside proof of registration in a safe place—one that you'll remember! Read Parts II and III of this book to help you understand the format and content of the test. Use your favorite PLT websites—the ones you bookmarked last month—to help you prepare for the test. Take a look at the table of contents, the glossary, and the index of your education psychology textbook to provide even more content information for the areas in which you are still learning.
One month (or more) before the PLT	Do you know where the actual building is for your PLT test day? Take a test drive there. Time how long it takes and note the traffic conditions. Take the full-length practice tests of the PLT in Part IV of this book to help you simulate test-taking conditions and assess which areas you still need to study. Use your websites and education psychology book to aid you in filling in any missing pieces of content.
One week before the PLT	Set aside your proof of registration, a few #2 pencils with erasers, a couple blue or black pens, and two valid forms of identification. Retake any or all of the full-length tests in this book. Review Part III of this book to refresh your memory on the test content.
The night before the PLT	Talk only to people who make you feel good and confident! Pack a water bottle and a small snack bag. While you can't bring these things into the test session, you'll enjoy the brain refueling after the test! Go to bed early. Don't cram all night. Relax. You've already put in lots of effort preparing for the PLT test.
The day of the PLT	Eat a good breakfast. Remember to bring your water bottle, snack, proof of registration, IDs, and writing instruments. Arrive to the test center at least 30 minutes early. You're confident, wise, and test savvy. In short, you're ready to pass the PLT test!

	If You Have a Shorter Timeline
When	**What You Need to Do**
One month before the PLT	Register for the PLT test. There is a late registration fee option and a standby option if you're registering within one month of the test.
	Complete paperwork and submit it to ETS if you are eligible for accommodations.
	Talk to your financial aid officer to learn if your school has a test fee waiver option for you.
	Read the Introduction and Part I of this book.
3 weeks before the PLT	Read Parts III and IV of this book.
	Do you know where the actual building is for your PLT test day? Take a test drive there. Time how long it takes and note the traffic conditions.
2 weeks before the PLT	Take the full-length practice tests of the PLT in Part IV of this book to help you simulate test-taking conditions and assess which areas you still need to study.
	Review content outlines in Part III of this book to help you shore up any areas that you are still learning.
1 week before the PLT	Set aside your proof of registration, a few #2 pencils with erasers, a couple blue or black pens, and two valid forms of identification.
	Retake any or all of the full-length tests in this guide.
	Review Part III of this book to refresh your memory on the test content.
The night before the PLT	Talk only to people who make you feel good and confident! Pack a water bottle and a small snack bag. While you can't bring these things into the test session, you'll enjoy the brain refueling after the test. Go to bed early. Don't cram all night. Relax. You've already put in lots of effort preparing for the PLT test.
The day of the PLT	Eat a good breakfast! Remember to bring your water bottle, snack, proof of registration, IDs, and writing instruments.
	Arrive to the test center at least 30 minutes early.
	You're confident, wise, and test savvy. In short, you're ready to pass the PLT test!